MW00561471

PRAISE FOR TAKING THE CAPE OFF

"This book kept me engaged and focused cover-to-cover. Chief Kenny has done something no one has been able to do. In tackling the most difficult human experiences using the profound tragedies of his own life—loss of a loved one to terminal illness, suicide, self-doubt, fear, helplessness, loss of faith, and perceived personal and professional failure—Chief Kenny has provided leaders in every profession with a handbook that can guide them through the darkest of times. This intensely personal book manages to connect the reader to the most devastating and desperate human tragedies of life in a way that gives the reader hope, guidance, and purpose. As Chief Kenny states in the book; don't hesitate to be the only one to stand up for someone in a desperate struggle for life. Show them you don't want them to fail. They may still loss the fight. But they will know you didn't want them to. You might be the only one, and that might be enough. Chief Kenny has stood up."

— **Colonel Royal P. Mortenson**, USMC (Ret.),
Director of the Illinois Fire Service Institute,
University of Illinois-Urbana/Champaign

"Powerful comparison of true-life experiences delivering a heartwarming message pertaining to the realization that mental illness is in fact a physical illness, even though it can't be visualized like other diseases. The author's words are written with never-ending love for his son, wife, family and friends."

— **Tim McElroy**, Assistant Chief (Retired),
Hinsdale Fire Department, Hinsdale, Illinois

"Grief, loss, and suffering are part of the human existence and every generation has had great thinkers share their insight and their personal experience to help those around them. Pat is one of those modern-day voices, there is no judgment, this is not an attempt at garnering pity, or self-aggrandizement this book was written for me and you.
In this book you will find no anger, you will find no silver bullet but you will find your heart, you will find yourself and you will find yourself connected to a man whose experiences and influences have molded an archetype of empathy and understanding. The complicated world of loss whether from disease, accident or other outside forces does not have to be destructive or debilitating. This book was written by a man who was faced with the option on numerous occasions to give up, to become a victim, or to become enraged, but who rather chose to endure and grow and share so that others faced with similar circumstances can know that there is hope, there is a tomorrow and that love,
in the end, is all that truly matters."

— **Bobby Halton**, Chief Editorial Director,
Clarion Fire Rescue Group,
Educational Director, FDIC International

"Chief Kenny's, Taking the Cape Off, provides a clear and effective message: mental illness is a physical illness. I have listened to Chief Kenny's presentations several times, so I am familiar with his life's work, yet I read for 3 hours before I realized how much time had passed. His conversational style of writing will keep you turning the pages. Chief Kenny tackles the subject of mental illness -what it is, what it is not, and provides real-life examples of how to navigate through the uncertainty as a flawed human, as a leader, as a parent,
in order to be the best version of you."

— **Heather Moore**, Division Chief of Training,
Springfield Fire Department, Springfield, IL.

"Firemen, Policemen, Doctors, Nurses, and Social Workers are just few of the professionals that are considered by many as heroes. And they are proud to be that hero, wearing a mythical cape and swooping in to save the day. But being a hero comes with immense responsibility to fix problems; so what happens when the hero is also a father/spouse who realizes that he alone cannot save his family?

As a Fire Chief and leader in the community Patrick Kenny wore a cape, always there to help his co-workers and friends through tough times. While Pat wore a public smile, few knew of his son Sean's struggle with mental health, depression, drugs, and suicide attempts. Believing they were protecting Sean, the Kennys kept his illnesses a secret, handling the struggles without support of friends and extended family. It wasn't until years later when Pat's wife Eileen was diagnosed with terminal brain cancer that he realized it was okay to take off the cape and accept help.

Through his personal experiences and strong faith, Chief Kenny gives insight into the stigma of mental health and suicide; discusses his helplessness during his wife's battle with cancer; and proposes suggestions on how to move forward after their deaths. His 'Lessons Learned' at the end of each chapter are simple and would benefit not only those in the helping professions but anyone living with the belief that a hero must keep the cape on and work alone."

— **Carol Cieslak**, Retired Coordinator, Social Work Department, Madonna University

"Reading this book will provide you with an entirely new perspective on how people in your life may be facing mental health challenges. Instead of looking away from a coworker, friend or loved one, let us embrace as a community how to help each other navigate through life. The people you least expect may be battling their own demons; lend your hand and help them up.

Pat Kenny demonstrates his thoughtful gift of writing; you can hear his voice with each turn of the page. His abundant love for his family, friends, profession as a firefighter, and the gift of life is inspiring. Make the time to read his heartfelt message."

— **Emily Palm Wagner**, Local government and human resources professional; granddaughter of a Chicago firefighter

"Pat Kenny introduces his readers to a topic that's often only whispered about, but seldom discussed. Pat writes about his son Sean, who was suffering from mental illness and shows how such a condition should never be looked-upon as a weakness or a personal failure.

Pat is a skillful public speaker who has delivered his message across the USA and foreign countries. I've seen his audiences give standing ovations as Pat explains not only how to recognize a person with a problem, but also how to get help for them. Other times, when his message touches something deep-inside but never dealt-with, I've seen audiences cry with relief as answers to hidden secrets are shown.

Pat is 'mister motivation' not only in his speeches, but also in his writing. Pat's book transcends his profession, the Fire Service, and shows business managers how to help troubled employees and friends find the inner peace that has evaded their grasp.

I believe Pat has a message not only for new managers, but also experienced bosses looking for knowledge and answers to personal and business relationships. This is a GREAT read that will have the reader looking on-line to find when Pat is speaking in their area. A Life Changer."

— **Robert Bruce Graham**, President, Graham Insurance

"I was proud to attend one of the pilot presentations of 'Mayday for Mental Health Program' from Chief Kenny and to see one of my personal mentors open up while discussing his growth, the loss of his son Sean, putting on the 'Superman Cape' and finally identify the challenges of maintaining one's own mental health was incredible. In the many times since that first presentation, I have had the honor of hosting, scheduling and recommending Chief Kenny's presentation and I always learn or refresh myself every time. If an attendee at a presentation or now a reader of this book takes one thing away from Chief Kenny's message it should be 'trust'. Trust in yourself if you might be having a potential issue, trust in someone to talk about your issue, trust in the message of 'Superman's Cape'; it cannot always protect you, but it's OK! Trust yourself and seek the help to protect yourself.*

Chief Kenny's words are simple and true – Have faith, trust in you, and it's OK to take off 'the cape' or if the cape needs some repair."

— **Tim Leidig**, Assistant Fire Chief,
West Chicago Fire Protection District

"One of my finest moments at the National Fire Academy was coaxing a reluctant Pat Kenny to tell Sean's story at an upcoming higher education conference. His presentation in 2009 unleashed a national urgency for fire fighter behavioral health and suicide prevention. Now, he's penned this groundbreaking book. Shed your Superman cape and heed Chief Kenny's message!"

— **Edward J. Kaplan**, Chief (Retired),
Education, Training and Partnerships
U. S. Fire Administration, National Fire Academy

"With a fire chief's valor, an Irish writer's gift of prose and a father and husband's worst nightmare, Chief Patrick Kenny burrows into the depths of loss in, "Taking the Cape Off: How to Lead Through Mental Illness, Unimaginable Grief and Loss". Not one to wallow in anguish, Chief Kenny offers very practical solutions to working through loss and prescribes a path of hope and encouragement to others on the same journey.
A 'must read' for uniformed and civilian alike."

— **Dr. Denis Onieal**, Deputy United States Fire Administrator (Ret.)

*"Taking the Cape Off: How to Lead Through Mental Illness, Unimaginable Grief and Loss by Patrick J. Kenny is **a powerful self-help book for leaders** who need help navigating the dark waters of grief and loss. Kenny honestly and bravely shares his personal journey and shows leaders how they can use professionals and their own faith to confront the social stigma surrounding mental illness in a variety of settings, from community, to home, to work, and elsewhere. Kenny also covers **how to maintain a healthy connection to your lost loved one's memory,** how to be more affective, and how to serve others."*

— **Tammy Ruggles**, Readers' Favorite 5 Stars!

TAKING THE CAPE OFF is a 2022 Gold Recipient of the Mom's Choice Awards® Honoring Excellence.

TAKING THE CAPE OFF won the Gold Medal Award in the Non-Fiction – Grief/Hardship category for the 2021 Readers' Favorite International Book Award Contest.

TAKING THE CAPE OFF is an Award-Winning Finalist in the Parenting & Family, and Spirituality categories of the 2021 Best Book Awards sponsored by American Book Fest.

TAKING THE
CAPE OFF

How to Lead Through Mental Illness, Unimaginable Grief and Loss

PATRICK J. KENNY

DISCLAIMER

The information contained herein is not intended to be a substitute for professional evaluation and therapy with a mental health professional. If you are experiencing suicidal thoughts, you need to seek professional help immediately.

This book is based on the author's personal experience and other real-life examples. To protect privacy, names have been changed in some cases.

TAKING THE
CAPE OFF

HOW TO LEAD THROUGH MENTAL ILLNESS, UNIMAGINABLE GRIEF AND LOSS

PATRICK J. KENNY

GLOBAL WELLNESS MEDIA
STRATEGIC EDGE INNOVATIONS PUBLISHING
LOS ANGELES, TORONTO, MONTREAL

For permission requests, send an email to Book@PatrickJKenny.com

First Edition. Published by:
Global Wellness Media
Strategic Edge Innovations Publishing
340 S Lemon Ave #2027
Walnut, California 91789-2706
(866) 467-9090
StrategicEdgeInnovations.com

Publisher's Note: The views expressed in this work are solely those of the authors and do not necessarily reflect the views of the publisher, and the publisher hereby disclaims any responsibilities for them.

Editor: Sarah Aschenbach
Book Design: Eric D. Groleau
Cover Design: Aldren Gamalo

Taking the Cape Off / Patrick J. Kenny. – 1st ed.
ISBN: 978-1-7333385-8-5 (Kindle)
ISBN: 978-1-7333385-7-8 (Paperback)

TABLE OF CONTENTS

Part 1
DEALING WITH MENTAL ILLNESS

Part 2
SUICIDE, GRIEF, AND LOSS

Part 3

LEADING WITHOUT A CAPE

Part 4

"SIGNS" AND FEELING THE PRESENCE OF THE DECEASED

Part 5

MOVING FORWARD

DEDICATION

This book is dedicated to the two people who have taught me the most in my life, my wife Eileen and our son Sean. Their faith in me as a husband and a father continue to inspire me to be the person and leader I am today. I carry their torch to illuminate the path and to bring mental illness out of the darkness of its stigma into the light of hope.

INTRODUCTION

Mental illness, suicide, and loss are deeply personal and traumatic. Although not often talked about, mental illness is a serious public health issue that affects millions around the globe, either directly or indirectly. I have unfortunately experienced this trauma firsthand as a firefighter and a father.

As a father, the self-identified protector, I experienced the pain and helplessness of watching my son struggle with mental illness for most of his life. Everything changed in our lives the day we got the call from a police officer, saying, "There is no easy way to say this. We are very sorry to tell you that your son has been found dead." His death devastated our family. It challenged the bond of a healthy marriage, and I felt a wide range of emotions, including loss, grief, and shame. How do you move forward after the death of your child?

Once called to be a firefighter, I've always believed that God gives firefighters a "Cape" to go places and do things that others cannot or should not do to protect and save lives. As a fire chief, my number-one responsibility is to protect my extended family, the members of my department. As a father and husband, that number-one responsibility is to protect my blood family, my wife, and my three children. I faithfully put on that "Cape" every day with both families in mind. However, when the person I wanted to save the most was in a battle for his life, the Cape failed me.

I could not protect my youngest son Sean from his struggles with mental illness or save his life when he died by suicide at the age of only twenty. I felt I had failed in my most basic responsibility as the leader of our family—to protect my wife and children from harm. I felt embarrassed that in my career, I was expected to save lives, but I could not save the most important life of all, the life of my son. What kind of leader did that make me? How could my firefighters count on me to keep them safe when I couldn't even protect my son?

The heroic persona of a firefighter naturally leads to a tough-it-out mentality. Your role is to save the day, to fix it. Sometimes it has to be that way. However, I can tell you from experience that there is no way to tough out losing your child, whether by accident or illness. As a priest friend put it, "You just joined a fraternity no one wants to belong to." There was no roadmap for dealing with the loss of a child from mental illness, and it wasn't included in the fictitious parents' handbook. My wife, our two sons and I had to find our way through the fog. It took us time even to find a path to face the next day, and each of us in our own way struggled to move forward. I am still on that journey today and will continue to be until I can hug Sean again.

A year after Sean's passing, various fire service and community groups approached me to talk about my experience with mental illness, suicide, loss, and grief. I declined, as the experience was still too raw and emotional to talk about. No one was talking about suicide in my field because of the stigma associated with death by that method, especially when the root cause was mental illness. No one wanted to admit they'd lost a family member to suicide, let alone share the experience.

Three years after Sean's passing, through the persistence of a good friend who was the editor of a fire service magazine, I reluctantly agreed to write an article about my journey and the lessons learned. My motivation was a direct result of having read an article by a young firefighter who was battling cancer. His article detailed with painful honesty the fears and challenges of facing a terminal illness. His courage to let people peek behind the Cape of a first responder and reveal the lessons he learned awakened me to what a gift it was to offer that experience to others with cancer. I wondered if I could do the same for mental health and suicide in Sean's honor. I didn't want his life experiences and his death to be in vain. So, I took a shot and wrote the article.

A few months later, I received a request from a close friend I had met years earlier at the National Fire Academy to speak publicly at a symposium for educators who teach firefighters across the country. He believed that the topic of mental health needed to be included in the educational curriculum of all firefighters.

That first talk was shaky at best. I couldn't get through more than three PowerPoint slides without crying. Although my emotions had interfered with my delivery, I was amazed at how many were touched in some way by mental illness. I could see the hurt in their eyes. Some came up afterward to profess their pain or share similar experiences. It was a profound shift in thinking for many participants. Sharing the information, even just speaking out about it, had challenged the stigma.

My message was this: Mental illness is a proven physical illness, not a character weakness, and indeed it is not a choice any more than one chooses cancer.

Honestly, I thought and prayed that first talk was my last. But to my surprise, the unsolicited demand for speaking engagements grew. "If you build it, he will come," as they say in the movie *Field of Dreams,* became "If you speak it, they will ask."

My wife Eileen was by my side, encouraging me to continue to proclaim Sean's story to help others and give meaning to his suffering by sharing the journey. It was draining and painful each time I presented, each time I exposed for all in the audience to hear what I felt was my failure as the leader of my family. I was comforted by Eileen's and Sean's presence. I literally could feel Sean on stage with me, bolstering my trust that his death indeed had not been in vain. His life's mission was to serve a higher purpose, that of educating those who couldn't grasp the truth about mental illness.

For more than ten years, I've been sharing Sean's story around the country and abroad, including Canada and the UK. The goal has been to provide resources and information to others in personal or professional leadership positions who may be dealing with mental illness themselves in their families or in the workplace. I focus on challenging people's views on mental health and in particular their attitude toward those afflicted with mental health challenges. Even more critical, I strive to combat the stigma that those who have mental illness are somehow different than any other person with a physical illness. Nobody chooses to suffer from a mental illness; it's no different from cancer—it chooses you.

Ten years later, just after our son Patrick announced his engagement, our family was again dealt a devastating blow. Without any real symptoms or warning, my wife was diagnosed with glioblastoma, an incurable brain cancer that consisted of nine inoperable tumors throughout her brain. Friends and family were unbelievably supportive throughout Eileen's battle with cancer. People rallied and prayed, not only to help her fight but also for my sons and me. Within ten months of her diagnosis, she went back home to heaven precisely one week to the day before Patrick's wedding. We had a wake on a Monday, a funeral on Tuesday, a rehearsal dinner on Friday, and a wedding on Saturday.

It took time to accept her loss. I was confronted with the same feelings of failure I had about Sean. The devastation of losing both my son and now my best friend and wife of thirty-five years was another massive tear in my Cape and a sickening reminder that it had let me down once again when I needed it most. My "protect your wife and children" mission had been dealt yet another blow; in my perception, it was another catastrophic failure on my part as the leader of the family. Whoever says you need to create a new normal after a significant loss has never been through one because there is no "normal" again. Instead, you must learn to adapt and survive in a new situation. You don't move on; you move forward.

There was irony in this loss. About three years before Eileen's diagnosis, I had shared with her my frustration that some in the audience didn't seem to comprehend and accept that mental illness is indeed a physical illness. Together, Eileen and I inserted a slide with a side-by-side comparison of mental illness to a physical diagnosis that people could recognize. We chose brain cancer, as it seemed the most logical. Cancer can physically affect the brain just as mental illness does. Feedback results revealed that including that slide comparison had proven to be even more effective than we had hoped.

I noticed a stark difference right away in how people reacted to my wife's cancer compared to Sean's mental illness and suicide, yet both were terminal illnesses. When my wife died, people were there to offer help, bring food, and embrace our family. Yet, when Sean died, people didn't know what to say, what to do, or how to act. I had to ask myself why people run to the aid of someone with cancer and yet ostracize those who suffer from mental health challenges, who are also in constant pain? Why the stigma around mental illness?

Our family counselor had warned us after Sean's passing that some people's reactions would border on rude or inappropriate. I, for one, didn't believe it. We were a popular family in the community with many wonderful friends and acquaintances, and yet some turned and went the other way when they saw me. I assume it was fear of not knowing what to say or how to approach me when all I needed was a hug. I learned the hard way that you can't fix the kind of pain I was experiencing, so don't try; just be present.

I am a spiritual guy, and all my life I have been fortunate to feel I have had "signs" sent from those on the other side to guide me or lend support. The signs came to affirm that I was on the right track, even amid failure and significant pain. That last week before my wife died, Sean appeared to her in our bedroom and said, "Mom, I'm coming to get you." That sign was both a relief and a warning; the end was indeed near.

During her last week, Eileen gave me a talk about several do's and don'ts when she was gone. One, I was to continue to spread Sean's message that mental illness isn't a weakness or a choice, but a physical illness. I was to continue to smash that stigma out of my Cape-wearing profession and others, as this prejudice is certainly not exclusive to the fire service. "If you touch even one person in the audience with Sean's story, with our story, it offers that person hope. If you let people know that they are not alone and give them resources and knowledge to help themselves or someone else, then you've made a difference. You are not a failure but a messenger." She made me promise to write this book. I flat-out said no, and I would not budge, even under those emotional circumstances. I told her I was no writer. So, we compromised. I said that I would at least try. She always was the smart one in our marriage!

I talk to both Sean and Eileen every day and know that they are together in heaven. As my son Pat has said, "We didn't lose Mom. We know exactly where she is!"

I have resumed the mission my wife and I began, sharing our story to reach as many people as I can. I think this is part of God's mission for me—to help others using Sean and Eileen's suffering to make them disciples of the message that having a mental illness is no different from being diagnosed with a disease like diabetes. You treat it, you manage it, and you live your life. I will not let the angels God gave me—albeit for a time too brief for my liking—to die in vain.

This book is for individuals who are leaders in their community or family, no matter how designated (i.e., Fire Chief, CEO, Dad, Mom, single parent) who have directly or indirectly dealt with or are currently dealing with mental illness, loss, or grief. Too often, we get lost in the designated role of leader. That loss of identity as a human being versus your role as a leader can cause you to stifle your right to the human emotions of grief, loss, and depression. And if God forbid, you allow yourself to feel these natural emotions, you may somehow equate feeling with failing. If you feel you always have to be "super" and struggle to see yourself as deserving the very compassion you give to others in similar situations, this book is for you.

This book is also for families with a loved one who is struggling with mental illness or who have lost that loved one to suicide. When your child is born with or develops a mental health illness, there is no parents' handbook on how to understand and support that child. And there is certainly no guidance on what to do when that child decides that no life is better than the daily painful life he is leading. For these children, suicide is not a matter of wanting to take their lives, but a choice to keep living them each day.

Finally, this book is for those seeking hope of something beyond this life, regardless of what you call it or where you think it is. Somewhere out there, are our loved ones again free from the anguish of mental illness, and do they wait for us there? Do they send "signs" to affirm or guide us in our lives, or is that my imagination or wishful thinking? I will share real-life experiences so that you may contemplate the answer to that question.

A few months after my wife Eileen passed away, a good friend gave me a plaque. She said, "I thought of you as soon as I saw this." The plaque read: *Real Heroes Don't Wear Capes.* It is the message of this book. You don't have to, nor can you, shoulder the heavy burden of pain and loss alone. As a leader in any capacity, you must accept that you will not be able to "fix" everything, whether at work or home, and that's okay! What you can do is offer your constant support and hope by embracing and acknowledging that others' pain is genuine and we welcome and support them, no matter what.

HOW TO USE THIS BOOK

There are many excellent books on loss and grief written by authors who are trained professionals in that field. I am just a Dad/Husband and Fire Chief, nothing special. I have a degree in psychology, but about that my mom always said, "What a waste of money that was. Smart people run out of burning buildings, and my bullheaded Irish son runs in!" I believe the power in this book comes from my willingness to open my heart to you in a completely honest and candid manner as an everyday Leader/Dad/Husband. I thought I could save the world and was brought to my knees because I felt I failed to protect two people I loved dearly, my son and my wife. What makes this book different is my willingness to hit head-on the reality that when mental illness is the catalyst behind the suffering, loss, and grief of one you swore to protect, your feelings of ineptitude and ultimately of failure are magnified.

I believe you will come to recognize that those who suffer from mental health challenges are beautiful and courageous people who are not weaker or more responsible for their illnesses than someone who is diagnosed with a terminal physical illness. Their disease is not something you can see, like a tumor on an X-ray, but it is just as real, and it needs your support and medical treatment.

The general population of leaders, fortunately, has not experienced the emotional roller coaster of losing a child and a spouse, so think of this book as a reference guide. Turn to a specific chapter to help you with what you or someone you know is experiencing. Give it to a fellow leader/friend who is suffering when you don't know what to say or do that might be helpful. That gesture alone lets them know that they are not alone in their pain. Establishing a connection is powerful.

So now, all you leaders, I invite you to discover how to take the Cape off without guilt.

ADDITIONAL MATERIALS & RESOURCES

Access your additional materials & resources
referenced throughout this book at:

https://patrickjkenny.com/bookbonus

Part 1

DEALING WITH MENTAL ILLNESS

I Wanted to Die

I was fourteen years old, my life had come crashing down on me, and I just wanted to die. What series of events led me to this?

I was nearing the end of junior high, and I was excited about an opportunity to attend high school and hopefully play both football and baseball. It was July of 1971 when this journey turned from a dream to real-life challenges. On July 20th, I was walking back from a shopping mall with a couple of my friends after buying new football spikes that I wanted to break in before high school tryouts. Two single lines of traffic were backed up at a busy intersection, and we crossed between the vehicles. I went first. What I didn't see was a shoulder beyond the second line of cars, and as I stepped out, a vehicle racing up that shoulder to avoid the traffic backup, struck me.

HIT BY A CAR

The car caught my right knee with its bumper, and it smashed violently into my left knee. I spun along the side of the vehicle and fell behind it. I remember seeing a yellow streak right before impact, and then I woke up behind the tailpipe. I looked up, thinking I was having a bad dream. A considerable crowd had assembled, looking horrified, and my friends were long gone.

Reality hit when I tried to sit up and couldn't feel anything from my waist down. I was rushed to a local hospital, and my Mom and Dad were called. Now, my Mom and Dad, having been born in Ireland, had never obtained their drivers' licenses, so they had to get a ride to the hospital.

I was diagnosed with trauma to both legs, but luckily, X-rays showed nothing but a little circular object shaped like a dime in my left knee. Otherwise, I was good to go. I was sent home with instructions for my Dad to periodically wake me up and walk me, hopefully, to negate some of the effects of the trauma on my muscles and to relieve the feeling that I couldn't use them.

So that night, we did just that. My Dad would get me up, and I would try to walk from the bedroom to the bathroom, but the pain was intense, and I kept passing out. I developed a fever, and in the middle of the night, my Mom called our general practitioner. "This doesn't sound right," he said, and had me rushed to another hospital. There, another series of X-rays were taken, with vastly different results. My legs were shattered, both kneecaps were in pieces, and the only thing left intact was part of one kneecap the size of a dime. My left knee had several torn ligaments, and the doctor was concerned that I would never walk again.

Imagine your typical smart-ass eighth-grader. I'd thought I had everything figured out: I was going to play both football and baseball in high school. I had pictured in my mind two different sets of cheerleaders at these games and me running out of the tunnel for football, the prettiest cheerleader of all calling out my name and wanting to be my girlfriend. And when I went behind the plate in the spring, a different cute girl would be watching, and she would care only about me. Now, instead, I was faced with the fact that I might not walk again and certainly would not be running out of any tunnel or getting into any crouch any time soon, if ever.

I believe angels are sent into our lives at times like this to mitigate pain and suffering and put you on God's track. That was the case for me. The doctor who was assigned to me, Dr. James Lambur, was a fairly new orthopedic physician at the time. After a few days of being packed in ice to reduce the swelling, Dr. Lambur performed surgery, and I was placed in toe-to-thigh casts and sent home to lie in bed for the next couple of months.

I had a lot of time to think, and my thoughts were never positive. I felt that my dreams had been crushed through one careless act, and this undoubtedly challenged my faith. Why me? When the casts came off, I saw that all the muscle I had built was gone. Nothing left but two bony legs. I was in a wheelchair for a while after that. It made me so angry to see the look of pity on people's faces as they passed by that I was determined to walk again.

I have several common themes in my life, and one is that if you tell me I can't do something, then you'd better get out of my way while I show you I can. Looking back now, I think those looks of pity might have been power pills sent by God to keep me going. To this day, I can recall some of those faces and sometimes use them as fuel to climb over what seems like an impossible challenge.

I started my freshman year in high school that Halloween, maybe appropriately. I was on crutches, academically two months behind everybody else, didn't know my way around the school, and truly felt like a fish out of water. As the holidays approached, I was doing intense physical therapy and I was able to get off the crutches. The ship seemed to be settling—at least it was not sinking anymore—and then my world got rocked again.

MY DAD'S SUDDEN ILLNESS

Dad enjoyed eating, and on special occasions such as Christmas, my mom made roast duck for him. That Christmas Eve, I received a tape recorder. On Christmas Day, we watched what would be the longest game in NFL history, between the Kansas City Chiefs and the Miami Dolphins, and tried to get Mom to speak so we could record her voice without her knowing. Later, we played it back. How heartily my dad had laughed, how much I enjoyed our time together!

Dad was a hard charger, a no-nonsense guy. He never really told me he loved me or gave me big hugs. His way was more of a push or a shove or a good-natured punch in the arm. But somehow, I always knew he did love me. I didn't understand until sometime later why he had put up that emotional distance.

The day after Christmas, Dad didn't feel very well. As I look back, I remember that he didn't eat much of the duck on Christmas day, and sometime early that evening I heard him throwing up in the bathroom. I knocked on the door and went in, and I remember seeing large blood clots in the sink. He was yellow, and for the first time in my entire life, I saw some fear on his face. I said, "Dad, I think we need to call the ambulance." He said, "You're right; tell your mom to do that."

My Dad had grown up in Ireland and was not very trusting of doctors. The last thing he ever wanted to do was see one. So, for him to so willingly agree that he would go in an ambulance should have been a bright-red flag that something was seriously wrong. But I didn't pick up on that at the time.

The ambulance came to get him. As he was being carried out on a stretcher, he stuck out his arms when they got to the front door, blocking the stretcher from clearing the door. My Dad had gained a lot of weight but was still a big muscular guy with large hands and massive shoulders. He had no trouble stopping the firefighters from carrying him out the door. I remember seeing tears in his eyes. I had only seen my father cry one other time, when he lost his brother. That night as he blocked the door, I vividly remember him saying, "I'll never be back here again." I ran up to the stretcher and told him in a stern tone, "You're going to be just fine. The doctors just need to take care of you. Don't worry." He let go of the doorframe, and they carried him out.

Mom took me to visit him a couple of days later. She had repeatedly told me that he was just a little sick and would be fine in a few days. When I arrived, that was not what I observed. My dad looked terrible, his skin was yellow, the whites of his eyes were also yellow, and he looked genuinely afraid. He made the sign of the cross over and over. I hugged him and said, "You'll be out of here in a few days, Dad. We'll get you all good."

On the ride home, I didn't believe he was going to be okay. Two weeks earlier, I'd had a dream of his wake. I saw him in a casket in a navy-blue suit, and I could smell the flowers. I woke up from that dream frightened and in tears and so thankful that it was only a dream.

Now I wondered if that had been a message to get ready for what was about to occur. On New Year's Eve, my mom specifically invited over a good friend of mine so I would not be alone. Barely after midnight, we were outside blowing off fireworks when my mom came out and said the hospital had called and she needed to go. I felt nauseated; in my heart, I knew what that phone call meant even though she had tried to sound upbeat.

There was no word in the morning about my dad's condition. My mom came through the door sometime in the very early afternoon. I took one look at her face and said, "Dad's gone, isn't he?" and she broke down. She said, "How do you know?" and I said, "I knew it a while ago."

SUDDEN LOSS

When you grow up Irish-Catholic, one of the things that comes along with that is guilt. I think it's in the genes. At that moment, even more than the sense of loss, I felt guilty. I felt guilty that I had not told my dad I loved him when I had seen him in the hospital. In my heart, I had known he was dying, and I just was too afraid to say it because I didn't want him to be frightened. Now, I had missed that opportunity.

Two days later, when I walked into the funeral parlor, the scene was the same as in my dream, down to every detail: the way my dad looked, the color of his suit, and the smell of the flowers. Looking back, I believe God was telling me, "Get ready, kid; you're going to need to get everything in order because here's what's coming."

After Dad was buried, the doctor told us that Dad had stomach cancer, that most of his stomach had been eaten away, and that he had died of a massive hemorrhage on that January 1st morning. The plan had been to operate and take out his entire stomach. It was the only thing they could do. He would never have been able to eat again and would've lived a much different life than he had previously enjoyed. We were told that he must have been in an incredible amount of pain, which reminded me that his drinking had increased a lot over the past year. He was self-medicating to treat that pain. I did not know at the time that this would not be my last experience with self-medication.

At that point, I didn't know how to feel, whether to be angry that he hadn't gone to the doctor or just devastated that he was gone. What was pretty clear, however, was that I was expected to step up. I had become the man of the house, starting at the wake. That day, I'd sneak off to the bathroom and sob and then come back out to the gathered mourners and be the dutiful, strong son, standing tall, the way I thought my dad would want. Yet, what hurt the most was overhearing a few people say after they passed me at the casket, "They must not have had a very close relationship. He doesn't even look like he cares." They could not have been more wrong.

VOICE FROM BEYOND

In the span of five months, I had been told I might never walk again and lost my fantasy of playing two professional sports, and I had lost my hero, my dad, who I envisioned being in the stands to cheer me on. Every dream and the things I loved had been crushed.

I went back to high school a week later. The school bus passed right by the cemetery where my dad was buried. After that first week back, I decided I needed to go to his grave. So, one day, on the way home from school, I got off the bus there.

It was a cold, sunny day after a snowstorm. The wind chill was in the single digits. I was nearing the end of physical therapy, so I could walk on my own, but not for long distances and not well. I had to walk about a mile and a half to where he was buried, and it took everything I had to make it there.

It wasn't hard to find the grave because it was the only one not covered in snow. As I stood there looking down, I was thinking that from July 20th to January 1st, my whole world had been destroyed. Gone were all my dreams of being a sports hero with a tremendous following and the biggest fan of all, my dad, standing in the stands, being proud of me, reliving his heroic sports efforts as an all-national hurler in Ireland. All I could see for my future was black. Dad was, I hoped, in a place called heaven, and I remained behind in a place called hell with no dreams and no hope.

I dropped my book bag and lay down on it on the adjacent grave and waited to die. I believed it was cold enough that I would go to sleep and literally freeze to death. I wanted to go where he was. I couldn't take the pain of my life, which in my mind was already over. There was no alternative for going on with life, so why not end it? I was going to die right there. I was going to die right next to my hero.

Let's step back here and look at this moment. This was about to be another devastating loss from my mom's perspective. Here's a woman who lost her husband suddenly, has only one child, and this child, if he gets his wish, is now going to present her five days later with another devastating loss, one he *chose* to make happen.

When people who are not familiar with suicide reflect on it, they categorize it as a cowardly and selfish act. The people who are left behind are devastated, and that part is true. The part about it being cowardly is entirely wrong and is a horrible stigma that follows mental health to this day. Here is the truth about it. At the moment you are in that spot, it is dark, and you can see no alternative to escape that pain but that one. You are not thinking about anyone else or any other effects from your action because, if you could focus on that, you would not be in such desperation.

So, I lay down to die, and I was all good with that. "Boy, I hope there's a heaven," I thought, "and I hope all that Catholic stuff is correct. But even if it isn't, at least I won't be in pain anymore. If there is a heaven and Dad is pissed with me, I'll deal with it when I get there." I remember thinking I was being quite rational. I lay down, and I started to get sleepy. I thought how great it was that I was only fourteen, but I had figured out that the sleepy feeling was the start of freezing to death.

My Aunt Mary was another mother to me. She had suffered multiple miscarriages and never had a child of her own. She lived with us from the time I was an infant. With my death, she would have lost the only son she knew and helped to raise. I didn't think about her. I didn't think about my friends and what it would do to them after they had helped me recover both physically and emotionally. All I cared about right then was that I was in incredible pain and I wanted it to stop. The world was dark. There was no hope. I wanted to find my Dad. I believed there was a heaven, and I was going to go there as quickly as I could.

I thought it wouldn't take long. I'll fall asleep, and that wouldn't be a bad way to die. I started to get cold and drowsy. Then, for the first of many times through the years, I heard an angel's voice, and this time it was my father, and I heard his voice say:

"You need to get up."

"This is good!" I thought. "I must be getting close to dying. I'm starting to hear things." Then I heard it again, except this time, it was precisely the way Dad would talk to me when he was very angry with me. In a stern voice, almost a yell, I heard loud and clear:

"You need to get up!"

Of course, there is no way you can hear a dead man yelling at you. I thought it might be oxygen deprivation since I was about to pass out from hypothermia. Whatever you want to call it, sign or hallucination, I no longer felt peaceful or good about my decision. Startled, I quickly sat up and looked at Dad's grave, and I was sure he was standing there and shouting, "You need to get up and get out of here!"

I stood up. I realized I had to leave, but I was already freezing and stiff. My legs hurt because I had pushed myself beyond endurance to reach the gravesite. Now, I had to make my way back out of that cemetery. I went from feeling calm and peaceful and wanting to die to being cold and afraid that I *was* going to die. Ironic. I went there to die, and now I was struggling to get out of there alive. (Plus, I'm sure I was scared that if I did die, I'd see my Dad on the other side and if I wasn't already dead, he would kill me!)

Somehow, I made my way out of there and into a little coffee shop across from the cemetery. There were no cell phones then, so I called Aunt Mary on a payphone. "I got off the bus to see Dad, and I'm going to need a ride home." Without question, she came, got me, and took me home.

INSIDE THE SUICIDAL MIND

I tell my story because it's a great example of what suicidal thoughts are like from the viewpoint of the suffering person. All I cared about was the devastating pain, and the only way I could see to get out of it was not to be alive anymore.

As the leader in your organization, whether your family or work, or in a support role for those suffering any terminal illness, including mental illness, you must realize that the focus is on the one who is struggling, not on you. It is not a matter of you saving them, because maybe you can't. Instead, the greatest gift you can give them is to love and accept them unconditionally. Even when you don't understand their illness, you can acknowledge that their pain is genuine and reinforce those supportive thoughts every day.

I FELT ASHAMED

In all the years since that suicide attempt, I never told Aunt Mary and Mom the truth about why I went to the cemetery that day. I felt ashamed that I had let them down. I had let my Dad down.

Things I didn't do: I didn't seek any counseling, which I desperately needed. I didn't let people know about my pain, which could have helped me see it as normal after what I had experienced. Could I have benefited from counseling? You bet I could have. Could it have helped me with some of the pain that I went through in high school, feeling bad about myself, who I was, and my purpose? Oh boy, it would have been an incredible help.

Back then, much like now, there was a stigma about seeking help. It was thought to reflect weakness. There I was, the man of the house at fourteen years old, so I certainly couldn't be weak. I was caught in that idea and consumed by the feeling that I didn't want to let my Dad down.

I went through this journey of considering suicide by myself, working through it alone as I rationalized that I couldn't tell anybody or seek any help. I just pushed through it because I was the "leader" of our house. I learned early on to don the Cape and lock emotions of loss and being powerless in the phone booth. In many situations the Cape carried me through the darkest moments to a place where I could at least function. It became a pattern of life in general, and in particular, it was a pattern of leadership that I adopted: Big boys don't cry. As a human being and a leader, that mode of operation was often effective for surviving traumatic situations, *but it was not always the healthiest choice.*

My accident and my Dad's passing certainly created significant bumps that tested my faith from an early age. I'm a big believer in signs, and somewhere in that voice of my Dad telling me to get up was the message: "You aren't doing what you are supposed to be doing, so we are going to figure out something else for you." I hung onto that message from that point forward. I had desperately needed a sign, and I got it. The sign gave me hope that there was indeed an afterlife and someone or some higher power was running the show. After all, my Dad was there!

EVERYTHING HAPPENS FOR A REASON

I think my suicide attempt was meant to be. I honestly believe that everything happens for a reason. I don't have to like the reason, and most of the time I don't understand the logic. Sometimes I see the "why" only after the fact, many years later.

Today, I see why I took that journey to the cemetery. I see why feeling so desperate that I wanted to take my own life was necessary. Now, when somebody tells me they feel that anguish, I understand. Everyone's perception is different, but deciding you would rather be dead than to live as you are—I get it. I have no judgment towards anyone who has attempted or succeeded in dying by suicide. I have lived it.

I went on to receive my degree from Loyola University in psychology. I met a wonderful woman named Eileen, and we got married. We were both teachers during the first few years of our marriage. Eileen's most powerful wish was to be a mother. We had decided before we got married that we wanted to start a family right away so we could enjoy our children in their teen years while we were still young enough to be active with them. When the time came, Eileen would be a stay-at-home mom, and I would be the breadwinner.

God blessed us in a short amount of time with three wonderful sons, Brendan, Patrick, and Sean. I was hired as a firefighter the month before our oldest was born, so all three boys were born into a firefighting family. When our last son, Sean, was born, life couldn't have been any better. I had three wonderful boys who brought various gifts to the family table, a great wife, and a career I was proud to be a part of and thoroughly enjoyed. That fourteen-year-old who almost took his life because he had no hope had climbed to the top of life's mountain where the sun shone bright.

I did not know at fourteen that the experience of being ready to take my life, despite having so many things to live for, is what led me to the education I would need as a leader of my family and the leader of my fire department. That horrible journey was intended for me. It was critical to understanding the excruciating mental pain that would drive a child to take his life. Without that, I'm not sure I would have had any empathy, much less understanding, of what I was about to face in my life as a dad and a leader when our youngest son Sean, who was mentally ill, took his life at the age of twenty.

13

LESSONS LEARNED

- **Don't be afraid to tell the truth.** If a parent is very ill, don't give a child false hope. Tell the truth. They are more durable than you think and can sense things you don't give them credit for, so address the situation.
- **As a child, it's okay to grieve.** If you are the child who loses a parent at a young age, you don't have to "take their place" and be a grown-up. It is okay and necessary to grieve your loss as a child.
- **Being present provides comfort, while words often fail.** The tragic loss of a parent, child, or spouse can cause people of all ages to say and do things that appear rude. It's not that they lack empathy for your loss; rather, they are acting out of ignorance. No one teaches us what to say or not say during such painful encounters. A silent hug is powerful; try it sometime.
- **Seek counseling.** Tragedy, compounded by a lack of support, can lead to deep depression and anxiety about even wanting to be alive. Regardless of age, you need to seek counseling to deal with that loss. Everyone grieves differently, and it helps to have a "guide" to get you on your path.
- **Grief and loss have no timeline or expiration date.** Whether you deal with these feelings at the time or years later, at some point you will have to face them. I believe it is best to get counseling right away and maintain the kind of relationship you have with a good mechanic. When your mind's "check engine light goes on," have your counselor's number available. Periodic psychological maintenance is a good thing.
- **Contemplating suicide is not a selfish act.** It is an act borne out of seeing no other alternative to pain.
- **Everything happens for a reason.** You may know it at the time, years later, or never, but there is a higher power in charge and angels on the other side to help guide you. You just have to believe.

Chapter 2

Child Diagnosis of Depression

When Sean was five, he was diagnosed with clinical depression. I didn't know that could happen. Yes, I knew a child could get upset if you took his bike away or he didn't get an extra scoop of ice cream, but I had no idea that a five-year-old could suffer from depression.

I have come to learn from reading that childhood depression is different from the normal sadness of adjusting to growing up and facing the ups and downs of life. Just because a child seems sad doesn't mean that he or she has significant depression.

However, it could be a sign of depressive illness when the sadness becomes:

- Persistent and
- Interferes with normal social activities, interests, schoolwork, or family life

It is important to know that while depression is a serious illness, it is also treatable.

THE SIGNS

A constant theme that you'll encounter in this book is that Eileen noticed the signs first. Two things were striking:

- Sean colored all in black; he never used the other colors in the crayon box.
- Sean had a pair of shoes with Velcro closures that he wore to kindergarten. In the late 1980s and early 1990s, these shoes were a big deal for little kids, so he wanted to wear them every day. I thought it was because he liked them. I had no idea at

that time of the significance. When Sean put the shoes on, he strapped and unstrapped one shoe and then the other maybe fifty times, no exaggeration, before he went to school. If you interrupted him for any reason, he'd have what I'd called a temper tantrum with inconsolable crying and anger.

Years later, I learned that what I had labeled a tantrum was an anxiety or panic attack. I didn't see it that way at all: I saw him as just a headstrong kid like his dad; needed to be disciplined; the child is not in charge!

Eileen didn't read it that way. She knew it was not normal, and so she took him to the pediatrician. The pediatrician then referred him to a psychologist, who ran some basic diagnostic tests. From the results, Sean was diagnosed and given medication and periodic counseling to deal with the diagnosis of clinical depression. Clinical depression is the more severe form of depression, also known as major depression or major depressive disorder. It isn't the same as depression caused by a loss, such as the death of a loved one. Also, the need to wear those shoes every day was an early sign of obsessive-compulsive disorder, a diagnosis that Sean would receive in junior high.

The literature on depression in children states that the illness often goes undiagnosed and untreated because "incidents" like what happened with the Velcro shoes are accepted as normal emotional changes that occur during growth. Early medical studies focused on "masked" depression, where a child's depressed mood was shown by acting out or displaying angry behavior. This display of anger did occur for Sean when he was interrupted, but many children display sadness or a low mood similar to adults who are depressed. After all, children are mini-adults. So, I didn't read it as depression, but as Sean's Irish temper.

The primary symptoms of depression revolve around:

- Sadness
- A feeling of hopelessness, and
- Mood changes

THE CAUSES

Now, think back to my perception of myself as the heroic persona that was this firefighter, the guy wearing the Cape. I couldn't possibly have a five-year-old child who's got depression, who's on medication. Are you kidding me? Not my kid. I mean, what could have caused this?

When I looked up the answer to that question, I found out that, just like in adults, depression in children can be caused by any combination of factors. Some of these factors include:

- Physical health
- Life events
- Family history
- Environment
- Genetics
- Biochemical disturbance

Remember, depression is a physical illness, not a passing mood, and if it persists, it is not a condition that will go away without proper treatment.

FAMILY HISTORY

Children with a family history of depression are at greater risk of experiencing depression themselves. Children whose parents suffer from depression tend to develop their first episode of depression earlier than children whose parents do not. My grandfather in Ireland took his life by suicide. As time went on, I dug into our family medical history to find that depression and other mental health challenges occurred on both sides of our families.

I had to ask many questions, because no one wants to admit they have a family member who is struggling with a mental illness. This is due to the stigma that it is a choice driven by weakness, and not a physical illness. Even when asked, families don't openly share mental health as a possible pre-existing medical condition as one would share a history of cardiac or cancer issues. This is because of the shame

17

attached to it. Also, children from chaotic or conflicted families, or children and teens who abuse substances like alcohol and drugs, are at greater risk of depression.

The sad part for me is that I can honestly say I didn't link any of those family history situations to Sean's symptoms until many years into his illness. One reason is because no one had ever talked about them. I didn't find out about my grandfather's suicide until I was in my early thirties, and then only because Mom "slipped" one day and told me.

Even very young children may show early warning signs of mental health concerns. These mental health problems are often clinically diagnosable and can be a product of the interaction of biological, psychological, and social factors. Half of all mental health disorders show first signs before a person turns fourteen years old, and three-quarters of mental health disorders begin before age twenty-four.

Unfortunately, less than 20 percent of children and adolescents with diagnosable mental health problems receive the treatment they need.

TREATMENT

Early in Sean's journey, the illness easily could have driven a wedge between Eileen and me, since she was "all in" and I was "all out" as to what was going on. She was always the smarter of us when it came to life. It tests a marriage when your child's well-being is on the line and you're not on the same page about it. If you are in this situation, please be aware that open, honest, and non-judgmental communication is crucial to the survival of that marriage.

I went along with the diagnosis and treatment only because I thought it would make my wife feel better. My attitude was that it would all go away, and "it's not a big deal." Thus, there wasn't a strain in our relationship in the early stages because I was in complete denial.

This pattern continued consistently through Sean's seventh grade. Now, Sean was incredibly intelligent and athletic, and he had a great sense of humor. From the outside, no one would ever have known what was going on; but on the inside, he was being torn apart. If you're an adolescent who struggles with mental illness, as your hormones change, it's like throwing gasoline on a fire. Things get worse and worse. He was diagnosed with obsessive-compulsive disorder, which I thought was just about washing your hands too many times. I had no idea about the power of intrusive thoughts and what they could do, not only then, but later.

We were heading into the teen years, and we had no idea that the worst part of the journey was yet to come.

LESSONS LEARNED

- **Children are not immune to disease.** Children of all ages can be afflicted with mental illness.
- **Be aware of signs in your child that seem extreme or out-of-the-ordinary.**
- **Children are little adults.** They experience the same emotions as adults, both positive and negative.
- **Speak to your doctor.** Talk to your family physician if you are concerned that your child might have a mental illness. Parental instincts should not be dismissed by the parent or the doctor, so if you feel your child needs help, push until they get it. That doctor can then guide you to a mental health professional if need be.
- **Early intervention is key.** As with any physical illness, the earlier a mental illness is diagnosed, the sooner treatment can begin, and a positive outcome becomes more likely.
- **Children who have mental illness are not weak.** There can be many causes for a child to have a mental illness, but being weak is not one of them. Don't let the stigma attached to mental illness keep you from having your child examined.

Chapter 3

Teen Years and Mental Illness

The day before high school was to begin when Sean was just short of his fourteenth birthday, he said to my wife and me as we were about to climb in the car, "I can't do this. I just can't do this anymore."

"Sean," I said, "it's no big deal. High school—being nervous on the first day—that's normal, and your two brothers are there, and they'll look out for you. Freshmen are usually targets of pranks, like paying for things that don't exist, like buying a pool pass when the school has no pool. So don't buy an elevator pass, because there is no elevator in your school, and you'll be just fine."

"No, I mean it. I just can't do this anymore." As was the pattern in our house, Eileen was always so much more perceptive. She said, "Wait a minute, Pat. Let him talk. What do you mean?"

"I don't want to live anymore."

Now, the fire department I worked on was only four blocks away from a hospital, and unfortunately, we responded to a lot of mental health emergencies. It was routine to be called at two o'clock in the morning; it was often a panic attack or somebody was upset. To dispatch, based on initial symptoms, it often appeared to be a cardiac event, but once we had assessed the patient, we would see that it wasn't cardiac at all, but something related to mental illness.

In this case, our patient care consisted of putting the person on a cot and taking him to the hospital. Once there, we got into one of a bank of four white elevators, went up to the fourth floor and got out. The patient was helped off the cot, had all his clothes and belongings taken away, was put in a hospital gown, and then disappeared behind a door.

I remember being frustrated and angry about these situations. Did the person have to wait until two o'clock in the morning to call? Couldn't he have had this attack at noon? I knew I'd be exhausted. I was anxious to go home because I had to teach or take care of the kids or whatever, and this person who had intruded on me was now in a group of other losers behind that door.

SCARED STRAIGHT DOESN'T WORK

Brilliant dad that I was in those days, I decided I would scare Sean to see just how serious he was. I said, "You do realize that by saying you want to hurt yourself, you are making it necessary for me to take you to the hospital. Once we get there, they have to lock you in and keep you, because you're talking about hurting yourself."

"Yeah, I know," he said, looking at both of us. He walked around to the front of the car, opened the passenger door, got in, and closed it. I stood there in front of the car, wondering what had just happened, and now that he had called my bluff, what I was going to do.

We took him to the hospital. We stood in front of that bank of four elevators. We went up to the fourth floor. He got out, he went into the other room, he had his clothes, shoes, and everything else taken away so that he wouldn't have anything like shoelaces or a belt to take his life, and then he too, disappeared behind that door.

This time was very different for me. For the first time, I didn't think of the people on the other side of that door as losers, because my son was not a loser. He was a great son, like his two brothers. It finally dawned on me that the people on the other side of that door were great people, too. Mothers and fathers, lawyers, doctors, accountants, plumbers, you name it, just regular people who are ill, physically ill. They are no different than anyone else in the hospital except that they were locked away as if mental illness was somehow a choice they had made or due to something weak about their character.

I felt sick to my stomach, not just because my son, at almost fourteen, was now behind that door, but because of the thoughts I'd had about those patients. I was also struck by the symbolism of the number 14. I was 14 when I lost my dad and thought about taking my life. Now, here was Sean, just weeks short of 14, thinking about taking his life. Still, the lightbulb didn't go on in this thick Irish skull about just how seriously ill Sean was.

At this point, I was Fire Chief, and I was considered successful. I led people out of danger. I couldn't have a kid with mental health issues. I had to fix this; that's what we firefighters did. After all, I had my Cape.

As a family, we worked diligently on this situation for the next few years as Sean completed high school. We were not very successful: constantly changing medications that had horrible side effects, all sorts of procedures, and numerous suicide attempts. It was a very, very painful time in our lives.

As the end of high school neared, we were exhausted, emotionally and financially. Insurance was useless when it came to mental health coverage. While others in my profession were buying summer cottages and boats, we were broke.

ILLEGAL DRUG USE

In the last semester of his senior year, Sean came to us and said, "I need help."

"Sean; I don't know what else we can do for you. We've done everything we can. What do you mean you need help?"

"I'm using drugs."

Immediately, I got angry. "You know, you can't do that. Those drugs sometimes negate the medications you're on, or sometimes they intensify them. You can't be messing around smoking that stuff when you're on those medications."

He said, "That's not what I'm doing."

"What do you mean that's not what you're doing?"

"I'm not using marijuana."

23

"So, what are you using?"

"Coke and heroin, among other things."

Now, we lived in a tiny house. We were a very close family; Sean had two great brothers and absolutely the best mom that had ever been put on the face of the earth, and none of us had seen it.

"Sean, why?"

"For that little time, I'm high, it's an escape from all the other pain. I know I can't go through life like this, but I need help to get clean."

TREATMENT CENTER

We put Sean in a dual-diagnosis treatment center called Rosecrance, some ninety minutes away from home. Dual-diagnosis treatment addresses both addiction and mental health problems. Frequently, the addiction is an attempt to self-medicate the pain of mental illness. Sean spent ninety days there.

During the time that Sean had been sick, which by then was thirteen years, I had never shared the extent of his illness with anyone. As I used to say many times, if he'd had brain cancer, I would have told everybody, and then my wife and my boys would have received support, and I would have, too. I liked to think it was my way of protecting him. I didn't want him to come into the firehouse or a family party and be looked down on, like, "Hey, there's the kid who's been in an institution. There's the kid who tried to kill himself."

I think there was some truth to that, but I also think it was partly because I didn't want the people in my fire department to know. If I couldn't even protect my own kid, why would they think I could protect them? Superman doesn't exist, does he? I'd be no more than a poor version of Clark Kent. I think I kept that secret to myself so I could still wear the Cape.

THE TATTOO

When Sean came out of rehab, it was one of those times as a parent when I learned about picking my battles, a lesson every parent and leader needs to consider. Sean wanted to get a tattoo, and I didn't want him to have it and was willing to battle on this even as he was getting ready to graduate from the program.

Eileen said to me, "Seriously, Pat? We've almost lost him how many times? He went through ninety-day rehab when he was old enough to sign himself out. He became a role model for other kids in there." That was Sean's pattern when he was hospitalized. He always took care of others, whether they were younger or older than he. He had a kind heart. He knew all too well that they were ill, not bad people. He just couldn't do the same for himself.

"And now we're going to quibble over a tattoo? Really?" As usual, Eileen was right. I wasn't seeing the big picture. He got the tattoo, and I hoped that his graduation from the program was a sign that we were moving forward. Now that he was clean, maybe those other medications that were supposed to help him would be effective.

THERE IS NO MAGIC PILL

Sean was again in search of that magic pill, the one thing that would make him feel better. You know what? So was I. Unfortunately, it just doesn't work that way because mental illness is a physical illness; it involves all these chemical reactions in your body. You need something that is a medication to help balance those chemicals. Yet, you must also have coping mechanisms. There is no magic wand. There is no Cape to save anyone in that situation. It's just not that simple. In fact, it is incredibly complicated.

Instead of coming forward, those suffering mental illness lock themselves out of any success they can have—and not by their choice: we have created that environment. We've created that negativity in the firehouse, at major corporations, in tiny shops, and in our own families.

We have created that stigma about mental health. We have boiled it down, simplified it to a "choice" that people make, and not an illness they suffer.

Sean's struggle throughout high school with mental illness took a toll. Our whole family went through four years of pure hell as he experimented with all sorts of different legal medications while he was trying many illegal methods that we didn't become aware of until he was eighteen. All of this was an effort to self-medicate.

TERMINAL

Once out of rehab, Sean started to get worse. He tried to go to college part-time, but couldn't, as he couldn't concentrate. I used to think it was baloney when I heard people who were depressed say that they were so tired they couldn't get out of bed. Well, this time I watched it. I watched him get exhausted just from going from our bathroom to the bedroom. He tried a part-time job, and because of the obsessive- compulsiveness he would do well in the beginning, work way too many hours, and then all of a sudden fall into exhaustion.

At one point in this journey, things were looking so dim by then that we took him to Mayo Clinic. The evaluation was not covered by insurance, so we had to borrow money to do it. He spent seven days there, where they did an extensive study of all of him, top to bottom, physically and mentally. At the end of it, they told my wife and me, "Your son is terminal."

I felt a certain sense of relief. "You found something. He's got a brain tumor, or what is it?" They shook their heads as if to say, "No, you don't get it," and they gave me an example.

"Let's say ten women come in with breast cancer. Same stage, same age, and we do the same treatment. Nine women respond incredibly, full recovery. One does not, and we don't know why, but the disease doesn't respond. We've looked at your son's medical record. He has tried every medication, every intervention, most of which he has researched himself, and none of them touch his depression, his anxiety, or his obsessive-compulsive disorder (OCD). You have no idea what his day is like, and each day he makes a choice to stay on this earth; each time he chooses not to go, but to stay. If we don't find something soon, something new that will give him hope; eventually he's going to die."

It was a long ride home from Rochester, Minnesota. Finally, when I got the courage up to ask Sean if the doctors talked to him, he said, "Yes, and for the first time, Dad, I believe that somebody believed me. They understood. They get it."

"But, Sean. You can't give up. You're too young. We'll find something." I was sure my Cape would rally at some time, in some way.

Later, he told Eileen, "Mom, when it gets bad enough, I'm going to do it for sure, because I can't take it anymore."

When we are in a struggle of any kind, whether it is mental health-related or just life, psychologists encourage us to journal, to write everything down and reflect on what we see, what we've done, what we might have learned, and where we might want to go.

I have included below a page from a journal I found just recently in Sean's room. The timeline clearly indicates the struggles he felt at an early age, the extremes to which he went for recognized treatment methods, but also his self-medication with illegal substances. It is painfully apparent how unsuccessful any method was in providing relief, as he also documents his multiple suicide attempts, including those he made after successfully completing his ninety-day treatment at Rosecrance.

SEAN'S TIMELINE

Sean created this timeline of all he had been through, including what occurred after his Rosecrance stay:

- Hospitalization locations: U of I, Cornell, Linden Oaks, Elgin, Hinsdale.
- Age 8: Anxiety, intrusive thoughts begin.
- Age 8: Diagnosed ADD, started Ritalin.

- Age 13: Depression sets in, suicide attempt, first psych ward Hinsdale Hospital, start anti-depressants and anti-anxiety medications.
- Age 13: Acne starts, intrusive thoughts become extremely bothersome, depression worsens, find relief in drugs and alcohol.
- Age 15: Drug use almost every day, start inhalants, overdose on clonazepam.
- Age 16: Outpatient drug rehab at Cornell.
- Age 17: Begin heroin use, then PCP, crack, cocaine, amphetamines painkillers, benzodiazepines.
- Age 18: Go into 90-day Rosecrance inpatient drug rehab.
- Age 18: Admitted to University of Chicago psych ward.
- Age 18: Go into Linden Oaks psych ward, get ECT treatments after a suicide attempt.
- Age 19: Go into Central DuPage psych ward after a suicide attempt.
- Age 19: Go into Elgin psych ward after a suicide attempt, undergo 16 rounds of ECT.
- Age 19: Outpatient drug rehab at Salt Creek.

We lived on this emotional rollercoaster as a family through three more suicide attempts after Rosecrance. Finally, I said, "Sean, you're going to have to be able to look me in the eye and say no more suicide attempts. I cannot have your mom find you. I can't have that happen to her."

He looked back at me with sad eyes. "I can't promise that, Dad."

"Well, then, you can't live here anymore."

The only alternative we had was to tell him he had to move out. I can't even explain the feeling of more or less throwing your child, who is very ill, out of your house, but we were at the end of our rope. We found an alternative place for him to live in a group home that provided a slight glimmer of hope because it offered a combination of treatment, counseling, and a supportive living environment.

A GROUP HOME

If you are looking for the easy way out by kicking your kid out and removing yourself from the problem, let me tell you it is not that easy or effective.

We weren't looking for easy; quite the opposite: we had tried every doctor, supported all the medication changes including the side effects that impacted not only Sean but our whole family: weight gain, extreme mood changes, anger, and sometimes just disappearing. In all of it, the hardest part was to watch him wasting away emotionally. You could see the hope drain right out of him.

When you have children, no one ever prepares you for the fact that someday you might have to tell a child they can't live with you. Now, there are a lot of things I'm going to refer to that are not in the "parents' handbook." Telling your kid that he has to move out while he's got a mental health illness is not in that handbook. But I knew he couldn't stay because I knew what was going to happen.

We researched and found a group home for him that had a counselor to monitor medications and provide some on-site counseling. The group home would provide a family atmosphere and would help to get residents schooling and jobs.

Needless to say, he didn't want to go, and this transition was butting right up against a big celebration that my wife and I had planned for our 25th wedding anniversary. We had been married on June 6, 1981, but we thought it would be awesome to go to Hawaii when the weather was horrible in Chicago instead of in the summer, so we planned to go during the first week of January 2006 instead of June. In mid-December of 2005, and we realized we couldn't go unless Sean was in that group home. We couldn't leave him at home. It looked like he was all set to be admitted. There were just a couple of things we needed to tidy up as we prepared to get on the plane, and we'd get them handled by the time we got settled in Hawaii.

Right after we landed, we were told that Sean had not been approved. We had just put our luggage away. I sat at the poolside bar, crying. "We need to go back home. We can't even celebrate our anniversary. We have never had a honeymoon; this is it, and we're going back home."

What I'm going to tell you provides the most accurate snapshot of Sean, the person—not Sean the person with an illness. Once he discovered he had not been admitted, he got his brother Brendan to take him out to buy a fax machine. Back then, it was unheard of to have a fax machine in your home. Sean then contacted the doctor. He got the paperwork he needed faxed to our home and then he faxed it to the group home.

Within less than twenty-four hours, he had successfully gotten himself admitted, and we knew we didn't need to come home. It was the greatest 25th wedding anniversary anybody could ever have been given. What he did was proof of the relentless love of a son who hated the thought of going into that group home but who put his parents' needs first. That was Sean Kenny.

We enjoyed that time. We felt Sean was in a safe place. We knew it was not what we wanted, but we had to refuel somehow, because when you're dealing with somebody who has a mental health challenge, it sucks the life out of you. The emotional bank account goes dry because you're not putting in any deposits. You're doing nothing but withdrawals. This was a huge deposit for us. We came back with more energy and with new hope. Unfortunately, this respite and feeling of hope was extremely short-lived.

LESSONS LEARNED

- **Mental illness does not discriminate.** Don't think just because you are a leader, your family or co-workers' children are immune to mental illness.
- **Believe they are in pain,** not just looking for attention.
- **You can't "tough out" mental illness;** it must be treated.

- **Mental Illness is a physical illness.** Realize and accept that those who suffer from mental illness are wonderful people who have a physical illness that needs treatment.
- **Mental illness can be terminal.**
- **Self-medication is a common by-product for those trying to alleviate their pain,** especially if they are hesitant to share their problems or if recognized methods do not work.
- **Pick your battles.** As a parent of a child with mental illness, know what hills to die on. There are so many challenges that sometimes you must allow things you never dreamed would be acceptable, and that is okay.
- **You may have to make tough decisions.** You may have to make the ultimate decision that your child is not welcome in your home anymore if the behavior they are exhibiting is self-destructive or harmful to the family.
- **It is key to always reinforce that they are loved.** The door remains open, and they are welcomed back if you can agree on what the boundaries are and a plan to attack the disease.
- **It's a marathon, not a sprint.** There is no magic pill to cure mental illness. To keep your child alive, you must commit to the marathon. You can't eradicate the illness in a sprint.

Chapter 4

Coming Out of a Coma

We got that horrible call on Saturday morning, March 11, 2006, from MacNeal Hospital. It is the call that no parent ever wants to get: that your child is injured or, worse yet, dead. Our caller reported that the hospital had Sean, who had been found down, nobody knew for how long, at a hotel. He was in very bad shape, and we needed to get to the hospital right away.

At the time, Sean had been living in the group home for about three months. That period was not without challenges, but he seemed to be assimilating into their routine. He was an advocate for his medications and was looked at as a kind of "dad" figure. While the group home had supervision, it was not a locked-down facility. Sean would come home on weekends so long as his behavior in the home stayed within their rules.

After the call, we thought, "Wait a minute! He was in this group home, what do you mean he's gone? What happened?" Nevertheless, at that moment, it didn't matter. Our son was critical, and I knew by the tone it was bad.

We raced to the hospital, and when we got there, I saw what I had seen before in my profession but with complete strangers, never my child. There Sean was, on a ventilator. He was gray; he was aspirating around the tube; he was all but gone. I looked at Eileen. "We need to call the boys and get everybody else here."

"We're going to take him up to ICU, and then people can come and say goodbye," the doctor said.

This is another situation that's not in the "Parents' Handbook." We had been through so much already; how could it get worse? Yet, now, I was being handed a Do Not Resuscitate (DNR) order and an organ donation form to sign. As I signed the last document, I said, "I just can't believe this is happening."

THE HAND-PUMP SEQUENCE

A nurse came in and said that there was a chaplain outside who would like to come in and say a prayer. I have to tell you, regardless of signs from the past, I was about as angry with God as I could be. Frankly, I was tired of feeling betrayed, and I didn't want to pray. I certainly didn't want some stranger walking in as I was trying to process what it was going to be like to bury my son and watch my wife suffer the loss she feared most.

From the time we had dated, Eileen had spoken of the horror of having to bury your child. She truly lived in fear of that, even before we had children. Now it was on the horizon, and I wondered if, somehow, she had known, just as I had known it before my dad passed away.

The chaplain came in. He was a black gentleman in a bright-gold suit that looked more appropriate for a 1970s' disco party with John Travolta than for chaplain work. He said, "Do you mind if we say the *Our Father*?"

"Okay, great, fine," I said, but I was thinking that I didn't care. Eileen took one of Sean's limp hands, the chaplain grabbed Eileen's hand and mine, while, with my other hand, I held Sean's limp, cold hand.

Sean was not a big churchgoer. We were blessed to have found a priest, Father Gavin Quinn, who said Mass on Saturday mornings. Saturday Mass was a little shorter, and Sean enjoyed it. Always during the *Our Father,* he held my hand and we played a game. He would pump my hand in a sequence: four pumps, then one, then two; or five pumps, then three, then four. Whatever it was, he'd look at me and expect me to repeat the pattern. If I didn't, he would give me what I called the "Sean look," which you had to see to understand. It made me smile and it does to this day. His look said, "Seriously, you can't remember three sequences?"

Well, as the *Our Father* was going on and our son was lying there on that table, dying, unexpectedly, the chaplain pumps my hand in a sequence. Did I imagine it, I wondered? Or was it Sean's way of letting me know, "Yeah, I'm here, Dad. It's okay. I'm going to be okay, no matter what happens?" It was surreal.

Eileen and I stepped into the hallway as staff prepared to take the cot upstairs. Eileen looked at me oddly. "Did anything funny happen to you during that *Our Father?*" she asked.

"Yeah, I swear the chaplain was pumping my hand like Sean does."

"He did the same thing to me. I felt like it was Sean on the other end."

We both felt a sense of comfort, like maybe Sean was already in heaven, and thank God he was not going to suffer anymore. Sign or wishful thinking? Maybe the chaplain had a nervous tick. Or, maybe, the other side was trying to provide at least a sense that we were not alone.

We spent the next twenty-four hours with family. My wife is from a family of thirteen, so loads of aunts and uncles, cousins, and friends came to say goodbye to Sean. We just stayed there next to his bed, holding his hand, feeling it getting colder and colder as his life slipped away.

About thirty-six hours into this vigil, the doctor came in and said he wanted to tear up the DNR order. I hadn't had any sleep. I was sitting there with my head on Sean's bed. I looked up.

"What? Why would I do that?"

"Because he's fighting. He's trying to come back. We want to give him a chance."

"All right, give me the paperwork." Were they kidding me?

I ripped it up. Maybe another eight hours later, it's hard to remember the exact time, the chaplain came back in, dressed in the same gold suit he'd worn in the emergency room. I wondered if the guy had another suit. He said, "You don't need to worry. I talked to your son. He's coming back." And he walked out.

Eileen and I looked at each other. I thought, "Okay, this guy is loony. Look at our son; he's dying. He's not coming back. There's been no sign of any type of improvement." So frankly, I blew it off. The next day, the doctors noted that Sean's condition had begun to worsen. He now had a collapsed lung. They inserted a needle to relieve the pressure. How much more could this child take? I prayed, "Lord, please come and take him."

The situation went on unchanged for another couple of days. Sean was critical. That was when the doctor said they would try to take him off the ventilator, to see if they could get him to breathe on his own. We were hopeful, but scared. It didn't work. They tried again the following day, and it didn't work. They said, "We're going to try it one more time tomorrow, and if it doesn't work, then this is the way he's going to be, and you're going to need to find a place for him."

Now, talk about being angry with God! I thought, "You put this kid through all of this, and you're going to leave him like this? What is this going to do to his mother? To his family? To watch him like this and find a place for him in this condition? This is wrong." Repeatedly, I had said to Sean in his coma, "Go. You need to go. This place is not good for you. You've fought like a champion with your illness, and you're not getting any better. This world is not a good place for you. Go to heaven. Go."

ST. PATRICK'S DAY

Day 7 since they found Sean was our last chance to remove the ventilator. It was St. Patrick's Day. An Irish theme runs through my family. Shamrocks are everywhere. St. Patrick's Day was one of Sean's favorite holidays. Green cupcakes and green cakes were everywhere, and everyone wore green. We had parties at our house to celebrate with a keg of green beer. The house was full of Irish music and joy with

36

family and loads of friends. Our sons may have struggled in mathematics, but when it came to pouring a beer from the keg with a perfect head, I'm ashamed to admit all of them could do it. Sean just loved that day, especially the tips!

I decorated his ICU room and wore my St. Patrick's Day tie. One of the nurses came in. "What's this all about?"

"Seriously? Don't you know it's St. Patrick's Day? This should be a national holiday!"

"Oh, is that what today is?" She was so indifferent that it was humorous.

When the time came time to take Sean off the ventilator, I left. Mr. Hero, Mr. Cape, the big-time leader, the guy who looked in the mirror and saw Superman, was too afraid to be in that room. In my heart, I knew what would happen. He wasn't going to breathe when he was taken off the ventilator, and we would have to find a facility where he could live out the rest of his days in a vegetative state.

I waited in the hallway while my brave wife and my niece, Sarah, stayed in the room. I had nothing but negative thoughts. There was no prayer. There was no asking for help or signs because I didn't think they existed, anymore. My "hope chest" was empty.

I heard coughing. I thought it must have been one of the nurses. When I heard it a third time, I peeked around the corner sheepishly. There was Sean, off the ventilator, his eyes wide open. He looked at me standing in the doorway and smiled that beautiful, Sean-little-boy smile.

"Oh my God, Sean! Are you laughing at me? Are you laughing at my obnoxious tie?" He nodded his head. I thought, "God—you know all those bad things I said about you all week? Forget it. Sorry about that. Just erase them away. I was only kidding because my son is back."

I ran in the room and threw my arms around him, crying. Eileen and Sarah were crying, in fact, all the nurses were crying. Finally, someone said, "You guys need to go home now. He needs to rest, and so do you. We've got him, and you can come back tomorrow and see him. He's back." We went home and crashed, so thankful for another chance, hopeful that this was the turning point we had prayed for.

THE SIGN FROM BEYOND

The next morning, the phone rang at about eight o'clock. We had caller ID, so I could see that the call was from MacNeal Hospital. My heart dropped. He must have died during the night. Or he had a complication. He was down too long. "I knew this was too good to be true," I thought. I barely mumbled hello. I had tensed up to hear bad news. Instead, I heard a hoarse voice. It was Sean.

"Dad, are you coming to see me today?"

"Oh my God, Sean! We're leaving right now. Come on, Eileen, we're going."

We shot down to the hospital. No shower, no nothing. When we walked into his room, he was extremely agitated. He sat on the side of the bed, trying to talk, not making much sense.

"Sean, we've got plenty of time to talk. Relax. You need to rest. You need to get it back together. Take it easy."

Again, my wife, the smart one, said, "Pat, be quiet. Sean, what do you want to say?"

"Sean Kenny. I saw Sean Kenny."

Oh, no, I thought. Here we go. He has brain damage. I knew it. "I knew this was too good to be true. He doesn't even know who he is."

Eileen said, "Be quiet, Pat. Sit down." Very calmly, she said, "No, Sean, you're Sean Kenny."

"No, no, no. Looks just like Dad, but younger."

"Who looks just like Dad?" Eileen asked.

"Grandpa Mike."

"You were with Grandpa Mike?" Eileen asked.

"Yeah."

At that point, it was either sit down or fall down. I sat down.

Sean described my father in detail. It was not the man whose photo he had seen. That man was in his mid-fifties when he passed; heavyset,

38

thinning hair, not even a shade of what someone would consider athletic. Instead, Sean described my dad in his mid-thirties: thick, black, curly hair; in great condition.

"He had these big hands," Sean said. "He held my hand."

I thought about my dad. When I was a little kid, he'd hold my hand when we walked, and my hand would be engulfed in his.

Sean continued, "We sat on a concrete bench, and behind it were all these ads."

My dad never had a driver's license. We took public transit. While waiting, we sat on concrete benches that had ads behind them for the companies that had sponsored them. Sean had never heard that story. He had never even seen a picture of those benches, yet he described them meticulously.

"Did Grandpa Mike say anything to you?" Eileen asked.

"Yeah, he said, 'Make sure you tell your dad that I'm sorry I had to leave him so early, and I'm really proud of him.' "

By then, I was sobbing.

Eileen asked, "Did he say anything else to you, Sean?"

Sean replied, "Yes. He said, 'It's not your time, Sean. You need to go back.' "

Sean told this story with great emotion and clarity. You can challenge me all you want about oxygen deprivation, various medications, the coma he was in, the drugs he'd snorted—all those ideas. I am telling you that no eighteen-year-old would know how it feels when a father has to leave his son behind. He described things he had never been exposed to, had never seen. I had never talked about any of it; yet he nailed the details. My father knew I would recognize the description, would know the bench, would know what it meant, and would know that I would believe he had been there. I had lived to make my dad proud since I was fourteen, and now that effort had been validated.

The message I received was, "I am someplace. I am watching, and it is good. I am sending your boy back." Inexplicably, I had received the ultimate sign straight from my dad!

I did not know it at the time, but not only had Sean been the messenger for the most powerful sign we had ever experienced, but someday, way too soon, he would take the place of my dad in delivering another powerful sign, again under the worst circumstances.

We were thrilled when Sean came out of his coma. We had our miracle, the miracle that I was sure would change all our lives. Maybe while he was in the coma, I hoped, the chemicals that tormented his brain had changed. A reset, if you will. Whatever it was, we had another chance.

The next day, he told the story of seeing my dad to Father Gavin when he came to visit.

Father Gavin asked, "Can I touch you, Sean?"

"Sure, Father. Go ahead. But why?"

"Because I want to touch someone who's been in heaven and see what that feels like."

Sean recounted the story of dad's message a few times to other people, always citing the same details. It was a clear memory. It wasn't a dream. He had been there. And so, we were hopeful. Still, we knew we were not out of the woods. Having been down so long, Sean had lost a significant amount of his hearing, and his ears rang constantly. The tinnitus added to everything else made his overall condition worse. He could be taken home to recuperate physically.

We then faced the dilemma of convincing the group home to take Sean back. Obviously, they were concerned that he would try to kill himself again, given his track record. I didn't blame them, but I knew he couldn't stay at our home.

Sean himself told me something about those who suffer from mental illness: "We can be the best con people." He could convince you that he was solid, had no mental disturbances going on, had learned his lesson, and was all good—but it was all an act. He convinced us all that

40

he would not try to end his life again and would follow all the rules of the group home. We all wanted so badly to believe him; he was a charming kid with a really good heart, and he had been a positive influence in that home. They relented and took him back.

Now, I wonder how I could have thought that his promise would hold up for long; he had tried every known intervention to treat his disease, with no impact.

For the first couple of days, Sean seemed better, and then he went right back into that depression, and the darkness returned for all of us.

LESSONS LEARNED

- **Don't judge the value of someone suffering from a mental illness.** You may not know what their life's real mission is.
- **Be open to the existence of an afterlife where those you love reside.** Just because you can't explain it does not mean it's not real.
- **Turn to your faith.** As a leader, you will be faced with situations you are not prepared for, like signing a Do Not Resuscitate order for a loved one. In those moments, turn to your faith for comfort. Understand that you don't have the power to fix some situations.

Chapter 5

Exhausting All Options

It is hard to describe the energy it takes to follow a path of trial and error, looking for the right psychologist, psychiatrist, treatment facility, and medication. The patient, along with the family, is repeatedly led to a ledge of hope only to see that it's a cliff, leading to a painful fall, and there is no end in sight. Prescription medications may make things worse or the side effects may be so paralyzing that the patient refuses to take them.

As the parents, you are not nearly educated enough even to have an intelligent conversation about this because most doctors talk over your head. They can be impatient with your questions. The truth was that Sean could keep up with their medical jargon better than we could. Frequently, they were infuriated because he knew of a new medication or intervention they did not know existed. OCD and the internet can do that.

On one occasion, we sat with a group of psychiatrists in the psych ward of a famous Chicago hospital. One doctor, annoyed with Sean's questions about new medications, told him, "Sean, your problem is that you are an addict. Fix that, and you will fix the problem."

"Doc, you don't get it. If you can get the obsessive thoughts to quit entering my brain, I can stop cold turkey tomorrow."

Eileen and I signed him out right after that meeting. As the advocate, you must be willing to fight for your child and believe in him. Not all doctors and facilities live up to their reputations, so even though it takes more energy to keep moving until you find a match, sometimes you have to make that change.

Here is some perspective: as a team, our family, Sean's psychologist, and Sean himself had done exhaustive research for therapies, medications, and treatments to help him. I have very limited knowledge of the science behind most of these, but I will briefly summarize some of the treatments we explored below. It is not an all-inclusive list, so I encourage you to continue to research any and all options.

ELECTROCONVULSIVE THERAPY (ECT)

Sean tried all the known therapies of the day, including ECT, a procedure that is administered under general anesthesia. Small electric currents are passed through the brain, intentionally triggering a brief seizure. ECT seems to cause changes in brain chemistry that can quickly reverse symptoms of certain mental health conditions. It is most commonly used in patients with severe major depression or bipolar disorder that has not responded to other treatments.

All I knew about ECT in those days was what I had seen applied to Jack Nicholson in the movie *One Flew over the Cuckoo's Nest*, shocking his brain and sending him into tremors. We begged Sean not to do this, but he was desperate and did it during two separate hospitalizations, once when he was eighteen and again at nineteen. The second time he received sixteen rounds but no improvement.

Like any medical procedure, ECT has some risks. It has been associated with short-term memory loss and learning difficulties. Some people have trouble remembering events that occurred in the weeks before the treatment or earlier. In most cases, memory problems improve within a couple of months. Some patients may experience longer-lasting problems, including permanent gaps in memory. Sean, unfortunately, suffered all those residual effects, especially after the last series.

COGNITIVE BEHAVIORAL THERAPY (CBT)

Sean also tried CBT, a common type of talk therapy (psychotherapy). He worked with a mental health counselor in a structured way, attending a limited number of sessions. CBT helps you become aware of inaccurate or negative thinking so you can view challenging situations more clearly and respond to them more effectively. CBT therapists focus on what is going on in the person's current life, rather than on what has led up to their difficulties. A certain amount of historical information is involved, but the focus is primarily on moving forward in time to develop more effective ways of coping with life.

CBT emphasizes helping individuals learn to function as their own therapists. Through exercises in the session as well as homework exercises outside of sessions, patients are helped to develop coping skills, whereby they can learn to change their thinking, unhealthy emotions, and behavior. I can't emphasize enough that work away from the counselor or the facility is critical to a successful outcome. CBT is a lifelong process, not a two-week investment.

Unfortunately, this therapy didn't work for Sean, either. He also explored meditation, biofeedback, and many other techniques. You name them, and Sean tried them with no tangible or long-lasting evidence of success.

MEDICATIONS

The list of medications Sean tried would be at least two pages long. Remember, Sean had been diagnosed with an obsessive-compulsive disorder in junior high. It causes you to fixate on things. It was the only "positive" by-product of his disease, since it made him hunger for knowledge.

In the beginning, some medications calmed the anxiety or depression, but not the obsessive-compulsive disorder. Side effects like acne, weight gain, hair loss did nothing more than add to the anxiety of the situation.

It struck me as ironic that the number-one side effect of many medications given to suicide-prone patients was suicidal thoughts. In frustration, I said to one doctor, "Did you get the f**king memo, Doctor? He's in here because he tried to kill himself, and now you're filling him full of things in which the number-one side effect is that they make him think even more about doing it?" To me, it was no different than filling a person full of lethal chemo to fight the cancer in their system! What is the result we are trying to achieve, to save or to kill? Sean always wanted instant results from a medication, but really, when trying any medication, the child and parents need to be fully educated on its effects and side effects and how long it will take to reach an effective level in their system. A drug might require weeks to work, but Sean would take it for only a week or two, and seeing no results, he'd stop. At all costs, no medication should be stopped abruptly, as that can intensify the side effects, which can be life-threatening. If they are going to stop, wean them off the medication under your doctor's supervision.

SELF-MEDICATION

Many people who have a mental health challenge that has not improved turn to self-medication. According to Sean's own timeline, he started drinking at the age of thirteen and then, by seventeen, he had moved up through various illegal drugs from marijuana to the hard stuff of cocaine and heroin.

Although we were a small, close-knit family living in a tiny house, none of us knew what he was doing or the extent to which he was doing it. It's called desperation. Just as a cancer patient will fly to Mexico or Sweden to drink some strange concoction or get injections of some serum they have never even heard of, all for the outside chance it might cure them or at least relieve their pain. On the other hand, because the treatment is by nature experimental, it might kill them, too. Whatever the outcome, the goal is to end the pain and suffering.

Sean was in pursuit of the same thing. He, too, wanted to find the counterbalance to his physical illness, something that would shut down the malfunctioning chemicals in his brain, and he was willing to go to any lengths. He was not a quitter looking for "the easy way out," as suicidal people are so inaccurately painted. Quite the contrary, Sean was relentless in his search.

TREATMENT RESISTANCE

Sean was fixated on this unending search for the magic pill or the life-saving technique. Unfortunately, as we found out at Mayo Clinic when they spoke of his "terminal" diagnosis, his series of mental illness challenges were treatment-resistant, just as some cancers won't respond to any radiation or chemotherapy that is aimed at them. The combination of therapy and medication were not touching his illness, and they certainly were not easing his pain.

HOPE

As you try to support someone who is ill with a mental health diagnosis, you realize quickly that the thing that has been robbed from them, the thing that they need most, is *not* their energy level and *not* their social contacts, but their hope. Once hope has been completely dashed, that's when you run the biggest risk of losing them.

In the beginning, Sean's hope came from one-on-one therapy with his wonderful counselor, Sue. They continued working together from his junior high years until he went to heaven. In fact, he stopped by her office the day he ran away from the group home, literally on his way to take his life, but she was with a patient. We all agree that he had stopped by not to be talked out of what he was about to do but to say goodbye. Unfortunately, just talking about how overwhelmed and hopeless you are is not enough. You need something tangible in the way of hope and pain-relief to keep you going.

As we were told at Mayo Clinic, there was no one medication or one intervention method that Sean didn't try, but the combination of his mental illness challenges had overwhelmed any treatment plan, no matter how ambitious or experimental.

EXPERIMENTAL TRIAL

In April of the year when he was twenty, only a few weeks after surviving the overdose and with no improvement in sight, Sean sought out and was accepted as a patient in a trial. An implant was put in his chest to block some of the chemical impulses sent to his brain. Sean was one of the first people in the state of Illinois to have this procedure. Eileen and I didn't understand it, but we went along with it because we didn't want to face reality: if Sean didn't get better soon, he was going to take his life.

I now know from researching this procedure that the implant was to transmit electrical pulses directly into the vagus nerve. Also known as the 10th cranial nerve, it is the most complex of the cranial nerves and in some ways the least understood. Experts have linked its activity to symptom changes in people with migraine headaches, inflammatory bowel disease, depression, epilepsy, arthritis, and many other common ailments. As scientists learn more about this nerve, they could unlock new doors to treatment. Since the vagus nerve is in charge of the parasympathetic nervous system, which helps control the body's relaxation responses, it was hoped that the implant would help with deep depression. This experimental treatment was reserved for people who weren't able to get control of their symptoms with medications or other therapeutic interventions, so Sean seemed a good candidate.

Unfortunately, the treatment only made Sean worse. On Easter Sunday morning, as we were getting up for a sunrise service at church, we heard a loud bang in the bathroom. It was Sean. He was down on the floor and Eileen was screaming, "What did you take!" because emotionally, we were scarred from all the years of trauma. We assumed the worst. We were caught between wishing for his survival, no matter what and wondering if death was not only inevitable but may be merciful. It is a frightening realization to contemplate. Who would ever think their child would be better off dead?

I grabbed him. "Sean, did you take something?"

He needed hearing aids at that point and had not yet put them in, so he did not understand. I could tell he had been groggy and was just coming out of it. I repeated myself, and he looked at me. "No, Dad. I didn't take anything." Even as I write this, that look of sadness on his face, as if he were saying, "what else, now?" makes me cry. He had been through so much, and his life had been spared for what? This?

We called the ambulance. For the first time, Eileen did not go to the hospital with him. She was emotionally bankrupt, her pain as a mother was just too deep. We discovered that the device had pulsed and, when it did, his blood pressure dropped so low that he passed out. Sean and our whole family could not take much more. The device that was supposed to help him had made him worse. Now, he couldn't hear, and his voice sounded like he was going through puberty again. He was going back to the group home. For all of us, life had gone from hope of a great second chance and back again to the endless darkness.

Eileen and I talked candidly about the situation. The clock was ticking, and it had sped up. Not only was Sean physically worse, suffering headaches, tinnitus, and loss of hearing, he had gotten no relief from the mental illness and was living away from us in a group home he hated. It was a recipe that was leaving him only one option for stopping the years of suffering—suicide.

LESSONS LEARNED

- **Be a mental health advocate.** As the leader, you must be an advocate for mental health and be willing to fight for your child, loved one, friend, or co-worker by believing that they have an illness, and not a character weakness.
- **If a doctor isn't a fit, find another.** Just because someone is a doctor or runs a treatment facility does not guarantee instant

success with the person suffering. It takes energy to keep moving from one mental health professional or employee assistance program (EAP) to another until you find a match, but you must commit to that effort. Failure to connect with the first professional the patient meets is not only normal; it is more probable than a home run on the first contact. It does not mean that the patient can't get help; it only means that they can't get it from that particular source. Remember, this is a marathon, not a sprint.

- **Exhaust all treatment options.** There are many treatment options available today to treat mental illness. Exhaust them all as you try to provide relief to the person suffering. If it turns out that the patient has a terminal case of mental illness and takes their life, it is the only way you will know that you, as the leader, did everything you could.
- **Be fully educated on the effects and side effects of any medication prescribed.** When trying a medication, be sure you are fully educated on its effects and side effects and how long it will take to reach a therapeutic level in the system. At all costs, do not stop the medication abruptly, as that can make the side effects worse. Only stop medications under a doctor's supervision.

Chapter 6

How to Parent a Child with Mental Health Issues

When you have a child who is suffering from a mental health challenge, it's very easy to focus solely on that child at the expense of your other kids. I think we were guilty of that as parents. I know I was. When the situation got really bad, our oldest son Brendan was already in the working world at a demanding job, where he had been elevated to a supervisor, and our middle son Pat was away at college, seeking his future, so we just left them on automatic pilot. It wasn't about not caring; we were in damage control mode, trying to shelter them from pain. We weren't so naive as to think that neither of our other sons was facing the challenges of growing up. We just prayed that they were strong enough to weather their storms without mom and dad holding them up.

It's easy to take all your energy and drive it into the child who is most obviously suffering. I wish I could tell you to balance the needs of all your children equally, but honestly, at least for us, that was not practical, so don't even try it. I believe it will just leave you more frustrated and feeling even more like a failure. I do recommend that you keep those other siblings on the radar. You will need to focus your goals on simple things, like scheduling time out with the others for a pizza or a movie or, if they're older, for just a sit-down-and-check-in over a cup of coffee. This is not a time to speak about the child who is suffering; so, keep the conversation about them.

If they happen to ask what's going on, then, obviously, you should share the details honestly; but if it doesn't come up, don't bring it up. Make sure your time together is about them. Remind them how much you love them. You can tell them that this is not how you pictured parenting, but you're doing the best you can. You might be surprised by their feedback, even if it's nothing more than a vote of confidence. We were lucky enough to get that at various times during Sean's illness. Brendan and Pat were awesome and way beyond their years in terms of the care and compassion they showed their mom, who was dying each day along with Sean. All three boys adored their mom.

This advice about your other children carries over to your significant other because it is easy to lose your identity as husband and wife and think only of yourselves as parents. Even beyond this situation, both of you will be dealing with other struggles. It might be your emotional and/or physical health. You might be dealing with an ailing parent, as both Eileen and I were at various times during our journey. It's easy for a couple to get torn in so many directions that the relationship is put on hold. You count on the fact that you have a strong and healthy marital relationship, and it doesn't need any nurturing. However, just like a beautiful flower deprived of water, a relationship will eventually die from lack of attention.

Schedule date nights, even if only for an hour, with the ground rules being no talking about family issues, not just those concerning the suffering child, but also those concerning your other kids. Make it all about you as a couple. Keep it simple, because the reality is that you won't have a four-hour block to go out for an extravagant dinner, but you might be able to sneak out to the pub and have pizza and a pitcher of beer.

I did a poor job of navigating my work life. Some people find work a good distraction, while others find it one more challenge they don't want to think about. Work certainly provided me a safe haven in which I felt I could put on the Cape, call for its powers, and know that it listened. In my mind, when I walked through the door of the firehouse,

I made a conscious decision to separate the pain from home from the challenge of the workplace. That was my time to slip into a phone booth and put on my Cape to escape the arena in which I had no power, that of being a father; and years later, I repeated the pattern when Eileen was so ill. Now, I know that my work life could have been so much more supportive if I had just been open about Sean's illness to all my firefighters, not all the details, but certainly an overview.

You can't expect others to be mind readers. If you're acting like a pain in the ass, they may assume that you are angry with them when nothing could be further from the truth. Frankly, some days when I came into work, I didn't even notice that other people were in the building because I was so totally focused on how I was failing.

Especially when you're the leader of an organization, you feel a tremendous responsibility for those who serve with you. Isolating yourself does not work. It drains your emotional bank account, tears your Cape to pieces, and it also sells short the people who work with you. By remaining secretive or silent, you're not giving them enough credit for understanding your predicament and allowing them the freedom to offer help. The complexities of mental illness cause you to push away the kindness others offer because you don't want to impose on them, even though you need it desperately. You may think that if you, as the leader and a parent, can't understand what is going on, how could anyone else?

Knowing that they can approach you simply and even without words gives co-workers an opportunity to be part of the solution. I'm a big believer in hugs. Sometimes, someone putting an arm around you and validating how much this situation you're in must suck can give you a bit of an emotional boost. Note that that the boost isn't about someone fixing the problem or offering suggestions about how to fix it. It's about having someone validate your feelings. Also, once co-workers realize the depths of the struggle you are enduring, they are less likely to add to it unknowingly by approaching you with trivial things they can handle at their own level.

Your journey with mental illness provides you an opportunity to enhance the culture in your organization. You are letting people know through your own actions that it is not only okay to have a loved one who is dealing with mental illness, but it is okay to talk about it. Talking about it plants the seeds to normalize the existence of mental illness. As the leader, I failed to do these things during Sean's fifteen-year battle.

Another benefit of reaching out and sharing your experience is that you may encounter a co-worker, a friend or even a relative—perhaps someone you least expect—who is or has been through something similar. That person may know the name of a doctor or a promising medication or a new intervention that's on the radar, and that will renew your quest for hope and maybe give your child something to hang onto. I know we were desperate to find medical solutions throughout Sean's journey, and others can be helpful. Quite often now, when I speak about Sean's journey to groups, I have had the opportunity to share medical information to others in similar situations.

Here is another trap that parents with mentally ill children can fall into, which is to expect them, somehow, to lead a normal life. I never believed that someone couldn't get out of bed until I watched Sean struggle to walk from his bedroom to the bathroom to brush his teeth and then need to go back to bed. I looked at this as a choice, not a symptom of his disease. Just as we tend to categorize mental illness as a *choice* rather than a diagnosis, we also treat the symptoms as something a person would *choose* to experience!

I would not accuse someone with dementia of faking it if they could not remember their address, yet I accused Sean of not trying hard enough to get out of bed. I mean, how hard could it be? That's how I thought of it. Well, I learned quickly after he passed and then even more powerfully when I was alone after Eileen passed. I experienced that feeling of trying to sit up in bed with a 500-pound weight on my chest.

Trust me, my friends, if you've never experienced feeling that you can't move due to the weight of any illness, I can tell you from experience that it is not a choice; it is a very real condition and as draining as those with mental illness describe. So, as parents of someone mentally ill, we must believe that their pain is real and then try to find a way to relieve that 500-pound gorilla from their chest.

Most of the journey is about survival. Not only survival for your child, but for you as the leader and you as the parent. Amid this fight for your child's life, consciously decide to make your relationship a priority, and that will make you stronger parents.

LESSONS LEARNED

- **Make time for other family members.** In the middle of the battle, don't forget that others are affected, too, and they may go off your radar. They could be other family members or co-workers. Schedule one-on-one time with them however you can.
- **Each of you must make time for your significant other.** As you are busy being the leader, your mate may get lost in your quest to fix the problem, and you can't see it because your Cape is flapping in the wind, blinding your view. Always keep your relationship as a couple front and center so that you stay refueled and connected.
- **Share your journey with co-workers.** You, as the leader, can be a role model for how to handle mental illness, showing by your words and actions that it is nothing to be ashamed of. This may encourage others to come forward for help. Also, it gives you support as the leader and is a resource for your family.
- **Look beyond the surface.** People dealing with mental illness do things you may see as choices (e.g., staying in bed, absenteeism), which instead may be symptoms of disease.

Chapter 7

Parent Survival Tips

When you have a child, two people who have been defined as a couple, as best friends, as husband and wife take on the role of parents. With that honorable title comes a tremendous amount of responsibility, and you feel that the first time you hold your newborn. That little life is in your hands, and you feel the weight of that responsibility right away. I'm not sure why that catches most of us by surprise, but it does.

When you lose a child, your relationship as a couple is stressed to the maximum in all those areas. The range of emotions that try to tear apart your friendship and marriage is unimaginable until you experience it. You may even question your spouse's parenting skills as well as your own.

Eileen and I had no specialized training in relationships. However, we had thirty-five years of experience as husband and wife, thirty-four of which were blessed with children, one of whom was very ill for at least ten years and eventually died by suicide.

My goal in this chapter is to provide some guidance for parents navigating the tough road of saying goodbye to your child. I will share with you the top two lessons we learned to help maintain the three valuable aspects of your relationship: remaining best friends; continuing your strong husband and wife bond; and finally, what is most important—maintaining your belief in your parenting skills as well as those of your partner.

Before you read these tips, I will state what must be obvious: the stronger your relationship is in those three areas before you have a child who is ill and eventually passes away regardless of the reason, the better the chances for survival of the relationship. We were blessed to have a healthy marriage before we faced Sean's challenges. We were best friends, and there was no one whose mothering skills I respected more than Eileen. Yet, we found that even though our relationship was strong, it still was put to the test throughout Sean's illness, and also after we laid him to rest.

TIP: STAY CONNECTED TO YOUR SPOUSE

As you go through an emotional marathon like this as a couple, you find that you do things you never thought you would, things that other people may think are cold or crazy. For example, when Sean was nearing the end of his life, our insurance coverage was exhausted, and he had attempted suicide, so we had no choice but to put him into a state facility in Elgin, Illinois.

I can't honestly say what that facility is like today, but at that time, it was a glorified prison where people who were mentally ill went to stay for a while to keep them off the streets. When Eileen and I went to see him there, our pain was incredible. It was the worst place he had ever been. We were searched like criminals just to visit him.

That was probably as low as we had been as a couple. Talk about feeling like failures as parents! We decided when we left that day that we would take a couple of days off and go to a hotel with a view in Lake Geneva, Wisconsin. We were going to pretend that we didn't have a child in a mental institution, a.k.a. prison. We were going to try to recapture the love that brought us together from the beginning.

When you lose a child, statistics about the divorce rate are all over the place, anywhere between 16 and 90 percent. Counseling had given us that heads up regarding the destruction of relationships, so our antennas were up, which is yet another good reason to seek counseling during, not only after, traumatic situations. Our counselor had warned us that the estimate was almost 50 percent. I don't honestly know what it is on that precarious path leading to eventual loss, but I can tell you that it is very easy to lose each other and to seek blame rather than unity if you don't make a conscious decision to fight for your relationship.

We decided that we would do what "normal" couples do. Now, think about two parents who just had their child locked away in a state mental facility. They were going to sit on a balcony overlooking the beach and drink a few beers. Sounds cold and calculated, uncaring, something done by people unfit to be parents, but I will tell you it was the only thing we could do to stay sane and refill our emotional bank account that was bankrupt from all the pain we had watched Sean go through.

It was a wise decision, and it gave us some energy to fight, but if you had told me at the beginning of Sean's journey that we would go out and have a beer while he was locked away in that prison-like facility, I would have told you that you were crazy. We were responsible parents. We would never do that!

If you are in a similar, unimaginably stressful situation where there is no Cape to save you, you and your partner need to be keenly aware that a fight for your child can destroy your marriage. That awareness must stay on the front burner. Make a deliberate decision to keep alive the love flame that brought you together and created this child in the first place. We lost a child in this battle, but we didn't want to lose each other, as well. It is a decision that may lead you to do things that others will not understand, and frankly, some may even condemn, but if it helps you refill that emotional bank account, you will be doing the best you can to serve your child well. I can't say that there are any rights or wrongs in this incredibly difficult situation, so seek counseling to guide you and sometimes frankly provide you a permission slip to act outside your previous norms. For example, something you might have once considered selfish might be the most giving thing you could do.

TIP: COMMUNICATE AND WORK AS A TEAM

Communication and teamwork are especially important for couples enduring a trauma involving their children, whether cancer, mental illness, or ADHD. It is vital that you and your partner are transparent with each other. That word *transparent* has become a kind of buzz word lately, but you really need to trust each other so that you can share specifically what's on your mind.

Sometimes it's not easy. Sometimes, those emotions you are expressing are counterproductive to the situation you're facing. For example, you may be experiencing hopelessness or fear, emotions that you are trying to keep at bay. If you don't express those feelings, however, your partner may mistake them for something else. One day when I came home after Sean had passed, Eileen asked me how my day was. I said it was good. Immediately, she started to cry and got uncharacteristically angry at me. How could anything ever be good again without Sean?

She had a valid point; it would never be good again. I was not saying I was good; I had meant to express that I was good, compared to how empty I felt every other day. Since that day had been less painful, in the grand scheme of things, it had been good but not the normal good of a normal life. As this example shows, don't leave it to your partner to guess what you're thinking or feeling. After the loss of your child, both of you will be feeling guilt anyway, and it's too easy to assume your partner is holding you responsible when they're just suffering. Call that suffering out for exactly what it is. Communicate it clearly, which takes that emotion's negative power away and gives it back to you as a positive.

The next part of the equation is teamwork. Sometimes, you just have to call out, "Tag! You're it," and let your partner carry the ball. Sometimes removing a burden from your partner results in a deposit in their emotional bank account, something as simple as, "I've got this hospital visit" or "I've got this appointment so you go out with your friends," or "honey, you go watch the football game and leave this aside for a while."

I have always wondered and still marvel at what single parents do when children are ill. It was tough enough for two of us to handle, so I can't imagine doing it alone. When you take turns tagging off as a couple, you build a strong bond. So, don't begrudge your partner having a social life; instead, encourage it, whether that social encounter includes talking about the illness or not. Your child's illness does not define either of you, so normal social outlets are crucial to giving you the energy to come back and fight.

Communication includes asking questions even about things you think are self-explanatory. Things like, "Are you mad at me?" or "Do you blame me for this? Do you think I was a bad mom or dad?" or "Is this why we are being punished?" or "Why did this have to happen to our child?"

Some questions have straightforward answers that will put the person at ease. Some are quite involved, and some have no answers at all, but getting them out on the table chokes them at the emotional roots and doesn't allow them to grow.

As I grew up, I played on sports teams. I transferred that team focus to my professional life, and I love the fire service because I'm part of a team. Any team is successful once you identify the strengths and weaknesses of each player and then maximize their strengths while protecting their weaknesses. A marriage or a business relationship is a team, as well. As a team, you can enhance your strengths and reduce exposure to your shortcomings, and this will empower you to take on things you didn't think you were capable of facing.

You are not helpless in this battle against mental illness. However, you as the leader and you as part of a marital team will be challenged, and you and your partner will need to stick together to create the atmosphere you need to fight.

"Divide and conquer" is a war technique, but it can apply to parenting through mental illness, suicide attempts, and eventually, even the loss of your child. Together, you must stand. Otherwise, you will be left feeling isolated and alone. Only a very small group truly knows your pain, and even then, their support usually doesn't arrive until the battle is over. Because of the many myths about mental illness, people are hesitant to approach you even if they know what is going on, so you must fight as a team until the cavalry arrives.

LESSONS LEARNED

- **Stay connected to your spouse/significant other during traumatic times.** Our counselor warned us that when a child dies, divorce rates can be in the 50 percent range.
- **Communicate your feelings and fears.** Communication and teamwork are everything, but they don't happen by themselves. Be aware that disconnects in these areas are threats to your relationship, so keep the line of communication open. You genuinely need each other; this is not time to go it alone.

Chapter 8

Mental Health Myths

Let me start by stating that there are numerous myths about mental health and suicide. You can Google it and come up with a list along with valid sources. I encourage you to do so if you are concerned about a co-worker, family member, or yourself. I am not a psychologist or psychiatrist and, as my mother said, my degree in psychology was a big waste of money as only dumb people run into burning buildings.

I can speak intelligently only to the myths I encountered with my son Sean. The reactions you see in the myths below were not always Sean's reactions, but I can tell you that they are on target.

MYTH 1: Talking about suicide with a person encourages the act.

Studies have shown that the first step in getting help is to admit that you're feeling suicidal and express it. Someone who dies by suicide is not doing it because you have discussed the topic with him; he is doing it based on how he perceives life. Encourage open communication, not the opposite. By opening the door to a discussion, you are encouraging him to evaluate what he is considering and other options beyond suicide. Silence will never make things better. Our open communications with Sean, I believe, bought us a few extra years to be with him, not the opposite.

MYTH 2: People who threaten suicide
are just seeking attention.

Anyone who goes so far as to use the word *suicide* is experiencing pain. Does it matter what degree of pain it is, whether it's just a call for help or a signal to you that he wants to end his life? Can you live with yourself afterward if you blow it off instead of making sure that he gets help? I wouldn't want to live with that. We never took Sean's suicide talks as anything but real. By taking him seriously, one thing we didn't have to live with after he passed was guilt that we didn't believe his pain.

MYTH 3: People with mental health
challenges have low intelligence.

Mental illness is the same as any other physical illness. Do we ever say that people who are diabetic are not very smart? No! So why do we do that to people who have a mental illness? Those who have mental illness come in all sizes and shapes and levels of intelligence, just like the rest of us, and they should be treated with the same respect. For the record, Sean was a B student; even during his hospitalizations, he kept up his studies. He could go toe-to-toe with any psychologist after his extensive reading on the newest medications and intervention theories. Don't sell your folks at work or at home short.

MYTH 4: Suicide is hereditary.

Frequently after I give my "Sean's" talk, I can see the look of dread on the faces of parents who have a child suffering from mental health challenges. Naturally, they worry that their child is destined to end up like Sean. We see that certain disorders can run in families. My grandfather killed himself, I almost killed myself, and then Sean killed himself. Even so, there is no direct evidence that an act as drastic as suicide is a foregone conclusion. As you would with any other physical illness, it is wise to keep your radar up if mental health illnesses are part of your family history.

MYTH 5: Mental illness is a sign of weakness. People with mental health problems can snap out of it if they try hard enough.

Mental illness is not a decision or a sign of weakness as the stigma suggests; it is a physical illness. Just as people do not choose to get pancreatic cancer, no one chooses to suffer from bipolar disorder, for example, and you can't just "snap out of it" one day.

It is vital to realize that cancer and mental illness are physical malfunctions and need to be treated the same way: seek professional help and medication and learn to cope with the illness. Sean was one of the strongest people I have ever known. He endured fifteen years of pain, and he survived until he was twenty years old because of his inner strength.

MYTH 6: People who suffer from depressive disorders and appear to be happy are no longer at risk for suicide.

A few of our friends as well as Sean's buddies saw him during the last few days of his life. All expressed that he appeared to be extremely happy. That was true. It was not because his pain was gone; rather, he was at peace with his decision that in several hours he would no longer be suffering that pain. One week prior to the night he took his life, I saw him get out of a car, singing as he ran up our side stairs into the house. I had not seen him so joyful in months. Now I know why. Just a couple of weeks earlier, on the last Mother's Day he was alive, Sean could barely get out of bed he was so depressed. We were going to his Aunt Rose's and Uncle Mark's house to celebrate. I begged him to try for Eileen's sake, and he eventually came for a bit. His Aunt Rose always understood and had a connection with Sean in which he felt he could be himself. I'm so thankful for that, as he took a picture that day with his arm around his mom, which we used on his Mass booklet. However, if you look closely, you can see the sadness in his eyes. Contrast that to his elation just two weeks later, only five days before he died by suicide. When I need a mental image of Sean to make me smile today, I remember his joy as he bounded out of that car, but I try not to think about what was motivating it.

MYTH 7: There is a magic pill or treatment that will cure mental illness challenges.

I wish it was true; certainly, Sean always sought it. The reality is that mental illness is chronic; it's a lifelong condition, one that requires a good doctor, possibly medication, and the ability to learn adaptive coping skills.

Remember this: if you don't feel a good connection with a counselor on your first attempt, or if the initial medication doesn't work, don't give up. It doesn't mean that another counselor or another medication won't work. It simply means there was no match that day, so please don't give up.

MYTH 8: Each mental health disease has only one successful course of treatment.

Nothing could be further from the truth. Certain courses of treatment appear to be better for making progress than others. However, what works for one situation may not work for yours, so exhaust all avenues until you find a connection. Some treatments work for years, and then you build a tolerance and need to adjust, but YOU CAN!

MYTH 9: Once people decide to die by suicide, there is no stopping them.

Riveting testimony given by survivors who have jumped from the Golden Gate Bridge revealed that all they wanted was someone to care about them and listen to them. They did not want to die. Yes, we did listen to Sean, and no, it didn't stop him; but again, his case was terminal. I believe there are many more people who have been saved by someone who intervened and cared than there are people who got help and still took their lives.

MYTH 10: Most suicides happen suddenly and without warning.

Often, after a suicide, you can find subtle warning signs, both verbal and physical. Sometimes the person shares something with a person who is close in an indirect manner. However, suicide categorized as an impulsive act is usually not the case. Sean's suicide, like most, was a culmination of years of suffering. Caught early, such cases can be successfully treated.

MYTH 11: Children don't experience mental health problems.

Even very young children may show early warning signs of mental health concerns. Sean was only five when his mother noticed that he was coloring all in black. He also had to tie his shoes over and over again before school or he would have a temper tantrum, what we learned later was an anxiety attack. He was diagnosed with clinical depression at five years old. Don't go into denial if you think your child may be suffering. Get an evaluation. If you are told there is nothing to worry about, go and celebrate. However, if there is an issue, early intervention is very successful. Don't let your Cape keep you from asking the question.

MYTH 12: People who die by suicide are selfish and have taken the easy way out.

If any myth angers me the most, this is it! Our basic human instinct is survival. It is wired into our brains chemically. It's the fight-or-flight instinct. When someone starts to see suicide as the only way to stop incredible pain, it becomes the only option for relief. *Suicide is not an end; it is a means to get away from the pain.* With that kind of pain, nothing else is on the person's radar: not how good life is around him or his wonderful loved ones. There is only the light at the end of the tunnel, and that light is suicide. The greatest love of Sean's life was his mom, and he would have laid his life down for her. If he had known how much it would hurt her to have him gone, he would never have carried it out. Instead, I'm sure he felt she would be better off.

Sean didn't take the easy way out; he was a warrior against his illness for over fifteen years. In his mind, he had no choice but to end that pain. In order to choose, you must have options; Sean felt that there was only one way to end the suffering. We are so much worse off now that Sean is no longer in our earthly world!

LESSONS LEARNED

- **Mental health remains a mystery.** So much about the disease is misunderstood, and we fear what we don't understand. Mental illness is not viewed as a physical illness; thus, it is not discussed. The only way to unlock the mystery attached to mental illness is to speak openly about the topic to friends, family, and co-workers. If you have any personal experiences or information from other credible sources, share them. Finally, be diligent in seeking answers to the questions you don't understand. Knowledge gives you the power to help others.

- **Education is key.** When people don't know the facts about something or are threatened by the subject matter, they tend to make up their own facts, and that leads to myths. As a leader, it is your job to take the extra effort to know what is accurate and disseminate the information so you can help those in need. When people don't feel connected, that loneliness and loss of hope can lead to suicide.

Chapter 9

Mental Illness Isn't a Choice

After I had been doing Sean's talk for about six years, I noticed that while the audience was very attentive and all felt sorry for me—which was not the point—some were not getting my key point, which is that mental illness is a physical illness, not a choice. Just as nobody chooses to have diabetes or ALS or cancer, people do not choose to suffer from mental health, either.

I sat down with Eileen to talk about how I could make this point more concrete for the audience. We decided that I would compare mental illness to a type of cancer, and we decided on brain cancer. I put together a couple of slides about exposure to both illnesses that were specific to the fire service. The irony was not lost on me when Eileen was diagnosed with brain cancer about two years later. We looked at each other. I said, "Did we somehow know?"

Obviously, firefighters are exposed to several dangerous by-products of fires, such as hazardous materials. And firefighters are also exposed to many stressful situations and, frankly, they see things that no human being should see.

When I go for my annual physical, the question of predisposition comes up. I have cancer in my family. I've had so many colonoscopies because my dad passed from stomach cancer that I feel like Swiss cheese. I'm on a first-name basis with the nurses, and that's all good. When it comes to mental health, there is usually no routine screening and or evaluation of mental health risk done as part of the physical, such as what kind of stress you are experiencing or have been exposed to or whether you have a family history of mental illness. You don't have to be a psychologist to know that someone going through a divorce or having to put their beloved father in a nursing home is at risk for a difficult time, but we usually don't ask those questions.

At the present time, there is more research on predisposition to cancer than to mental illness. There is no absolute proof that mental health is generational, but you often see that it runs in families. If that is true about your family, it can't hurt to keep your antenna up.

With cancer, there is always an initial denial of the condition, as silly as that sounds. Somebody finds a lump or a growth and comments, "It's just a cyst!" without having any idea what it is. It always drove me crazy when I reminded my firefighters to get their mandatory physicals and the ones who didn't, when asked why, would answer, "I don't want to know!" Seriously? You don't want to walk your daughter down the aisle because you don't want to get that lump checked out? Because of the annual physical, early diagnosis of cancer has been a lifesaver in my occupation. It is statistically proven that we firefighters are finding cancer early.

Certainly, denial is even more prevalent with mental health because of the stigma. People don't openly share that they are depressed or anxious. Instead, they say they're just a little more tired than usual or having a bad day or had one too many drinks the night before. People are quick to deny that stress of any kind could be creeping into their lives.

In the case of both cancer and mental health, unfortunately you can be given a terminal diagnosis. *Terminal diagnosis* is a term we use much more with cancer than with mental health, but as we learned with Sean, there can be a terminal diagnosis with a mental illness when the disease does not respond to any known treatment; and then it is just a matter of time.

Treatment for a terminal diagnosis in both cases is about the same. It is about trying to buy quality time and hoping that some new medication or treatment will show up on the horizon to give hope. The big difference comes when the patient passes away. A firefighter who dies of cancer is given a wonderful funeral as a hero, and his or her family is embraced. For a firefighter who is terminal and ends his life with suicide, the wake may be sparse, and the family shunned because people just don't understand.

Those slides comparing brain cancer and mental illness that Eileen and I added to my presentation have received more feedback than anything else I've changed or included to make it very real for people that mental illness is indeed a physical illness. Cancer can render you so weak that you can't get out of bed, and so can many types of mental illnesses. Medications that are supposed to make you better, can expedite your death, such as chemo or some of the mental health medications. Hope one day can lead to despair the next, when what you were promised would work does not. There is a helpless feeling in both cases as each day the family watches their loved one get closer to death, and there's nothing they can do about it. In both cases, the best you can do is to support and love those on their final journey.

Having watched Sean with his terminal illness and then Eileen with hers, I saw a difference. No one ever accused Eileen of faking her pain, while some people looked at Sean with a suspicious eye. We wouldn't accuse people who have dementia of faking it when that they can't remember their name, but we do accuse people who have a mental illness of being lazy or tell them to just "push through it." As Heather Armstrong stated in her book, *The Valedictorian of Being Dead,* sometimes all a person needs is "for you just to believe us."

I will finish this chapter with a description of how we prepare people who are entering fire service for a basic physical injury and translate that into a mental health injury.

We do a lot of lifting in our profession, and from rookie school on, firefighters are trained in the correct way to lift an object to eliminate a back injury. The truth is that the people we lift are usually in precarious positions, and it is impossible to use a perfect lift technique to get them life-saving help. That is, everything doesn't always happen as it should.

It's the same with treating a mental illness. Everything doesn't always go as it should. In the fire service, we hire people who care, and then we are shocked when they are impacted by a bad call or a series of traumatic events or something in their personal lives.

In the example above, it is just a matter of time before a firefighter gets a back injury or a mental health impact, so in training, we prepare the person that it's going to happen to them, and that it's normal!

In both cases, the first thing the person needs to do is to notify someone. That's not hard to do when you have a back injury; if you don't, you might not be covered by insurance. With a mental health issue, notification is extremely difficult because of the stigma. No one wants to tell a supervisor he is suffering; therefore, the suffering doesn't exist.

The next thing to do in both cases is to see a doctor who has been educated in what you do for a living. A back injury for someone who spends his day at a desk and for a firefighter on an engine company are two very different things. You need a doctor who understands the kind of physical stress you will be undergoing before he returns you to work. When you select a doctor to be your therapist, you need someone who understands the culture of your business. In the fire service, it's unique. Just as with a back injury, you may need some medication or therapy to treat a mental health challenge. In both situations, the goal is to return the person to 100 percent.

A back injury and a mental health injury are both physical issues that, if caught early, can be treated and resolved. The sad reality is that both go on longer than they should. Certainly, a mental health injury can go on so long that the person finds himself in a terminal situation that didn't need to be terminal. It's a shame, and it doesn't need to be that way if we can convince people that mental illness isn't a choice; it's a physical diagnosis.

Unfortunately, I can speak from experience on both kinds of illness. During the illness and after, Eileen and Sean were treated very differently. No one was afraid to hail Eileen as a hero, justifiably. Sean was tagged by many who didn't know the truth as someone who suffered from drug abuse, eventually took an overdose, and died.

LESSONS LEARNED

- **Cancer and mental illness have a lot in common:**
  1) Both are physical illnesses.
  2) Neither is a choice.
  3) Both can be diagnosed and treated with medication under a healthcare professional's direction.
  4) Both can be terminal.
  5) With both, people can go on to live a full life.
- **Terminally ill cancer patients have staged a heroic fight.** When they go back to God, they are hailed as heroes by family, friends, and co-workers. The surviving family is covered in love and support.
- **Terminally ill mental health patients are labeled cowards.** When they take their lives and go back to God, people say they were selfish and took the easy way out, and they avoid the surviving family. No one knows what to say, and people may even misdiagnose what happened and spread that rumor.
- **Education and communication are key to removing the stigma of mental illness.** When people are informed and share this knowledge, those who suffer from a mental illness have the opportunity to be viewed in the same compassionate way as someone with any other physical disease.

Part 2

SUICIDE, GRIEF, AND LOSS

Chapter 10

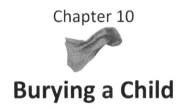

Burying a Child

How do you go on with your life after you have lived a parent's worst nightmare? Your child just died, and to complicate your grief, he died from suicide. I didn't know how to answer that question until it happened, even though my wife and I knew it was always on the horizon.

HOW DO YOU PREPARE FOR THE INEVITABLE?

On June the second of 2006, Eileen got a call from the group home asking us if Sean was at our house. Our routine was to bring him home for the weekend, and it was not the weekend. Eileen said, "No, he's not here. Why would he be here? We didn't come to pick him up. Isn't he there?"

"Well, no," they said. "He was supposed to be going out with some friends to a movie."

"Seriously? After what this kid went through, you didn't double-check what he was doing?"

It was a little after ten-thirty p.m. when Eileen got the call. I was out with my son Pat and his good friend, Kenny, for his birthday. Eileen tracked me down at the pizza parlor and told me what had happened, and I headed home, sure that Sean was experiencing his last hours on earth, if he was not already gone. His being missing was not a mistake; it was a calculated move on Sean's part. He was done with his life of suffering.

Not long after that, Eileen heard the phone ring, but by the time she got to it, nobody was on the other end of the line, and there was no caller identification number. When I got home about eleven, she told me the story and broke down in tears. She said, "He's gone. We just need to find him." She knew Sean was gone as only a mother could.

Throughout that night, we waited...and waited...and waited. The next morning, I went to nine a.m. Mass. I prayed, "Please, Lord. I know he's in heaven. We just need to find him." As I exited the church, I got a call from my mom's nursing home. She had been rushed to the hospital and I had to meet them at the emergency room. I wondered if things could get any worse.

You're not supposed to have your cell phone on in the emergency room, so I put it in my pocket on vibrate. It rang, but I didn't feel it vibrate. A bit later, I felt a reminder message come in. It was a Chicago number I didn't recognize. I went outside, and I listened to the voice message I will never forget: "This is Sergeant So-and-So of the Chicago Police Department. We found your son dead at a hotel on Washington Street, and he's been transported to the Cook County morgue. Can you come down and identify him?"

My first thought was, "Oh, my God! I've got to get hold of Eileen before he calls her!"

Unfortunately, it was too late. The sergeant called Eileen when he did not get hold of me the first time. I finally reached her and listened to the wail from her soul that her son was now in heaven. I called my brother-in-law Mark to sit with my mom. When I told her I needed to go and she asked why, I said, "Sean needs me." Truth be told, he didn't need me anymore; it was I who needed him.

I wanted to drive back home. It was only a twenty-minute ride, but Eileen, concerned about me, sent my son Pat and my brother-in-law Terry to pick me up. They had been at the house waiting to leave for a White Sox baseball game.

I sat on a hill outside the emergency room. I remember distinctly that it was a bright, sunny day, yet my world was all black. I didn't even cry. I just sat there thinking. For almost six years, we had lived in fear of this day. It certainly was not a surprise. Here it was, and I should be ready. Yet, I felt so numb, so lost. The only feeling I could recognize was relief; Sean had been found and was no longer suffering.

We went to the morgue later that afternoon to identify Sean. Up to that point in my life, several tragic events had occurred that had affected me personally and professionally, but going down to the Cook County Morgue was probably the hardest thing I've ever had to do.

To this day, I have flashbacks because of my own post-traumatic stress, which is not tied to emergency incidents, but to Sean's life. I can vividly picture him in the body bag, his hands tucked underneath his head in a very comfortable position. He looked peaceful. As a firefighter, I had witnessed many dead people, but it's a whole new ballgame when that person is your "Boomer," your little boy.

All my wife wanted to do was to kiss him on the forehead, but they wouldn't let her. Sean was part of a crime scene! I remember the crying and the despair that everyone felt, but I also remember a sense of peace, as if Sean were saying, "Hey, Dad. This time I got in for good. This time they're going to keep me home here. I don't have to come back. Grandpa Mike said so."

Now, that sounds great, but I will tell you that, even though I had spent twenty-four hours waiting to confirm what I already felt, that Sean was in heaven, seeing his body and the finality of it all was very different. The pain was numbing and deep in my bones, like nothing I had felt before. My brother-in-law Kieran had come with us to make the identification, and he said it best: "I never really saw his pain until the look on his face, now. Finally, I can see the pain of his illness." Sean was indeed at peace, but unfortunately, our suffering was just beginning.

THERE IS NO PARENTS' HANDBOOK
FOR BURYING YOUR CHILD

Eileen wanted to see Sean as soon as he was released to the funeral director. By then, it was a few days after his passing and post-autopsy. I begged her to back off, but she wouldn't and couldn't. I was afraid about how Sean would look and that it would be Eileen's last memory of him—not that the morgue view was any better. The funeral director, Brian, was excellent, and he convinced her to wait until he'd had a chance to take care of Sean.

We picked out a beautiful green casket in something we thought he would have liked. This decision had been directly preceded by a guy with a Notre Dame license plate cutting us off as we pulled into the funeral home parking lot. A big "signs" guy, I told Eileen, "Sean wants it green!" Even when you think you have prepared yourself for the inevitable, that, having no relief from his illness, your child will take his life, you are never prepared to pick out your own child's casket. Humor was my only way of coping at that time. All my other emotions seemed disconnected. This just couldn't be real.

The funeral director, Brian, called to say that Eileen would be able to come and see Sean hours before anyone else. Without her knowing, I called Brian, to make sure Sean was okay for her to view. He assured me.

We arrived a couple of hours before the viewing. Eileen got out of the car and said, "I need to do this on my own."

Now, I have to say that, at first, I was startled and upset. I didn't want her to go in there alone because I didn't know how Sean might look, and also, I wanted to be the first one to see my son. I compromised and walked her to the parlor door. The casket was open, and I could see the profile of our dear Sean from a distance. Brian, the funeral director, who was such a class act throughout, escorted Eileen to the casket. As she approached, I heard her say, "Oh, my Seany boy." I knew it was right to leave then, as only the mother who carried that child could feel worse than I did. I wept as I went outside to wait for her.

Sitting in that parking lot, I again tried to process what was happening. "Today is my son's wake!" I thought. Eileen's worst nightmare since we got married and even before children was coming true. Even when I had written the back page of the Mass booklet using Sean's words, a message I prayed to hear him speak, it still seemed like just a bad dream. Now, it was real, and I was caught between relief for him and the unbelievable fear of what life without Sean would do to Eileen and me as a couple and to me as a Dad. I had failed as the leader of my family to protect my son.

After what seemed hours, but was probably only fifteen minutes, I summoned the courage to go back in. When I walked in, I was surprised to see that Eileen was not alone with Sean. At first, I thought it was the funeral director, but, instead, it was Eileen's brother Terry. Terry had arrived early to support us, and when he saw Eileen alone, he went to her side. That is who Terry is! As I approached the casket, I walked at the pace of a 100-year-old man, knowing that each step drew me closer to the reality that I would never again get a "Sean" hug on this earth. I wanted to scream, cry, and vomit all at the same time. Finally, I reached him, and given what his body had been through, he looked quite similar to our Sean, but not 100 percent. When I kissed him on his cold forehead, I said: "This body did you no good, Sean. I'm glad you left it behind."

The wake was huge. Eileen was one of thirteen children, eight brothers and five sisters. They were a popular family in Oak Park, where they grew up. They all had many friends. There were over thirty first cousins of Sean's on Eileen's side of the family alone. My fire service brotherhood attended and friends of ours from many walks of life. As you can imagine, at one point there was a three-and-a-half-hour wait. People just kept coming. My brothers-in-law stood on the opposite side of the room from us as we greeted the well-wishers. They were like an honor guard watching over Sean and us, never leaving their places for the eight hours of grueling raw emotion. I will always remember that.

I do not remember two thirds of those who attended. I was distracted, worried about how Eileen and the boys were hurting both emotionally and physically. Standing up there for eight hours straight, consoling people rather than the other way around, was grueling. Father Gavin had told us that in that receiving line, we would be the consolers. I thought, "Well, that is B.S." I mean, we are the ones who have lost our son and brother! But he was so right.

I wondered what people in line were saying about Sean's cause of death. You see, most, including those who knew our family well, had no idea that Sean's mental illness was terminal or that he had tried to take his life numerous times before. Some just thought he was a drug addict who overdosed. That just killed me, but I was to blame. I had never shared his illness with them, his battle against this painful physical illness, because of the stigma of mental health; so how could they have known? Thus, they chose the easiest answer to the complex question of what had killed Sean Kenny. His mental illness, especially his obsessive-compulsive disorder (OCD) with horrible intrusive thoughts was indeed what had killed Sean Kenny.

That afternoon into the evening was filled with stories of Sean's goodness in deeds done for others. I had thought my Dad's wake was a terrible ordeal; this was so much harder, one wave of pain after another. I think what hurt most was to hear about Sean's positive impact on so many people. I was angry that this disease had not allowed him to complete his mission, to share his goodness with so many more, and to give his life more meaning. Little did I know that quite the opposite would be the case going forward.

ADVICE TO FOLLOW AT A WAKE

People do not know what to say when you lose a child, especially a child who died by suicide. They may say dumb things like, "He's so much better off." Like that's supposed to make the hole in your heart feel better. Some tried to share that they "understood" and could "sympathize" with our pain. No, they couldn't, not unless they had lost a child, too. These are things that grieving loved ones hear.

If you haven't lost a child, then you don't have a clue, and I hope you never do. Others say that "you will get over it" or "time heals all." I will *never* get over the loss of Sean, and while time has allowed me to move forward with that loss in my heart, it will not replace giving Sean a back rub as I did the week before he died. Please don't try to match or, worse yet, one-up the pain of those grieving by sharing your own stories of loss. A wake is not the time to put on your Cape and try to save them from this horrible pain, because words can't. It is not a contest to see who has suffered the most. "He is better off and with God, now" is something many people say. While I believe that, and I did indeed think Sean was healthy, finally, it wasn't the right time to hear it; the pain was too excruciating for divine intervention.

Others just gave a hug and cried with us. If you are ever in that horrible spot, a big hug with a tight squeeze is the best medicine you can provide. And let the grievers cry on your shoulder if they need to. You can't fix what happened, and probably can't fathom the depth of the pain either, but a hug that says, "I'm so sorry, and we loved him, too, and we love you" is powerful. Many in attendance greeted us that way, and those simple acts of kindness refilled my soul emotionally and got me through the most grueling day of my life. They were my life preservers.

THE FUNERAL

We gave Sean a funeral he would have loved, with an Irish theme and a wonderful celebrant of the Mass, Father Gavin Quinn, who understood Sean's battle with mental illness. He skillfully used his homily to educate all in attendance on Sean being in "the deep and the dark with no light to see a way out." The church was packed.

Eileen and I wrote our parts of the eulogy on that sunny morning, sitting separately on our driveway. Patrick had offered to speak, too. He went first. He began with what may have been the most powerful statement of the three eulogies. Pat said that he had not wanted to speak, that he had been afraid, but then he had remembered all those mornings when Sean woke up and did not want to get out of bed because he feared what the day would bring. Sean did it, anyway, so Pat was not going to let Sean down. His speech was short, but powerful. Pat truly captured Sean's fighting spirit. He was not some loser who had died of a drug overdose, but a courageous young brother afflicted with a horrible disease.

Eileen was next. I stood on the altar next to her. She spoke eloquently and kept her emotions in control. People heard her passion. She desperately wanted the audience to know what a fine son Sean was; that he had been so ill and not by choice, but with a physical illness. I kept my hand on her shoulder to steady her, but she didn't need it. She was on a mission, and boy, did she deliver. Afterward, many commented on her incredible strength. It was evident where Sean got his courage.

By the time it was my turn, I didn't really need to speak; it had all been said by Pat and Eileen. However, I thought it was my last opportunity to tell the world about Sean. I don't have a clue what I said. The Mass was videotaped, but it cut off right before I spoke, so I still don't know exactly what I said. I just remember that when I finished, people were all standing as I kissed Sean's casket and held our family in a group hug. I knew by their reactions that at least this group of people assembled knew Sean Kenny, his kind heart, what he stood for, how he battled, and why he died.

The procession to the cemetery was massive, and the gravesite was packed. While the service there is blurry, I remember two things vividly.

My brother-in-law Bob, who was in his final year of battling ALS, walked with assistance the 150 or so yards to the gravesite, over my protest. Bob couldn't have weighed more than a hundred pounds—his suit was nearly falling off his frame. He had known about Sean's journey as they both faced a terminal opponent that would ultimately send them home to heaven. He was *not* going to be denied, even though, for him, it had to seem like a marathon distance. And, by God, he did it. All stood at the grave watching, many with tears in their eyes and admiration, for this man saying goodbye to his partner in a terminal-illness battle. Often, over the years after Bob's diagnosis, they talked privately, as only two who were courageously facing insurmountable odds could. Bob always encouraged his co-warrior Sean.

The second thing I remember happened as they were about to lower Sean into the ground. I took off the tie he had laughed at back on St. Patrick's Day, when he was fresh out of the coma, and tied it to the rail on the casket. Finally, as they lowered his body, I lost it. My son was going into the ground, never to be seen again on this earth. The pain in my heart was so bad I was sure I was having a heart attack. You know, I wished I was, because I wanted to join him. It was just like I had felt when I lost my Dad, decades before.

We held the funeral luncheon in an Irish bar that Sean had loved. We had planned to have his twenty-first birthday there later that year. The wonderful owner and family friend, Rich, had hung Sean's picture above the bar, and a bagpiper led us in.

At that point, the family was so tired that there were no more tears. We made the luncheon a celebration of his life. I found out later that many who attended, including some family members, had disapproved of the location. They thought it was disrespectful to hold Sean's funeral luncheon in a bar when he had suffered from addictions and eventually took his life through an overdose. Good thing I did not know about it that day, or Sean would have had loads of company in heaven with him. When you lose a child, there are no rules. You make them up as you go, doing the best you can to honor that child. That is precisely what we did that day, and I would do it again in a heartbeat.

WHY DIDN'T HE COME TO ME?

It was a powerful send-off with much joy and great Sean stories his friends shared with Eileen and me. One exchange affected me more than others. A neighbor who was feeling no pain at the time, leaned in and said to me, "I get why Sean couldn't come to you guys, but all he had to do was come to me."

I got it, but did he think it was that easy? Did he think all Sean needed was another voice? Not in his pain, not by the end, and he had loads of voices along the way, all willing to help. People try to force some kind of logic out of a horrible situation like suicide when the reality is that it is too complicated to simplify. It was sad and ironic that, years later, that neighbor took his own life. He was a wonderful man, a good husband and father, and a good friend. When he got to heaven, I wonder if he told Sean, "Now, I get it."

AFTER THE FUNERAL

Beyond the heartfelt hug, what can you do? What happens after the wake and funeral is important. Don't shy away from the family. Engage them. Invite them to any event, just as you would have before. They may say no a hundred times, but at least they know they are not excluded because their kid "killed himself." Trust me, it happened to us. Sean was a "bad example," maybe a result of "poor parenting." "Poor kid was a drug addict; what did they expect?"

Remember the first anniversary of the child's passing, and if you can in the years to come, do the same every year. Send a card, make a phone call; any outreach is appreciated. The message is inconsequential; what carries the power is that you remember their loved one. To get a call or a card years later, remembering the anniversary of Sean's death, is a wonderfully uplifting moment for our family. I learned to do the same today as a direct result of that lesson I learned from Sean.

If you see family members in a store or at the local pizza parlor, approach them and say hello. We don't bite, and the disease is not contagious. As a family, we will be in pain from that moment of loss onward, and the only way you can make it worse is to ignore our son and us!

LESSONS LEARNED

- **You are never prepared to lose your child.** This might be the most obvious of all lessons learned: you are never ready to bury your child. Even when you know they are terminal, reality does not set in until you see that lifeless body. Be gentle with yourself. No matter how hard you try, you can't fully prepare for the grief until it happens.
- **There is nothing you can say to make a parent's pain go away.** That hole is eternal. However, some things you say will make it worse:
    - "I understand, and I can sympathize with your pain." No, you can't.
    - "He is so much better off." True, but I want to see him laugh again.
    - "He is with God, now." True, but I'm not, and it may be a long wait.
- **There are helpful ways to give comfort.**
    - **Give a big hug** with a tight squeeze and let them cry on your shoulder. This is the best medicine you can provide at such a moment. You can't fix what happened, and you probably can't fathom the depth of their pain, either, but a hug is powerful and clearly communicates, "I'm so sorry, and we loved him, too, and we love you."
    - **Invite them to events.** What happens after the wake and funeral is important. Don't shy away from the family. Engage them by inviting them to any event, just as you would have before this happened.
- **Remember the first anniversary of the child passing.** And, if you can in the years to come, do the same. Send a card or make a phone call. Any outreach is appreciated.
- **Engage.** If you see family members out in public, approach them and say hello. They won't bite. The family will be in pain

from that moment of loss on, and the only way you can make it worse is to ignore the life that existed and the family that remains behind.

- **Give comfort without expectations.** Don't have an outcome in mind. Remember, it is about them, not you. You may call several times and get no answer, and while that may be frustrating because you expect a return call, think of it like this: they know you care, and if they think talking to you will help, they will reach out.

Chapter 11

Honor Your Loved One

Death does not end a relationship. Keep that light burning.
Redefine their mission.

How do you go on when your child dies? From the day he went to heaven, Sean had told me clearly that while he was not here physically, he was certainly going to remain a part of my life. I needed to make sense of his suffering and his life's mission. How would I keep his memory alive instead of running away from the pain? Our counselor had told us people would literally run away when they saw us because they did not know what to say to address our loss.

Everyone approaches that challenge differently. Some establish scholarships, do charitable runs, or hold golf outings in memory of their child. In all cases, they honor their child's life; they do not bury him. Only the body is buried, not the soul of that child. Death does not destroy your relationship unless you allow it to occur.

You do need to try to keep the communication open with the "other side," and it is a conscious decision. The tough part is that you don't get the feedback in the way you were used to. The hearing part is altered. I can't ask and get an immediate verbal response. The answer you seek may not come at the time you desire, or it might come through signs rather than through vocal sounds. It takes effort and perseverance. I was listening for what Sean wanted me to do. "Sean, lead me!" I prayed, and he did.

The day we buried Sean's body marked the day I began my journey of realization that Sean's legacy was to save others through sharing his life's battles. His suffering would not be in vain, and I would not let him die with his burial. I would use his incredible energy for good, take that stigma of mental illness and put a beautiful, strong, kind face to it. Sean Kenny would be that face of mental illness, and he would live on through Eileen and me as we shared his message.

When you have lost a child, you notice that people avoid mentioning your child's name. They don't mention him because they don't want to upset you. However, as I told friends, you couldn't possibly make me feel any worse than I do except if you were to ignore Sean's life, his very presence. That's when you will see the real fire in my eyes. Yes, I may cry when you speak of him, but they will be tears of joy because you remember him for who he was, and not how he died.

When I was going through Sean's room months after he passed, I found a program he had filled out for school when he was ten-and-a-half:

> *"My name is Sean Kenny. I am 10-and-a-half. I'm an expert at fixing things and running. My favorite book is The Twits. My best school subject is spelling because I like it. What I like to do most is swim, and when I grow up, I will be a fireman."*

I never got to pin that fireman's badge on Sean as I had thought I might. It is one of my biggest regrets, because if he had been healthy, I can see that he would have made a great firefighter.

In truth, Sean Kenny has saved more firefighters by giving his life and teaching me lessons to pass on to them about mental health than anybody I've touched in over thirty-eight years in fire service. I could line up the careers of decades of firefighters back to back to back who have not touched as many people as he has. So, although I did not officially put him in that uniform and pin that badge on him, as God is my witness, Sean Kenny is a firefighter with his station in heaven. He will continue to be one until the day I die, saving lives, just in a different way.

LESSONS LEARNED

How do you go on with your life when your child dies?

- **You figure out a way to honor your child.** It doesn't have to be elaborate; it can be as simple as a balloon release on the anniversary.
- **You work hard to maintain that relationship.** Look for your child; reach out in prayer, thoughts, and deeds. Listen *really hard* for your child's voice and look for signs.
- **You run toward the pain through counseling, not away from it.** A counselor will warn you about traps to avoid. You CANNOT do it alone, and retreating to your safe zone as the leader only avoids the inevitable. That pain in your soul, ignored, does not dissipate. It intensifies, and you can't lead if you are too injured to function.
- **Talk about your child often and to all.** Initiate a conversation about your child. It gives others permission to not only talk about your child, but to ask questions like, "What is it like to lose a child? How do you go on?"

Chapter 12

The Loss of a Spouse

Days turn into months that turn into years as you try to move forward after any loss of a loved one. In the case of a child, you frantically search for ways to see what in this life can be used as a Band-Aid for that gaping wound. I hoped that one day Eileen and I might be blessed to have a grandchild. I knew, of course, that no one would replace Sean, but I hoped to see the joy on Eileen's face when a grandchild would be born. I assumed it would give her a gift of life and joy that Sean's physical absence was robbing her of.

The leader of a team often tries to "fix" problems with new and aggressive strategies that boost morale. As if with a crystal ball, you choose a plan based on how you think your employees will react. The problem is that you can't always control the mitigating circumstances around the plan, and those variables can drastically affect the outcome.

A BRIGHT FUTURE

In 2015, I thought I had a lot figured out, a clear crystal-ball view. On September 11, 2015, our son Patrick officially asked Abbie Rogers to be his wife. Eileen was thrilled. She and Abbie had hit it off right away, which was very different from the contentious relationship my mom had imposed on Eileen as a daughter-in-law, so the future was full of joy and hope.

The party we had on that day gave September 11th a new, and positive feeling for me. The world had been robbed on September 11, 2001—so many losses, and for me especially, 343 firefighters. Now, we could envision a day in the future when, God willing, we would have the grandchild we so longed for. Hoping to comfort Eileen, it was something I had prayed for fervently.

That year, I also made the decision to retire in May of 2017 on my sixtieth birthday. I would announce it in the oldest pub in Ireland, which is called Sean's Pub. It's in Athlone, a tiny town. With Eileen sitting on my lap, I planned to call in and announce, "I've retired." She had not wanted to go back to Ireland since our trip there with Sean in 2003 because it would have been just too painful to go back without him. However, she liked the thought of going back for this. She loved the idea of sharing it with him, so we agreed to do it.

A SHOCKING DIAGNOSIS

In October of 2015, Eileen started to have breathing problems. She had experienced a lung cancer scare in the late 1980s, which turned out to be sarcoidosis. This seemed different, so the doctor ordered a full scan, not just her lungs, and thank God, it came back all right.

Nevertheless, she continued to complain. She just didn't feel right. Her sleep was often fitful to the point that I had begun sleeping in another room to afford her more comfort. We celebrated the Irish New Year at six p.m., a perfect scenario for us old folks. On New Year's Eve in 2015, Eileen had tried to set a beer bottle on a table at the party we attended, but she missed the table, and the bottle broke. Of course, everybody laughed and said, "You need to cut her off," and blah, blah, blah. When we were driving home, she said, "I'm not drunk. I missed the table."

"Well, don't worry about it. It's not a big deal," I said.

Eileen was scheduled to go with me to Arizona in January to do Sean's talk, and then we were going on to California to visit my brother-in-law. That first week of January 2016, she said, "I'm starting to notice some other things. I'm having some trouble writing."

"When did this start?"

"Well, when I was writing Christmas cards, it seemed hard to write my name."

"We need to go see somebody. This is serious."

We went to a neurologist right before we left for Arizona. After a physical exam, the neurologist said, "I don't see anything here. I think you're just anxious. There are a lot of things going on. We just came off the holidays, and it's a very emotional time without your son."

"Is it okay for me to go on this trip to Arizona?" Eileen asked.

The neurologist said, "Absolutely. When you come back, just to be overcautious, we'll do an MRI, but don't worry about it."

When she walked out of the room, Eileen looked at me with a combination of despair and Irish anger. "She doesn't believe me!"

"Well, it doesn't matter. She said it was okay to go on the trip. We'll go on the trip. When we come back, we'll do the MRI right away." That was the plan.

We got out to Scottsdale, Arizona early in the morning. In the afternoon, we went out to a country-western bar and had a blast. My worry was on hold. We came back to the hotel that night and decided to order pizza. "I'm going to call out this number from my phone," I said. "Can you write it down, and then we'll call for the pizza?"

I called out the number, and I could hear Eileen start to cry. I looked over my shoulder, "What's the matter?"

She said, "I can't write."

"What do you mean you can't write?"

"I can't write the number."

Now, my wife was one of the strongest human beings I have ever met. I would put her up against any firefighter in terms of internal strength, yet she broke down and cried harder than she had since Sean's passing. I went to her and held her.

"What's the matter?"

She said in a somber voice that I can still hear, "There's something very, very wrong."

"We need to get out of here."

97

I left to talk to the chief who was running the symposium at which I was scheduled to speak. "I need to get her in for tests," I told him.

"Forget it, Pat. You don't need to talk tomorrow. You're going to go home. We'll get you to the airport and get her home."

All the fear and anxiety I had felt with Sean rose up in full force and shot throughout my body. Something horrible was happening to someone I loved, and once again I was just a spectator. Again, I had no Cape, no way to protect my wife from what this could be.

That night, we sat up, talking and crying through most of the night. I had never seen Eileen so afraid. Finally, she fell asleep. I went out on the hotel balcony. I pleaded out loud with God. This couldn't happen again. "I'm not strong enough to bury another family member. Please, whatever it is, give it to me."

In the morning, I got up, intending to go home. Eileen awoke and said, "Hell, no. You are not going home until you deliver Sean's talk. We came here for these people. There's somebody here who needs to hear that talk. I'll be fine. We're going home when we were supposed to."

So, I did. I did the talk with Eileen standing in the back of the room as she usually did to give me confidence. The whole time, I was distracted, looking at her, wondering what was going on. How serious could it be when we had just started to see symptoms? She'd had a full scan back in October that was okay.

We came home, and Eileen had her test. The morning after, I got a phone call at seven-thirty from the neurologist. Seeing the number, I took the call in Sean's room. "You need to get in here right away," she said.

"What are you talking about?"

"Well, your wife's tests have come back, and there are several shadows on the brain."

I put the phone down. I remember saying, aloud, "No, Sean, not again. I can't do it. You have to help Mom. I can't lose her, too." I wandered to the back of the house where she was sitting in our bedroom.

"Who was that?"

"It was the neurologist."

"Do they have my test results?"

"Yeah," and my voice cracked. "You need to pack a bag. We need to go. They found some things." I just started to sob. She did, too, but she said, "It's okay, Pat. They didn't believe me. At least now we know there's something there."

There she was, comforting me! Yeah, that's the kind of woman she was, always more worried about others.

We went straight to the hospital, and they ran more tests. Her brain was full of tumors. They were going to put her in the hospital and do more tests to see whether the tumors were malignant or part of some other disease, maybe even the sarcoidosis again.

They ran more scans and then did a biopsy. Even as they were fitting Eileen with a heavy, prehistoric-looking cage that they literally screwed into her skull to hold it in place for the biopsy, she was upbeat. She told the nurses I was a great husband—except for that one time.

Well, after thirty-five years of marriage, that "one time" could be a million things, some not so flattering. Eileen told the story of how I had hit her with a pitch after she'd gotten a hit off me in a schoolyard game of fast pitching when we were dating. It was true, but come on! It was only a rubber ball! I sat behind her out of sight and cried. My heart was tearing apart at the seams. There she was, praising me, staying in good humor all the while she was in that cage.

Our son Pat and I sat for what seemed like days, waiting for the doctor to come to the post-op waiting room. Finally, he did, and when he started with, "I'm sorry," I could feel my body go limp. The tests showed that Eileen had nine tumors in her brain that were malignant. It was terminal glioblastoma stage IV, an aggressive cancer with no surgical option. They could only provide treatment to buy what was referred to by her oncologist as "quality time."

HAD WE KNOWN?

Three years earlier, I included a slide in Sean's talk comparing a well-known physical illness to mental illness to show that both were, indeed, physical issues. Eileen and I had worked on it together, and we chose brain cancer. We felt that if Sean had suffered from brain cancer instead of mental illness, all would have believed and understood his plight, and we would have been able to share his fight more openly.

I looked at her after the diagnosis. I was crying as I said, "Did we know? Did we know that this was going to happen? Why did we pick that disease? Why was that the comparable?"

I have a lot of 'whys' in my life. This was the biggest why I had been faced with. Why Eileen? Why was our family going to be devastated at precisely the moment we saw joy on the horizon, especially for Eileen?

When I looked at the comparisons as she went through her treatments, the "beatings" that she took, one day feeling that a treatment was going to help and the next day it only made her worse. I thought about what Sean had been through, and the parallels got stronger. Except this time, we told people. This time the word was out that our family was facing another terminal illness. We held a pep rally for her before she started her treatment at the same Irish pub where we'd held Sean's funeral luncheon. It was packed with people cheering for her: "Go get this!" If we had done that for Sean with his mental health struggles, can you imagine how he would have felt to know that a roomful of people was rooting for him to battle something that was also terminal?

My fault. I was so afraid of how Sean would be looked at by others that I never shared his plight. As a leader of my family, I had failed to get support for my boys and my wife from an educated group of family and friends. But I had also failed because I didn't enhance the culture of my organization. I didn't "normalize" Sean's illness by presenting it as a physical illness no different than diabetes, high blood pressure, or cancer. At the time, I just didn't understand mental illness as I do today.

That lack of understanding coupled with feelings of letting Sean down in my role as his protector had left me emotionally drained and confused. I couldn't find my Cape and, frankly, I was ashamed I even had one.

In hindsight, Sean helped me learn and grow so much that I can now see what I could not before.

For eleven months, Eileen battled this horrible disease until Sean came to get her on November 5, 2016. On November 1st, All Saints Day, Eileen had had a vision of Sean in which he told her that he was coming to get her. We had a wake on Monday the 7th, a funeral on Tuesday the 8th, a wedding rehearsal on Friday the 11th for Abbie and Pat, and their wedding on Saturday the 12th.

I was faced with the fact that my wife, the mother of my children, the mother of the groom, and most important to me, my best friend, was gone at the most powerful, positive moment in our family's history. We—Abbie, Pat, both families, and friends—made it through the wedding because we had promised Eileen that we would. All in attendance, including our wonderful new in-laws and their friends, hit the day hard with their joy.

Eileen had warned me that last week after she had received Sean's message: "You can't be sad. They will all be watching you. Abbie has sacrificed this whole year when it should have been all about her, and instead, it was all about me."

I looked at her with disbelief. "We've been married for over thirty-five years. You have asked a lot of me, and I have always tried to oblige, but nothing as hard as this request. How can I be happy without you?"

She looked me right in the eye and said, "I'm counting on you."

I'm not sure how I did it except that I had promised. Don't miss this point: I enjoyed the wedding immensely because I was so happy for Pat and Abbie. I know for sure that Eileen helped me with that joy, as she had promised she would.

At the same time, though, sometimes I would sneak back to my hotel room, which was attached to the banquet hall. I would sob, wash my face, and come back out. I felt like a boxer coming out of the corner for another round. We didn't close the post-reception until almost three thirty in the morning. Eileen would have closed the party, so I was hell-bent to do just that. As I walked back to my room, I wondered what life would be like now, not only for me but for my boys, without the rock of our family.

LESSONS LEARNED

- **Want to make God laugh? Tell him your plan.** Don't count on life going the way you planned. Unexpected things occur all the time. God may have other ideas.
- **Be open to signs.** Signs you don't recognize or understand at the time may predict or warn what is ahead, both good and bad.
- **You can amaze yourself with your resiliency if you have faith that you are not alone.** I experienced burying my wife and best friend of thirty-five years on a Tuesday and attended a beautiful wedding for my son Pat and his wife Abbie that next Saturday. I only made it through because I believed Sean and Eileen were together again, and they had my back.

Chapter 13

Talking to Surviving Children about Death and Grief

It's always tricky dealing with surviving children about how you handle death and grief. Let's back up, though, and first talk about how to approach your children when you can see death coming.

Eileen's and Sean's cases were terminal, so we simply told them the truth and kept them informed. In Sean's case, that was a challenge. Half the time, we didn't know what the truth was, and we certainly couldn't predict how things were going to go. However, I would like to think both of our other boys, Brendan and Patrick, knew how ill Sean was, and also knew about his multiple suicide attempts and hospitalizations.

In Eileen's case, we knew from the time of the original diagnosis that the disease was terminal, and it became visibly undeniable as she deteriorated that death was lurking around the corner. Again, our communication was honest and, frankly, very painful. As a parent, you try to walk the fine line between honesty and not causing any more agony than is necessary at any given moment.

I looked back to my own father's illness, and from that, I learned what not to do. My dad got sick on December 26th and died on January 1. I had a chance to see him only once during his time in the hospital. He looked so yellow and afraid. My mom had repeatedly told me that everything would be okay when the doctors were telling her quite the opposite.

When she walked into the house that morning and told me he was gone, I already knew. I knew in my soul the day I visited him how ill he was, but no one had had the courage to let me in on the horrible secret. That was the hardest part after he passed. If I had known when I went to see him how ill he was, that he was really dying, I would've said some things that I still carry with me today. Things that a typical fourteen-year-old would tell his dad if he knew he was going to die in the next two days. Things like, "I'm sorry, Dad, I was such an ass. That was just a stupid teenager talking. I'm sorry, and I love you."

KEEP THE LINES OF COMMUNICATION OPEN

This is the best advice I can give you regarding your children, and it comes from my own experience. There's no wrong time to have a conversation, nor is there any content that's out of bounds. Feelings should not be debated or rationalized; they need to be vented. Find a good professional counselor who you see either as a family or as individuals to help walk that road.

There are loads of books out there on how to survive the grieving process and what it looks like (the stages, etc.). The authors know so much more than I do, and they are excellent guides, I'm sure. I am no authority on which ones are better than others. What I can say is that sustaining a loss and grieving are unique for each person as to what you experience and at how deeply the pain impacts you.

As the parent, be patient with your children. Try to understand their journey. Patience and understanding are imperative to keeping the lines of communication open for many things, not just for surviving this loss but for other life challenges in the future.

YOUR KIDS NEED SUPPORT AS YOU GRIEVE

After Sean passed, Eileen and I found that we were deeply immersed in our grief. I will speak for myself when I say I don't think I did a very good job of taking my own advice. Both Brendan and Patrick were suffering. We encouraged them to seek counseling, but frankly, that was about it. The struggle was to get through each day as Sean's mom and dad and that loss, and forgetting how blessed we were to have Brendan and Pat. But they had lost a brother. Parents tend to get all the attention while siblings, other than their friends, get little support. Please keep your kids on your radar when something like this happens. They, too, are devastated and are probably at a loss as to how to care for their grieving parents.

Grief affects every individual differently and also affects the family unit. Initially, nothing seems worth doing, and everyone walks on eggshells. *However, life is still there to be lived, and as a parent, one way to keep your family intact is to realize the value of the children you have left and encourage them to move forward and grow.* You can't push the pace; it is painfully slow with a lot of setbacks. Just keep your eye on the goal, that you are indeed moving forward as a family in honor of the person you lost, not despite the person you lost, and that intention will increase your chances for success.

LESSONS LEARNED

- **Grieving is unique for each person.** What each of you experiences and the rate at which the pain impacts you is different. Initially, nothing seems worth doing, and everyone walks on eggshells, but life is still there to be lived. You lost one person, not the whole family.

- **Be transparent.** Whether the loss was anticipated, as with Eileen, or sudden as with Sean's, the best approach is to tell your children the truth and keep them informed. They know more than you think they do about the situation and your distress.

- **Patience and communication are key.** When a parent loses a child and siblings are involved, it is imperative to be patient with your other children and try to understand their journey. This will keep the lines of communication open so they can grieve, too.

- **Value your remaining children.** Realize the value of your remaining children and encourage them to move forward and grow. This is essential to keeping your family unit intact and providing the motivation to move forward.

Chapter 14

Managing Social Relationships

After the death of a loved one, social environments and relationships may be altered for both children and parents. Sometimes, large events don't include your family because a person is missing from your family unit. Your family is "broken," and nobody knows what to say or whether just the very nature of an invitation will cause you more pain.

I cannot emphasize enough how essential it is to be included in gatherings by friends and family, how essential it is for the loved one you lost to be remembered and spoken about often—not the opposite. Along the way, you may lose friends you thought were very close. They can't understand, or choose not to understand, the grief your family is going through. Just because someone is a relative doesn't mean he knows all the tentacles of your grieving process. Misguided but well-intended words can be just as painful coming from someone you thought you knew well as they do when they come from an acquaintance or a complete stranger. If social environments and relationships are altered for you and your children, you learn to make new relationships.

EACH PERSON'S TIMELINE FOR GRIEVING IS UNIQUE

Some people have a timeline in mind as to what is acceptable as a period of grieving. I will tell you that people who think about timelines have never lost anyone they truly cared about, because there is no timeline when a loved one is physically gone from your sight. Everything is a timeless foggy gray. There is no special potion for healing loss or grief.

When someone advises me to find a new norm, I can only say that there will never be a new norm. Instead, there can only be an adjustment to the one who is missing.

To move forward, find ways to honor those who have passed. Keep your memories of them alive daily with positive thoughts. Try not to focus on what you've lost; instead, focus on appreciating the good fortune you had to be with them in the first place. It takes a conscious effort; it doesn't happen by itself, and it takes time to be ready to move the family forward. Even though you are a family unit, you are still a group of individuals, and you will heal and grieve at different rates. It's not only okay but healthy to talk about those differences out loud, so everybody is aware that there is no one right way to grieve.

You learn to live without your loved one because you don't have a choice! If I did, I would reach across that invisible barrier and retrieve my dad, Sean, and Eileen, but it's not that easy. That's why they call it faith.

WHAT YOU'RE FEELING IS NORMAL

The path forward is painful, but it is possible through both education and counseling. What you're feeling is normal. Find a counselor. Be patient with yourself, knowing that there will be good and bad days. Finally, the love and support of those around you will greatly assist your forward progress.

Your angels on the other side can only do so much. You still are in control here. They are just your support group as you make the effort to push the proverbial rock of grief back up the hill and bear the brunt of the pain that goes with it, because there is no way around it.

LESSONS LEARNED

- **Stay connected to friends and family.** It is essential to be included by friends and family in social activities.

- **Talk about your lost loved one.** The loved one you lost needs to be remembered and spoken about often and in group settings, not the opposite.
- **There is no timeline for grieving.** The process is too painful and complicated to put a number on the days, months, or years until "it will get better."
- **Lean on your faith.** The pain of your loss never goes away. That is the price for loving someone. However, you do learn to manage the situation, using your faith as your life preserver.
- **Seek professional help.** You learn to live without your loved one because you don't have a choice, so get professional help. My experience has taught me that trying to do it alone, while consistent with my Cape-wearing identity, was both frustrating and unsuccessful.

Chapter 15

Lessons Learned from Suicide, Grief, and Loss

The lessons learned from the grief that follows the loss of a loved one, whether due to natural causes or to suicide, are truly individual. There are many variables: your relationship with the person, the cause of death, the person's age, and so forth, and these variables affect what you take away from the devastation. I found one constant in dealing with grief and loss: there are no absolute rules to follow.

I will share some of the lessons I learned after losing my father during my teens to cancer in just five days, after losing a son to a fifteen-year terminal illness that culminated in a suicide, and after losing my wife of thirty-five years, after a courageous eleven-month battle with terminal cancer, just one week before our son's wedding.

EIGHT LESSONS LEARNED FROM SUICIDE, GRIEF, AND LOSS

1. **Never take the usual burial order for granted.** There is no guarantee that the oldest family member, routinely the dad, will go first, or that the children will bury their parents.
2. **Love your children.** Squeeze them tight every night because they may go first.
3. **Prayers are indeed answered, just not always the way you want.** With both Sean and Eileen, I prayed for them to be healed and not in pain, whether from mental illness or cancer.

In the end, that is true for them, just not in the way I had conceived it.

4. **Don't be afraid of grief.** By that, I mean don't try to hide your emotions, because they are inside you whether you like it or not. Don't worry about what others will think and keep the cellar door locked while those horrible emotions grow like mold until they break out, uncontrolled. Instead, kick the door open and let them out of the cellar despite what anybody else thinks, and watch them lose their steam, like a storm moving out into the ocean.

5. **Find a psychologist or psychiatrist you trust.** Don't be afraid to go regularly before, during, and after your loss. Counseling will help you understand your emotions as they leave the cellar where you have stored them. The pain is always there. My dad has been gone for forty-eight years, and sometimes it still feels like yesterday. That's why it's good to have someone on speed dial when the emotions return, and they will.

6. **Don't judge a person unless you've walked in his footsteps.** I thought I knew how I'd feel after Sean passed, but I had no idea how devastated I would be and how strong would be my sense of failure as a dad. Some others have said, "You wouldn't want him around with the life he had, would you?" That is not for you to say. During the last two months of her life when Eileen was so sick, I would sometimes wonder what it would be like to barbecue without her. It was something we had loved to do together, even in the depths of winter. As she lay in the hospital bed in the house, I would put her chair outside and pour her a drink. I thought, "This is what it's going to be like. I can do this." The very first time I tried after she went to heaven, it was not anywhere near as easy as I had practiced. In reality, it felt excruciatingly final, and you can't simulate that.

7. **Give a hug!** If you know someone who has experienced the loss of a loved one through suicide, you can't make their pain

any worse, and you can't fix it. So, don't be afraid to hug them. "Well," you may say, "I'm not a hugger." Become one! Sometimes that's the only thing you can do, and although it doesn't fix the pain, it gives some temporary relief.

8. **Don't be afraid to share what your journey was like with others.** This was my last lesson learned, and it is part of the motivation for this book. So many families have experienced devastating loss through suicide or cancer, and yet when it happens to you, you feel like you're the only one and what a failure you must be. When you are sharing your stories, both your good times and bad, your triumphs, and, most important, your struggles, you provide powerful support for people walking that same road.

Chapter 16

The Power of Professional Help

There's no question that I am an advocate for professional counseling for all, including leaders and their families.

All of us run into situations where we need guidance, somebody to help you navigate the road of life. Counseling can be an excellent tool for personal growth. Sometimes it is helpful to bounce your thoughts off someone else and hear them reflected in a different tone that leads to more clarity and success in whatever challenge you are facing. Sometimes you receive suggestions that help guide your decisions. Sometimes you may even receive a direct order.

I've had a counselor for many years but only started to go regularly after we lost Sean. Eileen and I had sought consultations on how we could help all our kids, specifically Sean, but not for how to help me personally. I didn't see the counseling as something for me, but rather as something that Sean needed. What I learned in counseling of any type, whether peer support, support groups, or one-on-one support, is that any of these counseling methods can be powerful tools for everybody, not just the person suffering the illness, but also others of your family and friends who choose to support that person.

Each form of professional help has its strengths and timing, and you match your personality and needs at the time to the format you chose. One-on-one might work great given certain problems, say self-doubt, and a support group may be appropriate when you need to know that you are not alone in your struggle.

SUPPORT GROUP FOR LOSS OF A CHILD

After Sean passed away, someone suggested that Eileen and I go to a support group for grieving parents. On the surface, it sounds like a great idea to be in a room with other people who know the pain of burying a child. Unfortunately, for us, it turned out to be a painful reminder that our child had chosen to take his life and we could be ostracized for that. I don't know if anyone in the room felt that way. Still, I know we internalized the feeling that there was a big difference between losing your child as the result of an illness or an accident he had no control over versus a child who chose to take his life, as Sean did.

Let me stop here to clarify what I have come to understand as it applies to suicide. Someone who gets to the point where death by suicide appears to be the only alternative to the pain really doesn't choose anything. There is no other option to choose. Instead, that decision is thrust upon them. However, there's no question that it's hard to look another parent in the eye who has lost a healthy fourteen-year-old son in a car accident, while there we were, talking about what appeared to be a handsome, smart, twenty-year-old with "so much to live for" who decided to end his life.

In both cases, the result is the same: the empty chair at the kitchen table or the bedroom door you close because you can't bear to walk into that room. No doubt, the pain is perceived differently based on the circumstances. Did your child make the decision, or was the loss beyond their control? We felt nothing but guilt sitting in that room, listening to the pain of parents who lost a child with no warning, or to those whose child had been ill and had no choice, but our child did. We felt that the grieving would not be the same as there would be anger about our pain being more self-inflicted than theirs.

So, if you decide to go to a support group, be aware of what you're walking into and what you want to get out of it. We were looking for the positive comfort aspect of being with people who felt the same as we did and might be able to provide some guidance on how to survive. With the group we chose, that would not be the case.

I can't emphasize enough that I don't know whether anybody in the group felt that way, but we sure did, and as we know, perception can be seen as reality. And when you are already reeling emotionally, it's even more likely that perception will be held as truth. In our case, perception was what counted, so we didn't go back. At that time, 2006, we were not aware of the existence of support groups for parents of children who had taken their lives. I'm guessing that is because no one wants to broadcast that fact.

I am glad to say there are groups now, such as Compassionate Friends, that do deal with the pain of suicide, and they will put you in touch with others who have gone through what you are experiencing. Everyone's journey is unique, but there are commonalities that will be helpful for you to hear so you don't feel these things are only happening to you, for example, being avoided in public.

There is an incredible value to that kind of painful sharing, and we did experience it purely by luck as we went forward. Other parents we met at social gatherings had suffered the same painful loss. You share a new fraternity/sorority that you hoped you would never belong to. However, sharing the feelings of loss and pain is truly a healing instrument and has great power.

It's about common ground. Just like two CEOs sharing what budget constraints and unfunded mandates have done to their operations, grieving parents talk about walking into a bedroom no longer physically occupied by their child. There is common ground. There may be no answer, but knowing you're not alone can offer a certain degree of comfort.

SUPPORT GROUP FOR LOSS OF A SPOUSE

My second encounter with support groups came after Eileen passed. The hospice counselor, who is not my regular counselor but an excellent resource, too, suggested a support group for spouses who have lost their significant other.

This was a much different experience from the group we tried after Sean passed. Eileen hadn't chosen to end her life, so unlike my experience of being the surviving parent of a suicide, I assumed I would find commonality. When I walked in, I realized that many of the people in the room, some who were five years down the road from their loss, were still grieving like it was yesterday. I had wandered in surrounded by a fog of uncertainty just two months after Eileen passed. The usually confident persona, the one I had always leaned on, had been stripped down to a wandering soul, my Cape long lost. I walked out after the meeting wondering if this was how I'd be five years from then. I felt more depressed than when I had arrived!

I hung on to one thing that gave me hope that I'd survive: Eileen and Sean were truly back together. In my eyes, the cover of this book is actually that sign of hope. I trust that when you looked at it, you saw the hand of someone in distress, reaching for a helping hand to give them aid and to affirm that they were not alone in whatever they were facing. Who and what it means to you is about your journey, and I do not claim to know what that is, for we are all individuals.

For me, the cover is about my journey. When Eileen was in the final few months of her life, she was unable to use her left arm at all. But her right arm was strong enough to put around someone's neck to help her stand and move from the chair to somewhere else. She loved to hold someone's hand, her right hand engulfing theirs with a powerful grip. Unfortunately, because of the tumors in her brain, she couldn't release her grip, so we would literally have to pry her fingers away from our hands.

When I opened the file for the front cover, I literally started to cry. The designer had known the book was about mental health but had no idea about the stories I have shared with you. My consultant told me that I'd know the right front cover when I saw it. After viewing many, this one was the right one, for sure.

The hand is pale, but it has an incredibly tight grip on that firefighter's gloved hand. Immediately, it reminded me of Eileen's hand. I held her hand at the moment she took her last breath, encouraging her to reach across home plate for Sean, because she was almost there.

As you've read, Sean wanted to be a firefighter. I always said that's what he would have become if he had been blessed with health. So, the firefighter's arm and gloved hand are not mine, but Sean's.

I picture Sean reaching across to pull his mom from her human pain into her heavenly reward. It's all about hope, and even though my Cape couldn't save Eileen, Sean could, and he came back and took her home. For me, the story behind the cover is that it is truly okay to take my Cape off, because Sean and Eileen are both healthy and together. Sean was indeed the firefighter I had hoped he would be; his station assignment just happens to be in heaven. I truly believe that when Eileen crossed, she walked right into Sean's arms. I believe this because Sean had spoken to her days before, telling her he was coming to get her.

That's how the cover spoke to me, as Sean grabbing Eileen's hand to pull her to her new life, leaving me in a much better place than almost everyone else in that particular support group. It gave me the hope that many others were still struggling to attain.

THE TRAP OF THE CAPE WEARER: TRYING TO FIX EVERYONE

The hospice counselor encouraged me to continue. It had been my first experience with the group. They were good people, and my pain was so acute that she felt I should go back and try it again. When I walked out after my second participation, I felt quite good. Unfortunately, I felt good for the wrong reasons.

As people shared their pain, I recognized that the counselor had been right; they were all caring, good people in distress. I recognized that I had done what I had been trained to do and had done instinctively for the past thirty-plus years: I put the Cape back on. Then, as each person spoke, I jumped in with, "Have you thought about this?" Or, "Have you tried this?" I shared some stories about Sean and Eileen and signs from the other side to encourage them. When I launched into the superhero role, it felt really good and comfortable. I was back in control. I recognized this person.

When I left, everyone thanked me and said they looked forward to me coming again. As I got in my car, I felt pretty good about myself for the first time since Eileen had been diagnosed. Just then, maybe the angels were in my ear or maybe I experienced a self-realization, but I knew the only reason I felt good had nothing whatsoever to do with addressing my pain in any way. Instead, I had fixed or tried to fix other people's problems while running from mine. I had not addressed my problems. That saddened me, but it also enlightened me, and when I shared it with the counselor, she said, "You're right. Support groups are excellent for many people, but the way you are wired, this is not something positive for you right now; maybe somewhere down the line."

I went back to our family counselor, and that was what I needed: one-on-one time where she could challenge my inner darkness in a way that forced me to find ways to move forward and acceptable ways of grieving. Now, don't mistake me. It took a long time—months and months of trying to navigate the dark feelings of depression and loneliness and my failure to protect Eileen, just as I had failed to protect Sean. The process was not easy or quick.

FINDING HELP

Some things I learned when picking a therapist include:
- To be successful, you need a connection. It's no different than asking a neighbor if they know of a good plumber. A referral from those who have had a good experience is so important.
- If you hit the wrong one first, it doesn't mean that the therapy won't work; it's just not the right fit.
- Ask the therapist:
  - Do you take insurance? If not, what is the cost?

- Do you have a sliding scale based on income?
- What are your hours/availability?
- Do you specialize in specific treatments that may be needed to handle my issue (e.g., couple therapy if a marriage issue, grief and loss)?

Finding a good match is the key to a successful outcome. The same is true if you are picking an oncologist. Doctors are doctors until you don't have a match. You must be compatible and able to trust the doctor as he pours poison into your loved one. All doctors may know what to do, but some don't know how to relate, and so keep looking until you find that good connection.

With Eileen's illness, we finally found our hero in Dr. Patrick Sweeney. The irony is that Dr. Sweeney is a leader in his field, and I believe he wears a Cape, too. He always did what was best for Eileen. If anyone could have saved Eileen, it would have been him, but he's not God, either.

Reconciling the gap between your talents as a leader, your desires, and your commitment against a failure you can't avoid in a situation that is out of your control can make that Cape a powerful choking mechanism. Knowing where you do have resources, even if they don't save your co-worker or family member, is at least a comfort that you did all you humanly—not superhumanly—could do for that person.

In the resource section of this book are just some of several organizational resources available that I hope you will find helpful. You need to know that your search for an answer has no boundaries. New resources appear daily as the quest to understand mental illness is being driven by the stress of day-to-day life. There is no guarantee that you will find the solution, but in many cases, you will be led to the assistance you need.

LESSONS LEARNED

- **Seeking counseling is a positive act.** Unfortunately, needing counseling is still seen as a weakness these days. If that's what's stopping you, consider this. If you wanted to learn about the newest diet, reduce the arthritis in your knee, train for a marathon, or find motivational techniques to lead your team, you would not hesitate to sign up. You might pay a hundred dollars or more to sit in an arena with five thousand strangers or to participate in an online course by a speaker who shows you how to improve some area of your life. If you are grieving and need counseling, go out and get it. It is not a sign of weakness. Actually, it takes strength.

- **Everyone needs professional guidance at one time or another.** Whether you reach out and engage is the real question, and that is usually driven by your view of mental health in general. Too many of us look at counseling as a negative instead of embracing what it can do for us. We are always spending money to improve the quality of our lives, and the financial investment you make in therapy provides tools that may help you survive.

- **A support program is successful when you are ready to talk.** The key is trust in those you are talking to, either one-on-one as in peer support or in a group. After Eileen passed, I went to a support group some four weeks after her death. Some people had been coming for years and were farther behind in their grief than I was. That made me feel even more hopeless. Did this mean I too would always be in grief? I tried it a few times and then chose to stay away. I don't think I gave it a chance because the people were strangers, and in hindsight, honestly, I wasn't ready. You need to be prepared to open up; no one can make another person talk.

- **Leaders should invest in counseling with the same zest they invest in financial advisors and motivational experts.** An effective real-life strategic plan includes having a counselor, whether you go once a year, every two years, or every other week. Everybody's makeup is different, and what you need to replenish yourself and when you need it are unique to you. What is common is that all human beings go through tough times that affect our mental health. So, wrap your arms around the concept of counseling as a human need, instead of treating it as a weakness. Now I see what counseling has done for me: I am stronger.

Part 3

LEADING WITHOUT A CAPE

Chapter 17

Experiencing Grief and Loss as a Leader

As a leader, a tough lesson I've come to grips with is this: The Cape doesn't provide every tool you need to be successful 100 percent of the time.

The goal of any leader is perfection. Leaders are typically type-A personalities, and as such, they think no challenge is too big. Bring it on—I'll don my Cape and find the solution! Granted, the only human being who ever walked the face of the earth that was assumed to be perfect (Jesus Christ) got nailed to a cross. I guess I should've figured out early in my life that perfection, while a worthy goal, is not attainable given our human constraints!

The Cape did not allow me to save Sean or Eileen, which left me devastated. I looked in the mirror as a husband and dad, and I saw a failure. For a leader, the fallout from that experience is that you don't allow yourself to grieve. You picture grieving as a weakness, and you're already drowning and choking on your Cape because you feel so inadequate; the last thing you need is to feel weak, too.

The only way you can save yourself from going down that rabbit hole, which can lead to deep depression, anxiety, or other mental health challenges, including suicide, is to give yourself permission to be human, and that includes failing and grieving. For me, the first step was to back away from the Cape and stop identifying myself as that fire chief who could lead people through the most difficult situations, and by whose actions, lives could be saved. The Cape kept the heroic persona intact, but the harder I clung to it, the more the Cape choked me. That leader who felt like a failure had to become a figment of my imagination. Instead, I had to get comfortable with the idea of going back into the phone booth, taking the Cape off, and just being Pat, the husband and father. I had to forgive myself for not having the superhuman powers I thought had come with the Cape.

I'm a big baseball guy. In baseball, it's remarkable that a player who is successful only one-third of the time as a hitter is considered incredibly talented. Yet, if you're successful on only one-third of your life journey, I don't think society is quite as charitable. And I know that most leaders wouldn't define themselves as a success with such numbers. Somehow, I had to realize that I couldn't do this on my own. I needed professional help. For many leaders, that step alone is a frightening leap into uncharted waters.

YOU WILL NEED HELP

Trust me: you must realize that you cannot travel this complicated road of grief and loss alone, or you will fail. So, I went back to the drawing board and sought out counseling. My journey down this path began with grieving about my dad and the pain of not saying goodbye. That was shortly followed by analyzing a career where I never felt what I did was good enough. It was always on to the next mountain top; no time to look back over my shoulder to see what had been accomplished or never taking time to smell the roses.

That feeling of never being good enough carried over into my parenting. I didn't smell the roses when I was reading a book to Sean or playing catch with him. I didn't smell the roses when the boys were on vacation with us and we went tubing or fishing. I was too busy looking for the next thing to validate that I was a good leader, a worthy husband, and a great father. I wasted that valuable time.

I can only speak for the fire service, but I'll bet that many retirees experience incredible identity loss. For thirty years a person is known as "Firefighter Joe," and suddenly they are "just" Joe. Stepping away from my identity as leader of the department, the fire chief people recognized, and become a flawed human being was like falling down the side of a mountain. Every bounce down that rocky terrain hurt worse than the one before it.

It was interesting that once I hit bottom, the Cape-wearing leader in me still wanted to climb the mountain. But there was a difference this time: I didn't know how. Therapy helped me examine who I really am; that I am not just a leader, but Pat.

It helped me to look at why I had such a strong feeling about being a failure. Where did those emotions come from? I realized that they originated in my childhood and my mom's negative attitude about everything I did. Critical therapeutic probing and self-analysis provided a way to tackle those demons.

As I was trying to ascend that mountain of my life, I can't say that those demons disappeared, but they were subdued. When they hit me about being a failure, I learned to recognize where they were coming from and try and fight them off using coping skills I learned in therapy.

The most effective coping skill for me was physical exercise. When those demons hit, if I could force myself to do something physical—a five-minute walk, a twenty-minute run, or a five-mile bike ride—the demons became smaller and smaller. It's a proven physiological fact that chemicals called endorphins are released during exercise that can lead to euphoric feelings, pain reduction, and/or a sedative effect.

When I was in a hotel room or other place where I could not easily exercise, I talked to the negative feelings or anxiety or depression and called it out. "I know what you are, and I know what you're trying to do, and it's not going to work this time." If you had been in the hotel room next to me, you might have called for hotel security, but it was the only way I knew to cope at that time. I used my sports brain to identify my opponent and tried to kick its butt. That may sound silly, but it worked.

Once you figure it out, you have the opportunity to re-enter the arena where you lead and provide a wonderful gift to your staff and co-workers as you share your pain and loss. No, I am not talking about walking in the first day after such a loss, filled with grief, and calling a department-wide meeting in which you bare your soul. But I am talking about establishing a culture where you educate your team to understand that mental illness is a physical illness that affects many people, including leaders and their families, and show them what they can do to support that positive culture.

As a by-product of sharing your own stories, you are creating an environment that invites others to do the same. Believe it or not, a lot of leaders are looked at as robots with no feelings or, worse yet, no personal struggles. I had the most wonderful wife and three awesome sons. That was the perception of my life, so I did not feel comfortable letting people know that my youngest was dying from a mental illness. Once I got back into the environment, and after months of counseling, I began to share the journey our family had taken over the past fifteen years.

Did my words make everybody want to run out and tell their stories? Not a chance, but it did provide a supportive environment if, God forbid, they or their spouse or their child was suffering. And at least they knew that the guy at the top had been affected and was open to the conversation. Once I resumed my leadership role, I didn't have all the answers, but I knew a lot of the questions and at least was aware of where someone should turn for resources, counselors, etc., some of which I've included in this book.

WHEN TEAM MEMBERS EXPERIENCE GRIEF OR LOSS

You can let your co-workers know it's okay to approach someone you think is struggling or someone who you know has suffered a terrible loss. A hand on the shoulder, a gentle inquiry, "Is there anything I can do for you?" is a good start.

The person may not have an answer that day, the next week, or the next month, but don't stop asking until they ask for help or you start to see the light return to their eyes. Just be warned that it could take a long time, but don't give up. Your co-workers need you, and not only you as the leader, but perhaps the support of everyone in that family/organization. Co-workers and even members of a family are naturally afraid to approach someone who exhibits signs they don't recognize or understand, such as withdrawal or behavior that's inconsistent with their normal behavior.

Here are some examples: people who suddenly stop being responsible drinkers, lose their appetite, or avoid other people. Connectivity is so important to us as human beings that when someone pulls away from others, it's a sign that something's amiss.

These may be simple life struggles, or they could signal mental illness. If someone tells us they have chest pains, we are not afraid to call an ambulance because we recognize it may indicate a possible life-threatening cardiac event. Yet the person who doesn't return phone calls or sits silently in meetings or stares out the window is not approached. It is not because we don't care; we simply don't know what such actions represent. So, if you're not sure, I encourage you to just ask. It's that simple. Just ask, "Is there anything I can do for you?"

LESSONS LEARNED

- **Failure is an opportunity to grow.** If you are a leader for more than an hour, you will fail at some point. You will step on, trip over, or get choked by your Cape. You may view failure as a weakness but it is an opportunity to grow and learn from your mistakes.

- **Grieving is not a weakness.** If you as the leader categorize grieving as a weakness, the grieving, combined with the label of weakness, can lead to deep depression, anxiety, or other mental health challenges, including suicide.

- **Leaders are allowed to grieve.** To be respected, leaders must give themselves permission to be human, to be vulnerable, and that includes failing and grieving.

- **Professional help is a tool, not a crutch.** Professional therapy, including self-analysis, can address failure and grieving and put them in the right context so that the leader can understand and grow. Using therapy as a tool in your leadership toolbox is not a sign of diminishing strength.

- **Be a role model.** Fellow employees are naturally afraid to approach someone who exhibits signs they don't recognize or understand, such as withdrawal or behavior that's inconsistent with how they usually view the person. Encourage your co-workers by being a role model in approaching someone you think is struggling or someone who you know has suffered a terrible loss.

Chapter 18

The Superman Syndrome

Did you become a leader because you believed you could make a difference? Did you believe you were capable of incredible accomplishments in your field, of becoming a modern-day superhero–Cape and all? Did you think that you could do what others can only dream?

Leaders have to believe that they can take their organizations to heights never seen before. In our profession as firefighters, we think that someday a life might be saved because of an action we performed. Ask yourself honestly, isn't that the goal of life in general, and specifically for a leader, to make things better than before you took over, to be just the right person to accomplish that? You bet it is!

Do we transfer that same sense of purpose from the public we serve to members of our department or company—or to our family? What if you, as the chief officer or CEO, are personally struggling to protect a member of your immediate family from harm? What if you learn a department member is having family problems? We all have experienced these situations or know of those in our organizations who are struggling with terminal illnesses or deaths of loved ones. How do we reconcile our "superhero" image when we cannot protect the very ones we love? The potential for devastation, both personally and professionally, is as powerful as a line-of-duty death in the fire service.

In the fire service, *brotherhood* is a term that lately has made me cringe more than embrace. It looks more like an excuse to hide behind the Cape than to meet apparent issues head-on. The same can be said of any organization. We tend to care for each other when it is convenient and comfortable. Well, that includes taking care of yourself! I challenge you, before you dismiss this chapter, to keep an open mind about where I am going.

An employee shows up for work and complains of extreme heartburn, shooting pain in his left arm, and tingling down into his fingers. There is no doubt that the next move is to call 9-1-1. Change the situation to an employee who is typically engaging and "the life of the party," but who now shows symptoms of being quiet, sullen, and sitting off by herself. Do you take any immediate action here? I hope so, but I bet not, in most cases.

I believe the lack of action is not due to indifference but is just a matter of not being comfortable with recognizing and acting upon visible symptoms that could indicate a mental health challenge. It is much easier to identify and act on a potential cardiac situation. This is because we are familiar with those physical signs and know precisely what to do: call 9-1-1. But in a situation where we have little or no training to recognize the symptoms of someone in trouble, or we feel so uncomfortable with possible mental health issues that we are almost paralyzed with fear of intervening. Ultimately, the person suffers in silence and the outcome can be as deadly as an untreated cardiac episode.

Leaders in general, and volunteer or career firefighters in particular, all wear the "S" on our chests. The Cape doesn't come attached to a W-2, but it does come with a firefighter's bunker gear when they choose this vocation. Leaders in other businesses also wear their own form of protective equipment. It may have the form of a suit, apron, or hard hat, but in all cases, leaders still have the "S" on their chests and the Cape around their necks.

What also comes with the bunker gear is that phone booth where we take off the Cape. That's where, in our roles as mom, dad, husband, wife, brother, sister, and so on, the stark reality hits that there are many times when we can't save anything! Worse yet is the situation where the one you are trying to save is someone you love, either in your organization, department, or your own family.

I learned firsthand that feeling of ineffectiveness after coming face-to-face with my inability to protect someone I loved. I lost my twenty-year-old son, Sean, to suicide after he had spent almost fifteen years battling mental illness. Throughout his illness, I believed if the department members knew of Sean's condition, they would have trouble understanding and accepting his mental illness. How could they possibly understand the whole mental illness concept and its ramifications when my wife, my other two sons, and I were living in that environment every day, and we felt lost?

I knew my firefighters had their crosses to bear, so why add to their plate? That was my reasoning. How could they trust me to keep them safe and "save the day" when I couldn't even save my own son? I confided in only a few people and, even then, never offered them the full truth. The irony is that if Sean had had brain cancer, I would have told anyone who would have listened, so that both Sean and my family would have received the support we needed.

In hindsight, that decision was a huge mistake. Wearing the Cape took a toll on my family as I tried to keep up this "super" façade. As Fire Chief, I also missed an opportunity to create an organizational culture more accepting of mental health challenges and, no matter how well-intentioned, it was a colossal error in judgment.

I continue to struggle today with the feeling that I was a failure at my most crucial responsibility here on earth—being a father. I would give anything I have been blessed with, personally and professionally, to have my son well and here for one more hug. Frankly, I would trade whatever time I have left of my life for that deal.

So now that you have a little perspective on where I am coming from, let's go back to my original thought. Faced with an employee who has become withdrawn, we wonder: *What am I supposed to do? It's none of my business. I don't want to intrude.* All of these excuses ignore the fact that the Cape won't work in these situations. We end up locked in the phone booth. It becomes very apparent that we are not trained or equipped to fix these challenges wearing our Cape, but we sure can lend some comfort and support in our Clark Kent way!

During Sean's painful journey, I never personally sought counseling. *No, not Superman! I don't need it because nothing is affecting me.* After all, the problem was with my son, and, by god, I would find a way to fix it. After all, that's what I did for a living—make things better.

Well, I didn't make things better, not for Sean or for anyone in my department, when it comes to mental health understanding. I missed out on that golden opportunity. As I stood next to Sean's open casket, I knew I was viewing my son for the last time on this side, and I was in the depths of a depression I never knew existed. For the very first time, I felt what he had dealt with daily for at least the last five years of his life. I thought about all those wounded souls I brought in by ambulance at two a.m. with anxiety attacks; those "weaklings" I was angry at because they got me out of bed. *Guess what, Superman? You are not only one of them now, but you may be in even worse shape than most. I wonder what others think of me now?*

I trust you to realize that the point of this chapter is not for you to feel sorry for my family or me. If you do, you are missing my point. My passion instead is to raise awareness that, just because we are leaders, our "Capes" do not protect us from the pain of mental illness in our work lives or in our families. It may even be affecting you.

In this superhero analogy, I view mental health challenges as Superman's kryptonite, which can penetrate our protective Capes and weaken us. So, how do we deal with the kryptonite? How do we forgive ourselves for being human while retaining those sacred "powers" bestowed on all of us in our professions? Better yet, how do we overcome the kryptonite so that we can provide understanding and assistance to our fellow staff, colleagues, their families, and ourselves?

In my vocation, the fire service, many states have answered the challenges of firefighters in need immediately after a critical incident through a network of response teams consisting of highly dedicated, educated personnel. You need to know how to bring in those teams locally. However, for mental illness, that is nowhere near enough. My concern is for the long haul of mental illness, not a quick-fix approach.

In my profession and in most occupations, there is nothing in place to care for those who suffer either long-term effects from a traumatic encounter at work or from a problem that is not job-related, as was my situation. So, what does your Cape do for you as the leader?

First, you have to understand that illnesses like post-traumatic stress disorder, bipolar disorder, or obsessive-compulsive disorder, to name just a few, are lifelong challenges that one swoop of your Cape can't fix, any more than you can cure someone who is a diabetic. However, the Cape can help you in one important way. It can provide the platform to lead through these kinds of crises. You do that by first enhancing the culture of your organization so that all understand that none of us is a superhero. We are human beings. We will have challenges along the way that are not indictments of our courage or strength; the reality is that we are indeed people who can and will suffer.

Your Cape as the leader gives you the opportunity to shape your culture, to encourage all to accept our frailties as human beings. You can model that it is not only okay to have these lifelong health challenges, such as diabetes or PTSD, but that you will embrace and support them as an organization.

Superman was called only when someone was in distress. The Cape allows you the access and financial support to seek out resources to help those in distress, both short- and long-term. The ability to respond is the essence of being truly a "Super" leader. You use your Cape in the most effective ways to help your employees.

LESSONS LEARNED

- **Leaders must possess self-confidence to succeed.** You need to believe that you can make a significant impact on your organization, that you possess some "super" insight or ability to be a leader. Many times, that confidence is based on being familiar with the operations of the organization and training to anticipate the next phase. Use your self-confidence to grow in areas you are not familiar with.

- **Leaders cannot and do not know everything.** Situations where they have little or no training to recognize the "what is next" or even the "what is this?" are challenging. Things like recognizing the symptoms of someone experiencing mental health challenges can almost paralyze a leader. Be okay with not knowing it all and seek out help to answer those critical questions.

- **Leaders, in general, all wear the "S" of the Superhero on their chests.** That may take many forms, such as a formal title or a certain uniform. In all cases, leaders still have the "S" on their chests and the Cape around their necks. It is an honor to have that "S" bestowed on you by people who follow your lead. Just be aware that the "S" does not stand for 'Solves everything,' which can lead to unbearable Stress and leaves you feeling worthless.

- **Leaders are defined by who they are.** With the Cape comes a phone booth where you take the Cape off and become Father or Mother, for example. Reconciling your roles is important to your success as a leader. You cannot be defined by *what* you do but by *who* you are. Some leaders are much more comfortable out of the phone booth with their Capes on.

- **Leaders aren't superhuman.** Mental health challenges, loss, grieving, and suicide are situations leaders must prepare for so they can support their families as well as their co-workers. The Cape provides the platform to lead through these kinds of crises. You lead by understanding that none of us is a superhero. We are all human beings. Accepting this fact comes with the realization that you will have challenges which are not indictments of your strength, but reminders of the reality that you are indeed a person first, who can and will suffer.

Chapter 19

The Cape Can Choke You

Leaders in any organization seek to define what shapes their industry. The number-one asset in any organization is the people who work there. As the leader, if I know what makes my people tick, I can hopefully motivate them more effectively and serve their needs more comprehensively, thus providing a better business outcome. It is a problem for leaders when their perception of the culture, which reflects the organization's core values, differs from those who work with them.

Firefighters, for instance, from the time they enter this vocation, are taught to be brave. The cover of *Reader's Digest* one year had a handsome firefighter on it, and in big, bold letters, were the words: *Born to be Brave*. I agree that firefighters must be brave. There's no question about that. All leaders, no matter what their walk of life, will be called upon to be brave in either their professional or personal lives, or both. What is important is how you define bravery.

Bravery means that when you're in trouble or can't save the day, when that Cape is too tight and is literally choking you, you're able to ask for help.

I'm challenging you to redefine the meaning of bravery. Does bravery mean that when you feel out of sorts and think something isn't right and you need help, you ask for it?

Could bravery be the ability and courage to say you need a little help because this life situation has affected you and you're not sleeping or you're having nightmares or the like?

Could bravery be the ability and courage to say you need a little help because you're just not processing things, and you know it doesn't seem like it's bothering anybody else, but it's bothering you?

Could this be bravery? Could we instill in our employees from orientation onward that reaching out to help a fellow employee or even helping ourselves is part of what it means to be brave? Sure, we can. Bravery can then be redefined to include, "Please help me."

It is brave to ask for help.

There's an incredible stigma around mental health across the country, in all occupations. When you're a first responder—police officer, firefighter, ER nurse, or the leader in any organization—you're supposed to save the day. The second part of that mantra implies that you're never supposed to need help yourself. You're always the helper, not the recipient. Therefore, it's easy to think that to show or ask for any type of help somehow indicates that you're weak, that you aren't strong enough to carry through your vocation, that the Cape given to you is defective, or you don't know how to use it. I think nothing could be further from the truth.

ACCESS TO COUNSELING AND PSYCHOLOGICAL SUPPORT

In 2004, the National Fallen Firefighters Foundation put together 16 life safety initiatives. These initiatives were supposed to be the "bible" of the fire service and were aimed at reducing and ultimately preventing Line of Duty Deaths. In 2004, I thought I was a pretty progressive fire chief, and I didn't even know that these existed. The 13th life safety initiative states explicitly: "Firefighters and their families must have access to counseling and psychological support."

THE CAPE CAN CHOKE YOU

Now there are two parts to that initiative, individual support for the firefighters and support for the families.

Individual Support

Firefighters have access to counseling and support. There's no question that there's a need for it because of who we recruit. Fire departments across the world:

- Recruit people who care. We want people who, at two a.m., will caringly respond to that eighty-year-old woman who consistently calls in the middle of the night because she struggles to get back into bed. We want people who will treat that person like she's their grandmother. We want people who will treat that person with respect and love, and you've got to be a caring soul to do that.
- Expose these people to the worst situations you can see: people burned, children dying, spouses who wake up in the morning to find they have lost their loved one. We are then shocked that these situations affect them. It is clear that they must have access to counseling and psychological support.

Yes, we bring in the person with the biggest heart, they get stabbed in it repeatedly, and when it begins to bleed a little bit, we are surprised! Really? That reaction in leaders is predictable, although we may tend to deny it.

Family Support

The second part of the initiative is just as critical. The families must have access to counseling and psychological support, too. Quite often, they are the ones who see the initial signs of pain in those first responders who recognize that the Cape has holes in it. Unfortunately, the firefighters don't share what's going on because, again: *I'm the superhero. I'm not the mortal being.* The families take that burden on themselves, perhaps think it's somehow their fault: *My spouse is upset with me. I must have done something wrong.* But it has nothing to do with them.

143

Leaders don't want to bring their work home, but the reality is, our families are the first to know when something is wrong. They don't want to ask the wrong question, as you might get upset or be mad at them. My wife would ask me the wrong question, and I'd get angry and tell her to leave me alone.

Ping-Pong Paddles

Families need this support, too, because you and they are working as a team. One young firefighter shared a way he had found to communicate with his family. He bought ping-pong paddles, one green and one red.

He hung the paddles inside the entry door to his home. When he came home after a bad day, he'd hold up the red paddle when he walked in. The family then knew that he was not mad at any of them but just needed thirty minutes alone to decompress.

If he'd had a good day, he'd hold up the green paddle to indicate that he was good to go to the water park or to buy a new couch. He learned quickly not to hold up the green paddle too often, or he would go broke!

MAYDAY

"Mayday" in the fire service is an emergency radio transmission. It means:

- I think I'm lost.
- I think I'm in trouble. Somebody, please come get me.

Unfortunately, a Mayday in the fire service is usually not called until:

- You think God is on the other side of that door; your life is almost over.
- There's very little time to save you.

The same thing applies to mental illness. We deny the need, wait until the last second to call for help, and many times it's too late. The only option we have at that point is suicide, and we haven't done anything about it. We have not been proactive about it; we have only been reactive.

CANCER AND MENTAL HEALTH

I'm comparing cancer and mental health throughout this book because I think it's vital that we move from a reactive to a proactive approach to both. It's funny, but sometimes as a fire chief I'll get in an argument with a firefighter about his physical.

"Why haven't you gone for your physical? You were scheduled two months ago."

"Well, I don't want to know."

"You don't want to know what? That there's something wrong? That you could be in a situation where you may not be able to walk your daughter down the aisle because you denied it?"

"Something can't happen to me. I'm a firefighter. I can't get cancer. It's supposed to bounce off me. I've got a Cape."

That denial is consistent across a couple of different physical illness platforms. The firefighting profession is no different than any other walk of life. It is not unique to the challenges I have outlined, not only in this chapter but throughout the book. Whether you own a small repair shop, manage a large retail store, or are a high school principal, you will be challenged to help those in need in your organization. The key to your Cape being a positive and not a hindrance is in your ability to discern what you can control and what you can't.

As a fire chief, I can order someone to take a physical, but I can't order someone to share the pain in their heart because of a sick child or a broken marriage. I can, however, provide the culture in which it is not only acceptable but laudable to reach out for assistance. I can provide access to the resources to address those issues.

Knowing your limitations as a leader is sometimes as critical as knowing your strengths. Self-acceptance keeps the Cape a positive symbol and not a choking collar.

LESSONS LEARNED

- **Brave leaders ask for help.** Bravery can be defined in many ways, but when it comes to mental health, it should be defined as the willingness to ask for help when you need it.
- **Always being the helper may not serve you.** Realize that your mindset as a leader can predispose you to think that you're always the helper and you're never supposed to need help yourself. Unfortunately, your Cape may not serve you well long-term and in all cases.
- **Lead by example.** Ask for help when you need it.
- **Support employees and their families.** As a leader, you must realize that your people have lives outside the organization. They can't leave their problems at the door on the way to work and pick them up on the way back. Your job is to support not only the employee, but also their families. That's how you build a cohesive team.
- **Teach employees that they need to communicate with their family members.** Whatever form that takes, whether it's a ping-pong paddle or calling a Mayday, is fine when everybody understands it's about the stress, not about the individual.
- **Accept limitations; embrace strengths.** Accept your limitations with the same enthusiasm as you embrace your strengths. This will keep the Cape from choking you and keep it a positive tool to support you as the leader as well as the mission of the organization.

Chapter 20

War Veterans and PTSD

In a 1995 study, Lieutenant Colonel David Grossman showed that Vietnam veterans had a higher instance of post-traumatic stress than their World War II counterparts. Why? Because they had no time to talk to their fellow Vietnam counterparts before being thrust back into society.

WORLD WAR II VETS

World War II veterans came home by ship as entire companies. They were on ships, not luxury liners. It took weeks. They didn't have loads of chaplains and certainly no psychologists down in the hole to help them work through their challenges. They talked to each other. It was the beginning of what we now recognize as peer support. They asked each other questions like:

- What are you going to tell your wife about what you saw?
- What are you going to tell your mom about what you had to do?
- What will you not talk to them about?

VIETNAM VETS

Vietnam vets flew home alone, and some were back in the United States the very next day. I remember reading reports about service members who came through Chicago O'Hare Airport in their dress uniforms. People spat on them and called them baby killers. And the following day, they were expected to pick up their lives where they left them. They were plumbers or electricians, teachers, and firefighters. There was no time to process the horrors they had seen. They were just supposed to assimilate back into life minus a mechanism for processing, even something as simple as a comrade to talk to. It didn't work.

LEADERS AND PTSD

Leaders of any kind can experience post-traumatic stress. Just like those returning World War II veterans, you need to talk to about it, but many leaders wait until they're drowning before they ask for help. We must change that stigma. We must inform people and convince them that mental illness is no different than cancer, a physical illness. It is not a weakness; it is not a choice. People are struggling through the worst day of their lives because something chemical in their body has changed impacting the way they look at things, the way they feel about things. Without help, they have no control over those chemical reactions. They can't will them away. Eventually, those people perceive only one option for dealing with the pain, and that may be to take their lives.

Be aware that there are loads of resources out there that you can look up right now about mental health, and I've included some at the end of this book.

It is important to note that post-traumatic stress disorder is only one of many mental health challenges, just as there are multiple forms of cancer. Mental health education and cancer prevention are truly critical components of overall safety for anyone, and both are physical illnesses. When we can look at mental illness in the same way we look at cancer, we will have vanquished the stigma of mental illness.

LESSONS LEARNED

- **PTSD can affect anyone.** Post-traumatic stress disorder has received much attention lately, and for good reason, as it has impacted so many of our heroic veterans. The reality is that

PTSD can affect anyone. Just as there are multiple cancers, it is one of many mental health challenges. Anxiety, depression, and bipolar disorder are just a few examples of other mental health illnesses.

- **Cost-effective therapeutic methods are available.** Helping our workers in need does not have to create a significant financial impact. Something as simple as creating an organizational climate that fosters discussion on all fronts is very effective with little financial outlay. Army Lieutenant Colonel Grossman (1995), who wrote a book on PTSD, stated that World War II veterans had a lower incidence of PTSD than Vietnam veterans. Why? Because they talked to each other! Training and implementing peer-support groups is not costly and has been quite effective in all kinds of settings.

Chapter 21

When the Cape Fails

It is hard to describe what happens when the Cape fails. Sometimes it happens in one significant, tragic moment that makes you aware that the Cape doesn't always work. Sometimes it comes as a series of events to remind you that, as a leader, you're human and not gifted with the superpowers you think come with the Cape.

In my case, the Cape's failure was revealed when Sean passed, and then it was reinforced when Eileen passed. My faith was hugely influential as it guided me through feelings of being abandoned and falling short as the leader of my family. Let me explain.

Earlier in my life, I was in the seminary, studying to be a Catholic priest. I did very poorly in my Bible studies. There were too many stories I couldn't relate to; they seemed embellished. Every Good Friday, I was dragged to the Stations of the Cross by my mom, and I continued to go when I was an adult, probably out of guilt. The Stations of the Cross are a series of pictures or carvings of fourteen incidents during Jesus Christ's progress from condemnation to crucifixion on the cross.

The teen group from our church re-enacted the fourteen stations every Good Friday, like a play. It wasn't until the first Good Friday after Sean passed that their performance made a huge impact on me. I won't go through all of the stations with you, as I may lose you if it turns you off, so let me recap just the parts crucial to me at the time.

As Christ carried his cross to the hill upon which he would die, he fell several times. Each time, with no help, he had to pick himself up, physically and emotionally, and stand back up again. Now, if you believe that he indeed was God, you might think he could just ascend into the clouds. He could have told the crowd to shove it: "Look, I am God." Instead, he saw the value of people seeing him vulnerable, of seeing him accepting the pain because he truly was human, also. The story includes his mother watching her son's torments in horrible emotional pain.

That first Good Friday after Sean's death, I could think of nothing but all the years Eileen watched Sean's painful battle and fall in excruciating agony, like Christ's, and yet somehow, he stood back up and continued on the path.

At the end of his journey, Jesus was nailed to the cross, and while he was hanging there for what must have been an excruciating amount of time, he cried out for help. If you believe this story, this was the only human being we know of who knew that there was a heaven, an afterlife, and a God. Yet, as he hung there, he finally said, "My God, my God, why have you forsaken me?" Arguably, he was the greatest leader ever to walk the face of the earth; still, he fell along the way, and he felt abandoned at the end.

So, how does it feel when the Cape fails? It feels like you've landed on a gravel road, face-down, and some people in your organization are watching to see if you'll get back up. Others are hoping that you have fallen from greatness. As the leader, there will be many points when you feel that people have abandoned you, even though you know you can still do wonderful things.

From this story of the Stations of the Cross, I take permission to be vulnerable. I take permission to fall flat on my face, pick myself up, and keep going. And finally, I take permission to feel abandoned and forsaken, to ask for help, and to be human!

If you accept that the Cape does fail at times and it is not your fault, you will be fine with failure and what you can take from that experience. Jesus was hanging on the cross when he passed, appearing to be a failure for many of those who thought he had brought the promise of being the new king, the supreme leader. He knew, however, that he could only do so much as a human being. He didn't look back on a lack of effort or being weak in that last moment when he reached out for help to his father to take him home. His strength came in asking for help. I figure if it was okay that the Cape did not work for Jesus all the time, and if it was okay for him to ask for help, then so should I.

LESSONS LEARNED

- **You won't have all the answers.** Leaders who think they will always have the answers and that the Cape will never fail them are fooling themselves.
- **The Cape will fail you, and that is okay.** Embrace the fact that the Cape will fail you at times and that it is not your fault. Failure is a learning experience, an opportunity to spread your wings as a leader.
- **Doubt and vulnerability are part of being a leader.** The only human who knew for sure that, no matter what happened, he would succeed, was Jesus Christ himself, and fell from greatness and allowed himself to doubt and be vulnerable. If it was good enough for him, then maybe great leaders should embrace that, also.

Chapter 22

Mental Health Myth Busters for Leaders

The following myths are from credible sources that, as a family, you may or may not have experienced but are good to have on your radar as leader of a business or family.

MYTH: People with mental health needs, even those who are managing their mental illness, cannot tolerate the stress of holding down a job.

People with mental health problems are just as productive as other employees. Employers report good attendance and punctuality, as well as motivation, good work, and job tenure on par with or higher than other employees.

When employees with mental health problems receive effective treatment, it can result in:

- Lower total medical costs
- Increased productivity
- Lower absenteeism
- Decreased disability costs

MYTH: Someone who develops a mental health problem will have it for the rest of their lives. They will never recover.

Mental health doesn't stay the same. It has ups and downs throughout your life, just like your physical health. Many factors can influence how you feel. If any of these factors change, your mental health can also be affected.

Many of the problems you may develop as the leader or witness in co-workers and family members are temporary. A good treatment plan will help you work through the problem and recover. This doesn't necessarily mean the problem has gone away, but you can find a way to manage it and still be a productive member of society. At the same time, feeling better might not mean that you're cured. You may have to continue with your treatment plan even after you feel better. Some mental health problems never go away. These usually are more severe conditions, such as schizophrenia or bipolar disorder. Others, like some cases of depression and anxiety, are temporary, quite normal, and resolve after treatment.

MYTH: Therapy is a waste of time.

Some people are not comfortable with therapy. They're afraid they'll have to go back and rummage in their childhoods, like some character you see lying on a couch on television declaring he hates his mother! For that very reason, it took me forever to go. While this scenario might occur, minus the couch, modern therapy is designed to be short-term and focuses on problems and solutions. Research has shown that modern therapy methods are very effective in treating mental illness. Those methods are usually most effective when used in combination with medication. Studies found that 70 percent to 90 percent of people reported improvement in their symptoms when both therapy and medication were part of their treatment plan.

MYTH: You can't prevent mental illness.

You can't always prevent mental health problems, but you can address risk factors.

- Try to minimize exposure to trauma. If you or someone else experiences a traumatic event, get help right away. Early treatment can prevent worse problems in the future.
- Reduce stress. A highly stressful job or home life can reduce the quality of your mental health.
- Put yourself in positive situations. Avoid negative people. Instead, surround yourself with healthy people who have a good outlook on life.
- Establish healthy habits. Eat a healthy diet, exercise, and get plenty of sleep. These basic self-care methods can go a long way to improve how you feel about yourself and how you function.

MYTH: There's nothing I can do to help someone with a mental health problem.

Friends and loved ones can make a big difference. Only 44 percent of adults with diagnosable mental health problems and less than 20 percent of children and adolescents receive needed treatment. Friends and family can be important influences to help someone get the treatment and services they need. There are many things you can do to help.

- Reach out and let the person know you are available to help if they need you.
- Learn about what the person is going through.
- Express your support in ways that are understandable and tangible.
- Help the person access mental health services.
- Don't give up on them.

- Learn and share facts about mental health, especially when you hear something that isn't true.
- Treat the person with respect, just as you would anyone else. Refuse to define them by their diagnosis or by using labels such as "crazy and nuts."
- Get help for yourself if you need it. You can't help your family or your staff if you are struggling, too.

LESSONS LEARNED

- **Share facts.** Human nature dictates that when we don't understand something, we make fun of it, and in the absence of facts, we make them up. A good leader clarifies the distinction between a myth and a fact.
- **Dispel myths.** Most of the myths about mental health go to the extreme: the person is weak, treatment won't work, the person is doomed to pain, and the person somehow has less worth as a human being than the rest of us "healthy people."
- **Use cancer as a comparison in myth-busting.** You can destroy a myth by applying it to a physical illness, like cancer. If the same person was experiencing cancer instead of mental illness, does the myth hold up? I think you'll find that your answer clearly challenges the validity of the myth.

Chapter 23

Leadership and Spotting Signs of Mental Health Issues

The stigma that surrounds mental illness prevents people from getting the help and support they need. They are afraid of what people will think or say about them. Shame controls them, and they don't seek treatment. Like any physical condition left untreated, it often gets worse.

SIGNS OF MENTAL ILLNESS

With mental illness, there are no absolutes. So, when people ask me how to know if someone is suffering, I usually tell them to look for changes in behavior.

When someone behaves in a way that prompts others to comment, "That's not like so-and-so," it can be at least a cue to ask if there is anything you can do for them. Below are some signs that you or a co-worker or a loved one may be experiencing that may signal mental illness:

- Excessive worry or fear.
- Excessive sadness or low mood.
- Confused thinking or problems concentrating and learning.
- Extreme mood changes, including uncontrollable highs or feelings of euphoria.
- Prolonged or strong feelings of irritability or anger.
- Avoiding friends and social activities.

- Difficulty understanding or relating to other people.
- Changes in sleep habits or feeling tired and low energy.
- Changes in eating habits, such as increased hunger or lack of appetite.
- Changes in sex drive.
- Difficulty perceiving reality (delusions or hallucinations in which the person experiences and senses things that don't exist in objective reality).
- Inability to perceive changes in one's own feelings, behavior, or personality (lack of insight or anosognosia).
- Overuse of substances like alcohol or drugs.
- Multiple physical ailments without obvious causes (headaches, stomachache, vague and persistent aches and pains).
- Thoughts about suicide.
- Inability to carry out daily activities or handle daily problems and stress.
- Intense fear of weight gain or concern with appearance.

YOU CAN'T JUDGE A BOOK BY ITS COVER

The adage "you can't judge a book by its cover" is so true when dealing with those who are struggling with mental health challenges. Sometimes, frankly, they present as not very happy and occasionally nasty people.

After one of my Sean's talks, a fire chief in the audience approached me. "Your talk gave me a whole different perspective. I'm in the process of firing someone who, frankly, I would term a jerk. No one wants to work with him; he's belligerent and not a team player. I now realize that he may have mental health challenges that need to be addressed. Instead of just putting him out on the street, I am going to go back, and I make a promise to Sean that I will have him evaluated and see if that's the issue. Certainly, if it is, I need to get him help; if not, then discipline will run its course."

I can't even begin to tell you how good it makes me feel when someone tells me how Sean's life has made a direct impact. In this case, it was even more powerful because the chief was kind enough to e-mail me a few weeks later to say that, indeed, an evaluation indicated that, unknown to anyone, the person was dealing with several issues causing depression and anger. He was getting help with the hope that, number one, he would be returned to duty, and number two and most importantly, he would be in a better place in his personal life.

Often people who seem to be mad at the world are angry at themselves instead, or at least it is part of the problem. I know I have presented in that way myself at times, so looking beyond the surface is critical if you genuinely care about your people.

"I'M FINE"

As the leader, sometimes you are acutely aware that something is wrong with someone because he is acting out of character, and not according to his typical behavior pattern. Now, if you ask someone who is struggling with a mental health challenge, "Are you okay?" a hundred percent of the time, especially in the fire service, the answer is, "I'm fine." But if you ask, "Is there anything I can do for you?" the scary part is that the person may open up and ask for help. It is critical that you, as the leader, know what resources you have available if someone in distress has the courage to admit they need help. The last thing you want to do is to discourage them in any way because they may never do it again, and the next step may be suicide.

As leaders, we may be afraid to persist when our gut instinct is still telling us there's a problem because we don't want to pry or interfere with someone's personal life. Also, we aren't trained to know whether something serious is brewing or it is just a bad day. A good friend and one of my most respected fire chiefs had a firefighter who had become very withdrawn. Instead of just asking if he was okay only to get an "I'm fine" in response, the chief trusted his instincts. He said, "I'm going to get a cup of coffee and when I come back let's talk about what's going on and how I can help you. And if you still tell me there's nothing wrong, then we're going to take a ride to see somebody who's better trained to find out what's going on." This took a tremendous amount of courage on the fire chief's part. He was stepping out on thin ice.

Obviously, as the leader of a fire department or a company, you need to know what your labor management rights are as well as where to take somebody if you have that ability. I have found it's much better to have a rational discussion about why it's good to seek help instead of ordering a person to go, but this chief made it very clear what he was going to do. When he returned with that cup of coffee, the firefighter confided that he had just been notified about a deeply personal problem that would have thrown anybody into a depression. The two of them were able to talk and indeed get him help to work through the problem.

Almost every book I've read about how to lead has stated that leadership is not about doing the easy thing; it's about doing the right thing. Many times, although doing the hard thing is difficult and uncomfortable, it also can provide the most powerful results.

HEARING SEAN'S VOICE

I returned to the firehouse in late June, about three weeks after Sean was buried. I needed to find my Cape, because I wasn't comfortable in the phone booth as Clark Kent, the dad who had failed to protect his son. It is not uncommon for leaders faced with a crisis they can't control at home to pour themselves into their work. People on the outside, including family, will judge that you don't care. The opposite is the case: you care so much, but you can't take the constant pain of being reminded that you can't change the outcome. I should not have returned when I did, because I went back against my wife's wishes. She always knew best, and I was about to learn that lesson once again.

A few days later, the crisis hit. It was a day on which the emphasis was entirely on the family. It was the Fourth of July when we usually recall all of our people and have an open house for the community.

Eileen begged me not to go. It had always been a huge day for our family in the past. My nieces and nephews would come and ride on the fire truck, along with my boys.

On this holiday, like most towns, we had a Fourth of July celebration. I didn't need to be there. All my firefighters knew what needed to be accomplished. My motivation was not to supervise but to put that Cape back on. I needed it. I couldn't exist as Clark Kent, and as a dad, I felt worthless. The one thing a father is supposed to do is protect his kids, and I had not carried out that mission. I intended to go back and be that firefighter hero. That was the role in which I was successful.

So that is what I did. Fourth of July is mandatory attendance, and I was no exception. I watched all the families of my firefighters and community members climb up on the engines, just like Sean had loved to do. In fact, whenever he was there when I was on shift, he drove me crazy: "I want to drive the truck. I want to drive the engine. I want to drive the ambulance!" I shook everybody's hand bravely, greeted them with, "Hi, how are you? Nice to see you," and pretended that nothing was wrong. As usual, Eileen was right. It was incredibly painful for me. I could visualize and hear Sean running around the firehouse.

I went to my office and cried for the next three hours. I didn't think I had that much water left in my eyes. Out I came at the end of the day, all puffy-faced and red-eyed with prominent dark circles around my eyes. Looking like a raccoon and pretending nobody would notice, I said goodbye to everybody and went home. The following day at work, I was faced with a lieutenant who stood at the door with that statement that no fire chief wants to hear, "Chief, have you got a minute?"

"Sure, what's the problem?"

"Did you happen to give anybody time off yesterday, tell them they didn't have to come for the mandatory Fourth of July detail?"

"Not that I remember, but of course, I'm pretty foggy at this point."

"Well, firefighter so-and-so didn't show up, and on the last couple of shifts, he's had some altercations with shift members, and the last one got physical."

"Is he here today?" When he said yes, I said, "Send him in."

Now, I would love to tell you that I welcomed the opportunity to connect, to be the reassuring leader. "Come on in; I'm going to take care of you; things are going to be great whatever your problem is." It wasn't like that. Instead, to my mind, he was going to get every painful emotion I had bottled up unloaded on him. All my anger and self-loathing. He had given me the opening, and I was going to use it.

Now, a leader's office generally has two chairs in front of the desk, one for the "victim" and one for the "witness." I didn't look up when the firefighter came in and sat down. I had the paperwork the lieutenant had prepared in front of me.

"I want to know about this, this, and this," I started, and he interrupted me.

"Chief, do you want to know where I was yesterday?"

"I don't care where the hell you were yesterday. I want to know about this first incident."

Then, for the first time, I heard Sean's voice: *Dad, you need to look up.*

Startled, I did look up, and what I saw was a man in tears. I pushed the paperwork away and said, "Where were you yesterday?"

"You know, for the last month, Chief, we've sat here, and we've talked about Sean. We all feel terrible. We didn't know about his struggle and could have maybe helped him. We sure could have helped your family. We all believe he's at peace now; he's not suffering anymore, and that's a good thing. So yesterday, I sat at home with a gun in my mouth and thought about wanting to join Sean. I don't want to be in this pain, anymore."

Again, old Superman here would like to say I saw that one was coming, but I didn't. And, I'd love to tell you that the extraordinary Cape-wearing leader in me came through, that this perfect example of leadership under fire stood up. Not so. My first thought was, *if I could trade your butt for my son's right now, I'd send you to heaven and bring him back. How dare you come in here and want me to save you when I couldn't save my kid.*

Again, Sean was in my ear. *Dad, you know what to do. Just do it.*

So I said, "Will you go in the ambulance to the hospital?"

"No."

As a next step, I called Sean's psychiatrist and explained the situation. She said, "Will he go with you to the hospital?"

I asked, "Will you go with me?" and he said he would.

I took him off the line, drove four blocks to the hospital, stood in front of that same bank of white elevators that I had taken Sean up in, back when the horrible suicide journey began, and went up to the psychiatric floor. He took his uniform off and disappeared behind the same door Sean had entered, along with the other people who were suffering, who were physically ill.

We were a small, close-knit fire department: one station, twenty-eight people. We knew each other's wives and kids, and probably almost every intimate secret you should not know. Yet, none of us knew that for the past few years, this firefighter/paramedic also suffered from the Superman syndrome, so when he lost a patient, even if the person had been deceased for hours before his arrival, he felt he had let them down. I found out later that anytime he lost a patient on the ambulance, he took personal time to either go to their wake or funeral and sometimes both. I'm not talking about somebody who died in his arms; I'm talking about somebody who could have been dead for twelve hours. He had done this for a span of several years.

None of us in the fire department knew the hell this man had been through. He had to leave the job because of post-traumatic stress disorder, as there were too many triggers in the firefighter position for him to remain. This person was a tremendous firefighter and paramedic, the person you would want working on your kid if they were seriously ill.

That brave young man's willingness to work through treatment, including therapy and many trials and errors, led to his leaving the fire service, but he is an exceptional and successful person. I feel regret, because maybe if I had shared Sean's illness and our family's struggle at the firehouse kitchen table as I would have if he'd had brain cancer, it might've saved this great guy's career in the fire service. I'm happy to say that he is doing well today. This proud father of two beautiful children is to be recognized and given credit for the courage it took to face his demons and get help. Without Sean's passing, there would have been no discussion at the kitchen table about mental health and suicide. I didn't model that behavior myself. As the leader, I had not created in the firehouse a culture of openness about mental health as a physical illness one is afflicted with through no choice of their own. It is not a weakness. If I had shared Sean's story, I don't know, but maybe that firefighter would have come forward earlier than he did, and we might have been able to save his career and indeed save the pain he went through.

That's what I have to live with. But Sean taught me through it. The lesson is this: a leader needs to know it's okay to be vulnerable, it's okay to be human, and that sometimes, by not wearing that Cape, you indeed show more strength than when you wear it.

That firefighter likes to say, "I appreciate you helped save my life."

I always say, "I didn't save your life. Sean saved your life by what he taught me; it brought you forward. The discussion of his life and suicide opened the door for you to save your own."

How often do we have the courage to reach out to employees we see in distress or those we have a gut feeling are troubled? How often do we recognize behavior patterns outside the norm and ask the simple question, "Is there anything I can do for you?"

The truth is, many leaders simply do not. We may be afraid because we don't know what to do if they start to open up. We may rationalize what we notice because we don't want to intrude. However, "It's none of my business," has nothing to do with our work. Truthfully, it's because the Cape doesn't have the answers to these difficult questions, but that is no excuse not to ask. Use the Cape to be ready to provide resources or help with the problems, not ignore them. It is your responsibility as a true leader to care for all facets of your workforce, including you!

LESSONS LEARNED

- **You can't judge a book by its cover.** Those who suffer from mental health challenges present differently from those with other illnesses. Unlike cancer, mental illness is not visibly apparent. You must be willing to ask the tough questions to those who are in need.
- **Be ready with resources.** Use your position as the leader to be ready to provide the resources for help instead of ignoring the problems you see and hoping they will resolve by themselves.
- **Ignorance is not a virtue of leadership.** Passion to provide knowledge to all is leadership.

Chapter 24

The Question to Ask
and What to Do

**It is a myth that talking to someone who is suicidal might make
things worse. Most people who are suicidal say, "You can't
make my pain any worse by talking to me. You might be
able to make me feel a little better, though."**

There is a misconception out there that if you discuss suicide with
someone who is thinking about it, you might talk the person into it. I
used to believe that myth, too. It has never been proven; quite the
opposite, asking about it may be the most effective way to prevent
suicide. Thus, all branches of the military have a 'don't-beat-around-
the-bush' approach. You ask the question directly: "Are you thinking
about killing yourself?"

All of the military models currently out there, as well as those used
by peer support groups, agree on how to approach someone you think
is going to die by suicide. It's to be as blunt and clear as possible about
what you are asking.

The question is: "Are you thinking about killing yourself?"

The question is *not*: Are you thinking of hurting yourself? Since
many people who are in mental health pain use cutting as a mechanism
to relieve the pain, that can be a misleading question.

You want to go straight to the heart of the matter. Someone who is genuinely thinking about suicide may say yes, and if so, you need to get the person help immediately. Who exactly do you call? That should be common knowledge—not on a bulletin board or hidden under some papers—but in everyone's cell phone. Have everyone pre-program the number so if they encounter a potential suicide situation with a family member or a peer, they will have it. In the event, call that number and hand the phone to the person as you're standing there. Find out where to take the person and get directions.

MILITARY MODEL FOR SUICIDE PREVENTION

Military branches are unique, yet they follow a consistent model. Two examples are below. The Air Force protocol first and then the Army.

- Ask.
- Know where to go.
- Escort the person to safety.

This is the model that every organization should adopt. You have to ask the person directly, "Are you thinking about suicide?" Be on the lookout for behavior that shows a change in the person's regular activities: suddenly drinking more, acting reckless, eating less—any drastic change can be a sign of mental unrest that may lead you to ask that question. If the answer is yes, all models agree that you must know where to take them for help. That resource needs to be vetted in advance. It can't wait until you face the crisis. Finally, the models agree that you should take the person to the resource. All the models start with peer support. Sometimes all the individual needs is a conversation with a peer.

THE ACE PEER CONCEPT

- Ask your buddy.
- Care for your buddy.
- Escort your buddy.

Now, you may be thinking that if somebody wants to kill himself, why would he tell you? Yes, if he is so far in the dark and the deep, he may indeed deny that feeling, even when confronted directly. However, it could be he is not sure and is just looking for someone who cares. People who have survived the jump from the Golden Gate Bridge all expressed that once they let go, they were sorry they jumped. They just didn't think anyone cared.

It's that simple. Sometimes, a person just needs to get a load off his chest. That can help so much. The challenge for you as a leader is the tendency to feel you have to save the day, you have to make it right when they tell you.

No, you don't! Usually, you can't! However, even when you're just listening, your Cape is still flapping in the wind. It still works. You don't have to be the end-all, be-all. You just need to get the person to someone who can treat that illness. It's just like when someone tells you they have cancer; you know you can't save them by yourself. You're not a doctor, so you get them to professionals where they can get the help they need.

This is how we need to deal with mental health. We need to get the person to help from trained professionals. We need to make it happen. We need to make it a priority, and we need to make it real for our employees. They must believe in the process we set in place as leaders, from education through the application of the help they are seeking.

The Cape is a good thing. The challenge is knowing when to put it on and when to take it off. As leaders, we have a responsibility to stand up and do the right thing so that people know we believe their pain. By being present to them, we send the powerful message that they are valuable, and we don't want to see them fail. In a family, an open line of communication is critical to the right environment for sharing tough issues.

WHAT IF THE ANSWER IS NO?

Again, remember, I am not a trained mental health professional or an expert. Still, because of Sean, I have been around several people who have thought of death by suicide, and sometimes No is the honest answer. They may be very depressed but have not yet reached that drastic point. Still, by asking, you open the communications door and make them aware that you see something that worries you. By this, you keep a line of communications open and a life preserver in place. Just showing compassion for a fellow human being and leaving the door open may save a life.

Of course, some people may lie to you because, indeed, they do wish to die and don't want you to stop them. In this case, the truth is, such people *will* take their lives.

It is critical to point out that you can do all the right things, ask all the right questions, have all the right resources in place, and you're still going to lose people to suicide. When someone is in the kind of deep and dark depression that Sean experienced, when there is no sign of hope, in their mind there truly is only one way out of the pain, and you're not going to be stronger than that pain.

However, if the answer is no and you still believe there's an issue, there are a couple of different ways you can handle it. First, be insistent. Challenge the person. "I don't believe you." Follow that by explaining what a loss it would be to you personally, to the organization, etc., if something were to happen. Don't try to tell them how great their life is; it wouldn't be on their radar. Remember, perception is reality. Even though you can see that a person has a beautiful family, an excellent job, and is a great person, when they look in the mirror, that is not what they see. So, don't insult them by trying to conjure up a picture that they can't perceive.

On the other hand, they do not control your emotions, so sharing how you would feel if they took their life can sometimes address feelings of not belonging or of being a burden. We will talk more about these concepts of not belonging and being a burden and how they play into the risk for suicide later when we examine Dr. Thomas Joiner's theory of suicide, *Why People Die by Suicide.*

It is critical that you continue to reinforce that the door is always open if they change their mind about wanting help to deal with these desperate suicidal thoughts. Make sure you mean that. Don't make false promises that you're going to make everything all right, because your Cape doesn't have that power. However, you certainly can provide resources that may give them some hope.

If your bells are still ringing, if you still think the person lied to you, make sure you check back with them. Be relentless about checking-in regularly. What is regularly? Again, I'm no expert, but in my own experience with Sean, sometimes that was an hourly question, sometimes daily or monthly. There is no right or wrong answer; just keep asking until you stop feeling that way or the person has told you they need help.

Will it save them? The answer is maybe or maybe not. However, you will have the peace of mind of knowing you did recognize something and tried to do something about it. Your genuine caring for your fellow human being, fellow employee, or family member, if indeed they decide to end their life, is the crucial and the one thing Eileen and I hung onto after Sean's passing. We experienced many negative emotions, but we did not feel that we hadn't done everything we could to try and save him. Just as important was that he knew daily that he was loved, even when the situation was one that made us angry and left us feeling powerless.

Peer support groups and trained psychological professionals know how to ask questions that will elicit responses to indicate whether someone is really in trouble. There are training courses in Motivational Interviewing. I am not familiar with the technique, but it could be an excellent resource for you and your staff. Remember also, as it was in Sean's case, when someone has made a final decision to take his life and for the first time in years is at peace and appears very happy, the person may look you in the eye with honesty and say that.

Yes, sometimes they lie about whether they are thinking about death by suicide, but they are not lying about how they feel. Mental illness is just like cancer; it comes in many forms and is incredibly complex. All you can do is care enough to be prepared, provide resources for the people you lead, and care about them both at home and in the workplace. Keep your radar up for those who look like they require help, and that also includes you.

WHAT IF THE ANSWER IS YES?

This is the question I am asked most often when I do Sean's talk. If I notice or am worried about someone and I ask them directly, "Are you thinking of killing yourself?" What if they say yes?

You may only have one chance to get this intervention action right, so you need to know your course of action beforehand, as the situation requires immediate attention. Make a simple start.

- Put a 24/7 suicide-prevention app on your phone (Suicide Hotline, etc.) (suicidepreventionlifeline.org, 1-800-273-8255 [TALK]). Research who is on the other end of that line.
- Call a counselor you know right away.
- Put the person on the phone with the hotline and escort them to a designated location.

Don't give a person who has opened up their soul the chance to change their mind. When the illness door opens, try to provide relief. The person will feel better just for having told someone. It's a bit like getting ten days of antibiotics; you may feel good after seven days, but you still have to take it for ten. With mental illness and suicide, the situation is far more severe. You've only opened the door; the demons haven't come out. With no professional follow-up, they could come out with brute force.

LESSONS LEARNED

- **Be direct, "Are you thinking of killing yourself?"** People who are suicidal are already suffering. You can't make their pain any worse by asking if they need help or be direct and ask are they thinking of killing themselves.

- **Know your resources ahead of time.** Know what to do if they say they want help or are thinking of suicide. That is not the time to tell them, "I'll get back to you." As the leader, know your resources ahead of time. Make sure they connect with the resource, even if you have to take them there.

- **Ask questions.** Be ready for them to say no to your suicide question. That may be precisely how they are feeling at that time. They may be distraught, but not at the point of taking their life. That does not guarantee the thought to take their life by suicide won't occur in the future. That could be the next day, week, or year. At any time, if you feel in your gut someone is at risk regardless of previous denial(s), continue to ask the question of "Are you thinking of killing yourself?" By asking the question, you open the lines of communications that they may revisit another time when they are indeed suicidal. You show you care, and that can sometimes be just enough to save a life.

Chapter 25

It's Not About You

When you are dealing with the loss of a spouse or a child due to terminal illness, mental illness, or cancer, you have to deal with the pain head-on, as difficult as that is. Perhaps the most important part of managing this horrible situation is to recognize that it's not all about you!

That's tough to do when you are in the middle of the pain. You, a leader, are helpless to protect the ones you love. You must literally stand by and watch them die. Whether it is a suicide or terminal cancer, it's not a death anyone chooses. It's a death that was genuinely chosen for them, and you are not empowered to change the course God has laid out. We think the Cape that has served us so well in other situations somehow makes us truly supernatural. Nothing could be farther from the truth; instead, it exposes your frail humanness.

What do I mean when I say it's not about you? Let's take the case of suicide. Many times, people asked me about our situation. "Are you upset with Sean about what he did to you? About what he did to your family? About what he did to your wife?" My answer was always straightforward: No. I realized that it wasn't about me.

Sean did not make a choice that day to take his life thinking about the pain his parents, his brothers, his friends, and his extended family would go through. You see, when your loved one is in that kind of pain, all they see is one solution, and that is to get out of the pain, to get off this earth and go someplace else where hopefully they are healed.

Sean had tried every known medication and treatment with no response. Like a cancer patient whose disease does not respond to known treatments like chemotherapy or radiation, his life clock was ticking down.

AFFIRM THIS TRUTH FOR LOVED ONES

As a bystander, either a leader in an organization or a family member dealing with someone you care about who's lost a child due to suicide, you can reaffirm:

- It wasn't about you.
- It wasn't about a family member not doing a good enough job, because in that final moment, family members weren't even on the radar.

Because in many cases of suicide, there's no answer to the nasty question of "why?" People don't want to have that conversation. That's a tough one to get your arms around, and instead of giving a complicated answer, often family members blame themselves. Just by supporting that family, you will be doing a great service.

PEOPLE WHO DIE BY SUICIDE
WANT TO ESCAPE THE PAIN

The fact is, they want to get away from the pain. It's not debatable, as much as parents and loved ones would love to argue it. We are trying to put some meaning to a devastating loss that can't possibly be that simple. It's almost comical to say, but you would rather blame yourself than accept it wasn't in your control. After all, somebody must be to blame, and someone must be held accountable for this terrible loss! It's just not the case. You couldn't have "fixed" their pain, or you would have.

The pain was just so overwhelming that suicide became the only viable decision, regardless of the hurt left to those behind. They needed to get away from that pain, and that is what drove the decision. It is so important to recognize that they did not do it to get away from you. They needed to get away from their earthly life, so please don't personalize that action. Don't go back and build a case against yourself that this is your fault because it's not. You did the best you could. If love could have kept your loved one here, it would have. My wife used to say that all the time. It was the single most powerful statement to reconcile losing Sean:

> *"If love could have kept Sean here, he'd still be here because so many people loved him."*

So true. He just couldn't feel it. The love didn't negate that black hole and pain.

The story is the same when you have a terminally ill spouse or a family member or friend who is dying. Make sure that you reach out to them in every way you can to let them know that you care. You can't fix it, but by being present, you are doing something! It is so uncomfortable because you don't know what to say or what to do, but don't let that stop you.

SHARE A HUG

Another way to symbolize for a mourner that it's not about them is to share a hug, and a, "This just sucks." You may feel it's not much, but indeed it means a lot to someone in that situation. Always ask permission first, as not everyone is open to being hugged. Just looking someone in the eyes to let them know you care goes a long way even if you feel inadequate. Remember, it's not about you.

It truly is lonely being the leader whether the loss is in your family or in your workplace. No one can own the pain the way you do. That's always been your role, so why pass on it now? Because it's not about you. It's about the disease and realizing that both cancer and mental illness are physical illnesses, and both can rob good people of their lives. This is paramount to your own survival as the leader. It is not what you failed to do as a leader. It is what you do for others to make them feel whole, giving them their dignity in the worst imaginable situation that will allow you to continue to move forward as a leader.

THE RABBIT HOLE OF SEARCHING FOR WHY

Another lesson to be learned, specifically from the loss of a child, begins the moment you're notified of that horrific news. Your child took his life. Going forward, you will search and search and search for signs you missed. You will go back over weeks and months, thinking, "This was coming. Why didn't I see it? He did this, or he did that, or she didn't do that, or she said that word to me..." and frankly, that is useless energy. It won't change the outcome, and it really is a search to take the burden of guilt off you as the leader. In a roundabout way, some people use it for justification: "If I had been a better leader, I would have seen that, and I could have done something about it." Either way, all you're left with is the same result, so as hard as it is, please let it go. *It was about your loved one and the search to end their mental pain, not your lack of foresight.*

Most of the things you remember couldn't possibly be tied to the fact that your loved one was going to take their life. Hindsight truly is 20/20, and in the case of losing a child to suicide, it can indeed send you into a spin you don't want to go through. And that child who took their life wouldn't want that for you. I know Sean didn't want that for his mom or me. Again, it's not about you. They didn't do it to make your life a mess. They want people who are healthy to enjoy their lives, more so than anybody. They get it, what a gift it is to be able to live your life and navigate it with as little pain as possible.

THE PERSON WHO DIED BY SUICIDE
MAY HAVE SEEMED HAPPY

With a terminally ill person, it's easy to see the pain they suffer and their decline. That is not usually the case with a person who is terminal from a mental illness. They are the best at conning you. They are the best at putting on a front to make everybody think things are wonderful. You get fooled as the family member, too, so again, you can't look back and think you should have known because the person seemed too happy. I remember feeling that way after stories shared by our family friends recounting the weekend before Sean took his life. He had seemed so happy at a local festival.

Well, of course, he was happy. He knew what he was going to do, and in seven days, he knew he wouldn't be in pain, anymore. I remember seeing the joy on his face as he sang, getting out of a car full of his close friends who had stuck by his side. Never in my wildest dreams did I realize that it was a sign that he was about to take his life. Looking back, I didn't see that coming, certainly not at that moment. I've learned not to waste my energy wondering why I, as a leader, didn't pick that up and save him somehow. I couldn't control the outcome.

YOU AREN'T SUPERHUMAN

The message "It's Not About You," allows you to be human. Truly, you don't have a Cape, and you don't possess superhuman abilities. You can't see the future. You can't look into people's hearts or minds or even their bodies to see what's really going on. All you can do is accept the authenticity of their pain, support that, and help them deal with it as best you can.

ENDING TREATMENT

"It's Not About You" really hits home when you decide you're done with treatment, and you don't want to deal with it anymore. Sean brought that reality to my attention when my mother-in-law decided she didn't want treatment for a medical condition. She refused treatment for an infection which could have been rectified but would have led her to a nursing home. My mother-in-law didn't want that. She said she was okay with dying, okay with seeing God. She passed away two weeks later.

Sean had asked my wife how come it was okay for Granny to make that decision but not him. I can still picture her in the kitchen, saying,

"Sean, you're only twenty years old. Granny lived a full life. You've got so much more to give."

His point was that he was in precisely the same degree of pain, but nobody got that. He had exactly the same terminal diagnosis, but nobody got it. Why? Because it was all about us. We weren't listening to his pain. We were trying to save him, not understand his feelings.

That's right. It wasn't about us, at all. Just like it's not about you; it's about the person who is suffering. It is a difficult leap for leaders to realize it's not about them, that it's always about the other person. Usually, leaders feel that the primary responsibility for their organizations falls on their shoulders, and, thus, responsibility for their personnel. To indeed have the strength to be a leader, you have to let that go. You must keep your eye on the target: it's about the person who is suffering, and you can't control the outcome. You can, however, create a culture in your organization that supports that view and removes the associated stigma.

I repeatedly said that I got that. "Look at all we did for Sean. Look at all we did for Eileen." But when they reach that crossroads, when they are on the runway preparing for the final journey back home, do we know it really was about them. In the aftermath, do we know it, or do we still focus on what we are left with? Is it still all about us?

The decisions we make need to be about them, not about us, because honestly, the only chance you have to put that Cape back on and move forward instead of just moving on is to follow their wishes. Because when they are not here, you can't tell them anymore how much you love them and would give anything to save them. Instead, you're standing in that funeral parlor, and you don't get a second chance to tell them to their face. It's really about them, and they are now safe and whole. Their suffering is over.

In the meantime, to reduce the guilt you will inevitably feel because your Cape failed to protect them, say, "I love you," often and say it loud. While I am not devoid of wishing I could have somehow saved both my son and my wife, it has helped me more than anything to know that when each of them passed, they knew that I loved them so much and felt so bad that I couldn't save them.

I miss my son, and I miss my wife; there is a void that will not be filled until I see them again. I know they're healthy, strong, happy, and free, and that's what counts. Because it's not about me.

LESSONS LEARNED

- **Reaffirm to survivors of suicide that it wasn't about them.** It wasn't because they didn't do a good enough job as a parent or loved one, because, at the moment of taking their life, they weren't even on their loved one's radar.
- **Hindsight is 20/20.** When you lose a loved one to suicide, it can send you into a terrible spin that your loved one would not want for you. You remember things and wonder if they were signs. Why didn't I see it coming? Most are things you couldn't possibly have connected to your loved one taking their life. *You can't predict the future.* You can't look into people's hearts, minds, or even their bodies to see what's going on. All you can do is accept that the pain they're in is genuine and help them to deal with it as best you can.
- **It's not about you.** It's about the person who is suffering. Usually, whether real or perceived, the responsibility to protect people from failing falls on the shoulders of the leader. It is difficult to let go of this idea. Keep it firmly in your line of sight that this is about the person who is suffering, and you can't control the outcome.
- **Move forward.** Finally, when your loved one has gone, do you know in the aftermath that it really was about them, or do you still focus on what you are left with? Moving forward means you accept their fate and will go forward to build on how they lived, not on how they died.

Chapter 26

Why People Die by Suicide

No matter the resource, mental health in general and suicide in particular are complicated issues. You have a better chance to address these issues as the leader if you can get some basic understanding. I knew how ill Sean was, and I knew that suicide was his decision to get out of the pain, but I still couldn't get my arms around it until I heard Dr. Thomas Joiner of Florida State University speak at the National Fire Academy. He wrote a book, *Why People Die by Suicide*.

THREE FACTORS COMBINE TO MAKE A PERSON SUICIDAL

His model is based on three things that must occur, and they all must be present at the same time for a person to be suicidal. The first two are psychological states: A perceived burdensomeness and thwarted belongingness. The final factor is what is called an *acquired ability to enact lethal self-injury*. Let's start with the first two of these factors.

The suicidal person sees himself as a burden to his loved ones and work colleagues, for example, and also feels that he doesn't belong. Dr. Joiner emphasizes that need to belong. Sean never felt that he belonged; he felt like a burden to our family, emotionally and financially. This is something we see a lot in the fire service and other professions with a strong "identity title." We see it when people retire because firefighting is so much of their identity, and now, suddenly, you are not one, anymore.

When I was the chief, I often invited retired employees to come back for coffee. Too often, they said, "Thanks, Pat, but I can't do that, because I don't belong."

"You spent thirty years here! What do you mean you don't belong?"

"No, I just don't feel like I fit."

Couple this fragile sense of belonging with the fact that, as we get older, we don't usually get physically healthier. Typically, we get worse and have to be a little more dependent on people. The feeling of being a burden along with the feeling that you don't belong can come together quickly with a retiree. However, it can certainly be that way for people who are on the job. "I'm too distracted. I'm too depressed, so I'm a burden to the people on my shift. I can't respond with them. I can't carry my weight. I'm a lousy husband. I'm a miserable wife. I'm a horrible dad. I'm a lousy mom. I don't belong here. They'd be better off without me." I'm sure Sean felt we would be better off without him, instead of realizing the harsh reality of just how devastated we were and remain to this day.

According to Dr. Joiner's theory, if either of those states occurs in isolation, it is not sufficient to be a trigger for suicide. However, if they occur together, along with the final factor, the desire for death is powerful.

The final factor is an acquired ability to enact lethal self-injury. In firefighter's parlance, it means that you have to devalue your life enough that you're willing to lose it for somebody else or something. Now, in the case of firefighters, police officers, ER nurses, the military—we take an oath. We raise our right hands and say we'll do that. If there is a life to be saved, we will put our lives on the line. So, we can devalue our lives in that way.

The other way you acquire the ability to enact lethal self-injury is through repeated attempts to take your life. Eventually, the will to turn back is gone, and you complete the act.

DR. JOINER'S MODEL

Dr. Joiner's theory is that firefighters already have the third factor, the ability to enact lethal self-injury. So, when the perception of being a burden and not belonging come together, the third factor is already locked in the chamber. The person feels they can't take it anymore and the only way out is to die by suicide. So, again, we can match mental illness with cancer. When people are so ill with cancer and we realize it is terminal, and we pray for them to die.

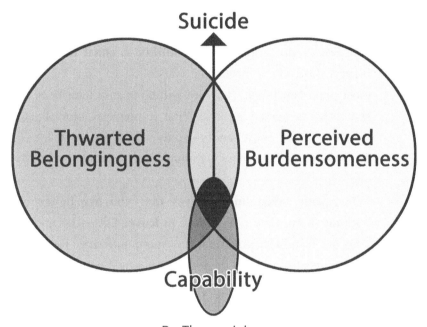

Dr. Thomas Joiner

Now, how does this apply to you as a leader when you ask the question directly, "Are you thinking of killing yourself?" Just caring enough to be brutally honest may be enough to relieve a person's feeling that he does not belong and that some people would be lost without him in this world, not better off.

In Sean's case, we did ask, and sometimes he did tell us that he was going to kill himself. On that final attempt, he didn't. I guarantee you that if you never ask, you will never have a chance to save that life, and you will live with it forever.

LESSONS LEARNED

- **Learn about the suicidal mind's components.** Seeing Dr. Thomas Joiner's model, I finally understood how Sean could get to the point of suicide. The three components of the model must all occur at the same time.
- **The first two are psychological states: a perceived sense of being a burden and thwarted belongingness.**
- **The last factor is an acquired ability to enact lethal self-injury.** Basically, it means that you do not see your life as the most important thing. They are willing to lose their lives for somebody or something else. First responders automatically have this factor, but it is not the only way to acquire this trait. The other way this occurs is through repeated attempts to take one's life.
- **When your loved one believes that you are better off without them, they will choose to leave.** This is not to hurt you, but to protect you from any more suffering. Reinforce three things that support the idea that you will *not* be better off without him.
- **Love that person unconditionally.** It can be a real challenge at times, especially when there is deception or when the mental illness lasts for years without improvement. However, no matter what they do or say, never let their actions control your response. In our worst times, we never failed to tell Sean we loved him.
- **Do not stop trying to get help for them.** That may mean financially, by overextending your family budget, or it may be emotionally, by not running out of energy to research treatment options.

- **Believe that the suffering is real.** Never question the effort your loved one is putting forth to battle the illness, using words like *lazy* or *quitter*. For many in a deep state of depression, just getting out of bed is all they can manage that day. Every day, they decide to live instead of taking their life. Supporting them and making them feel wanted may determine their decision that day.

Sean knew to the day he died that we held these things in our hearts. Sometimes, despite this, people still believe their death will set the family free. In that case, the only consolation for the survivors is to know that you did all you could, and they died knowing they were loved.

Chapter 27

Listening and Leadership

Most leaders are involved in strategic planning, a process of identifying strengths and weaknesses as well as opportunities and threats that you may face. In the fire service, the formulation is based on dire emergencies.

Assessment centers test the ability of firefighters to think on their feet. We call it pre-planning. Frankly, some of the scenarios are laughable. For instance, you may be told that there are three of you on an engine, and you pull up to a train derailment where a train hit a bus with thirty orphans inside and there is a hazardous material spill. There are five nuns on the bus who are supervising the orphans, but they are all blind and disabled! You are told to fix the problem. You have five minutes. Believe it or not, somehow, we figure out a way to do it because we pre-plan far ahead of time. But how do we face such impossible odds? We do it through reliable communications and knowing where to get resources.

HUMAN MENTAL HEALTH PRE-PLANNING

Sadly, we don't do human pre-planning in the area of mental health. We hire people who care and expose them to the worst things you can see without anticipating that they will indeed have a crisis. Yet, we have not prioritized and acquired the ability to clearly communicate our empathy and the resources we will suggest to assist in their care, recovery and return to the job. We need to embrace a model in which we teach our people and our organizations to be better communicators along the mental health continuum. Specifically, their job is *not* to fix the problem, but to identify that someone is hurting and know where to send them to get that help.

Good leaders do not just hear an employee's issue; they truly listen. They don't try to formulate an answer before they understand the entire problem. It is a challenge. Most of us involved in long-term, loving relations with a significant other suffer from this problem all the time. We may hear the noise that's coming our way, but we're not listening; we are already forming a response. That's not a good thing to do in a relationship, and it is a critical error when you are dealing with someone who's suffering from mental health challenges.

Ask firefighters how their life is going, and they will usually say, "It's fine," even when they have emotional turmoil in their lives. They reason that we all have burdens to carry, so why would anybody want to hear about theirs, especially if they think you can't do anything about it? What is frightening is that when they do start to open up, you may not know how to respond because you've done no personal pre-planning on what to say or where to send them for help. These are not insurmountable tasks. It's just a matter of preparation, and good leaders pride themselves on being prepared. We need to start doing this in the area of mental health.

Remember, your job as a leader is not to fix employees' problems, but instead to show empathy for their pain. Instead of trying to fix it, tell them:

- I'm sorry for what you're going through.
- I can't imagine being in your situation.
- Would it help to find resources for you?

This is genuine leadership, not fixing.

LEADERSHIP COMMUNICATION

Leaders must address the topic of communication. As a fire chief, when I look at our line-of-duty death reports, the issue noted in every report—and usually the number-one concern—is communication. I don't think as a service we ever do a perfect job of examining what exactly communication means. As a company leader, or even as the leader of your family, I am sure you can relate. Misunderstandings or wrong sense of direction or purpose can sometimes boil down to communication issues.

That's not always as simple as noting faulty radio transmissions. Sometimes the issue involves the sender and/or the receiver. Is everyone on the same page? As firefighters, we have it drilled into our heads from the start that when you receive a communication while on an emergency scene, you are to repeat it back to make sure that it's understood and everybody's on the same page.

When dealing with mental health issues, even at the extreme where somebody's feeling like hope is gone and suicide is the last and only option, how you communicate and how it's received are crucial components of a successful outcome.

I don't think we do a very good job with that in the fire service, specifically in the area of mental health, because the stigma associated with this disease is complicated when you wear our Cape. How do we communicate our concern for one another? It's awkward, at best. Why is that? First of all, it's because we're not very aware of what to do with a person who needs help.

ASKING THE RIGHT QUESTION

As I mentioned before, when you ask firefighters, "Are you okay?" the answer is always, "Of course, Chief. I'm okay." They could be missing an arm or an ear, but the response is always, "I'm okay! I got it." The problem is, we didn't ask the question the right way!

Instead, ask, "Is there anything that I can do for you?"

We're afraid to ask the question that way, because someone may admit, "Well, yeah. I'm feeling..." Immediately the communication stops because that's not the answer we were expecting. We haven't trained ourselves to know what to do once the communication hits that point.

193

PREPARATION

As the leader, I don't know what you're going to say when I ask you, "Is there anything I can do for you?" I have to be open-minded, and I have to expect the unexpected, which means I have to expect that you might say almost anything. I have to shut off my normal defense mechanisms so that my force field goes down. As the leader, when you do that, what are you doing? You are making yourself vulnerable, and that is scary for so many reasons.

As leaders, we try to avoid being vulnerable. We always have that shield up to protect ourselves. That is necessary to some extent so that being challenged doesn't hurt you, but when you're communicating with somebody who is struggling with a mental health challenge, that force field has to be down. The person talking to you must feel that there is a straight pathway to your heart and soul so they can communicate the pain they're in, and you have to be ready just to listen and hear them, hear what they're saying.

HOW TO LISTEN

Do not prepare a response while they are speaking. Do not jump immediately to fixing. If the first thing said was reasonably simple to comprehend, take it at face value, at the level of raw emotion, and don't analyze to find an answer.

Let's say somebody tells you they are very depressed because they have to put their dad into a nursing home. It may be a story you have heard before or even something you've been through yourself. Your immediate reaction is to fix that, so before they get through their sharing, you say, "Well, have you looked at good facilities, have you looked at the insurance, have you taken them there for a visit?" Too often, we think we're supposed to know all the answers. Instead, slow down. Maybe that was just the tip of the iceberg.

Back to those pre-planning fire scenarios from my profession: I pull up, I look, I survey the whole building by walking all the way around it. I give orders that communicate what I want. There's an immediate response from those on the receiving end. They trust that I know exactly what I'm doing, the direct orders are precisely correct and safe, and all the receiver has to do is repeat it back and carry it out.

When you're dealing with a mental health struggle, you can't give orders to fix it immediately. You have to survey the whole scenario; let the person share everything he wants to, if only for the relief of dumping. Take it in, let him know that you understand he is in pain even if it is nothing you have been trained to deal with. If people feel they can trust you enough to open their hearts because you've lowered your shield and allowed yourself to be vulnerable, you have started to create a culture of being open to mental health discussions.

As the leader, you can't give an answer, but you can give empathy and validate a person's feelings: "This sucks. It's terrible. I can't imagine being in your shoes."

Next, communicate exactly how you can help, starting with questions like: "Would it be helpful if I found you some resources?" or "Would it be helpful if I found somebody for you to talk to?"

Now, you've opened the dialogue, you've heard what they said, and you listened. You didn't try to fix it; instead, you communicated as one human being to another. Position titles, or what in fire service we call *bugles*, must be in the off position! The formal leadership position has to be put aside; this is now peer to peer. That means I am "Pat." Chief Kenny had better not be in the room because that can intimidate or set a different stage. This communication has to be peer-to-peer, friend-to-friend, teammate-to-teammate. It communicates that you will do the best you can to listen to what you say and to hear it and feel it. As the leader, you must fight the feeling that you're going to fix it. Instead, you will lead them to some place, some person, or some resource that can provide the help you need.

To truly heal, people need to help themselves, and you're going to have those resources they need to get better. As a leader, the best thing you can do is to give your people the tools for them to heal themselves.

One of the hardest things about getting promoted in any organization is that everybody likes to do the things that made them outstanding. In my case, they took the hose away from me! I would much rather have had the hose in my hand to extinguish the fire myself. I knew that task, and I was good at it. Once promoted, I had to delegate that task and stand back and supervise. Dealing with an employee who is struggling with mental health challenges is similar. Leaders would rather be the one who can fix the problem, but instead, they have to hand over the tools and let others do it.

Still, how you approach those in pain and how you make them feel when they come to you is critical and will make the difference between a successful outcome and one that will only frustrate them. An awkward encounter either convinces them not to talk to anybody at all or at least to feel that you are certainly not the one to approach. That's not a position you want to be as a leader; instead, you want to be someone who everybody wants to approach.

Sharing and educating the person who approaches you in pain is the right way to support them. Remain aware that even if you do everything in your power to help, it does not guarantee a successful outcome. For a leader, where mental health is concerned, success is defined by the effort put in, not necessarily the outcome.

LESSONS LEARNED

- **Make handling mental illness issues part of human pre-planning instead of disaster-recovery.** Gather information and resources. Educate yourself and your team about the challenges of mental illness. Look at ways to address these challenges and create a backup plan. Work through sample scenarios. If something doesn't work, don't fear going back to the drawing board. Instead, embrace the opportunity to be ready to help someone.
- **Ask the right questions.** Instead of, "Are you okay?" ask, "Is there anything I can do for you?"

- **Listen.** As a leader, you can't fix everything and you can't fix someone's pain, but you can show people empathy, listen, and validate their feelings. "This sucks. It's terrible. I can't imagine being in your shoes."
- **Communicate exactly how you can help.** Begin with questions like: "Would it be helpful if I found you some resources?" or "Would it be helpful if I found somebody for you to talk to?"

Chapter 28

Leadership Lessons

A good friend, Tim, gave me a wall hanging that I put in my office as a reminder of good leadership. It has three tiers to it. The top-tier indicates the mission, the second-tier the men, and the last tier is about me.

Mission

Men

Me

It faces me every morning when I walk into my office, reminding me that it's not about me; it's about the mission, and to get to the mission, I have to take care of my people. When it comes to mental health, leaders need to take care of their people. However, sometimes you do have to think about yourself first. That probably goes against every leadership principle that exists, but if you're not mentally healthy, you can't take care of those who serve next to you. If you fail in the fundamental area of self-care, your mission will never be accomplished.

The ability to stand back and realize you need to put yourself first sometimes is what separates real leaders from pretenders. I call them pretenders because they always have to pretend they're in control, and they have all the answers. It's their way of proving their own stature. They exhibit strength and bravery when, in reality, real courage is knowing when to reach out for help. Honestly, it took me a long time to understand that revelation and then put it into practice. I wouldn't say I've totally mastered it, yet. I'm a work in progress. Still, I see the value of putting my physical, emotional, and spiritual health first to take care of my family, my firefighters, and to accomplish the mission.

I can tell you from experience that if you wear a Cape in any profession and you lose a child, a spouse, or a loved one, you need to seek professional help. The heroic persona of most leaders comes from a tough-it-out mentality. Sure, you can try to go back to "normal," whatever that is, but you will find the pain too overwhelming to handle alone. After Sean passed, for the first time, I actually experienced a glimpse of the deep depression he felt every day. The pain is just as real as a toothache. It is a deteriorating condition, and the same result will occur if there is no professional intervention.

SEEK PROFESSIONAL HELP FOR
YOU AND/OR OTHERS

Do you and your business have a therapist you can turn to when faced with mental health concerns? Someone you have met, not just a name at the end of an employee assistance program business card? Contact that therapist and consider inviting that person to come in once a year and meet with your employees. This is not for a group therapy session but rather to acquaint the therapist with precisely what your folks do. How about asking the therapist to spend some time observing your people at work as another tool to benefit all as to the day-to-day stressors?

I turned to a therapist who knew Sean and, even more critical, she was familiar with the fire service. She made me face my demons of guilt and self-doubt through understanding that my profession and my own heroic persona were adding to my difficulty with beginning the healing process mentally. She hit me head-on: "Take the F…. Cape off!" I had to put my Cape down and realize that I was not Superman, and I was also not God, and both of those realities were okay!

Her experience with my profession was instrumental in opening my heart to hear what she was saying. I believed that she knew how I felt. You need to seek out mental health professionals who have at least a basic knowledge of the challenges you and your employees face daily. If a firefighter feels no connection with the therapist, the likelihood of success is severely diminished. From the therapist's viewpoint, I would imagine it also is challenging to treat people when you do not understand what their occupation entails.

One month almost to the date on which I lost my son, one of my firefighters had the courage to come to me with a severe mental health challenge. Unfortunately, I had a good idea of what he was struggling with; more important, I knew a trained professional to call. You never know when that call for help might come at home or at your business.

YOU AFFECT YOUR BUSINESS CULTURE

You can affect how accepting the culture in your business is with battling mental health issues both at work and at home. When I did not share with my department my struggles and those of my son, I sent a message: don't talk about mental illness because it is a dark secret and something to be ashamed of. I am big on role models, and I had an opportunity to model the progressive notion that mental health is just as important and as real as any of the physical challenges we all face. Instead of seizing that opportunity, I shied away from it. I rationalized it by thinking I was "saving" everyone from experiencing that pain. I would go it alone! I can tell you that the reactions I've gotten since my son's death have reinforced the fact that many people in various professions suffer similar mental health challenges in their families.

If I had been more public about my son's illness, I could have nurtured the culture of being open about mental health issues not only in my department, but also in neighboring organizations. I am not proposing that everyone should bare their most private challenges every morning in the break room. I am simply saying that the concern for and maintenance of the mental health side of most professions lags way behind the physical side. We had better wake up and understand that it is a worthy challenger for our employees' well-being as well as our own. Just the increase in documented cases of PTSD across many vocations should raise our antenna.

It has been more than fourteen years since I last hugged my son. My road to recovery is ongoing. Although it has been painful, I have made great strides. That is in no small part thanks to my faith, my therapist, my wife, and my sons. Also, I need to recognize the members of my department at the time, the Hinsdale Fire Department, and my friends throughout the fire service. The existence of that support group across many spectrums for you or one of your people will be the result of how your organizational culture looks at and reacts to those with mental health issues.

WHEN SOMEONE YOU KNOW OR LEAD HAS A MENTAL ILLNESS

I understand those feelings of depression and powerlessness that you feel when you're dealing with mental health issues. I have watched what the ravages of cancer can do. Stand up, so people will know you don't want to see them fail, whether it's a physical or mental illness. It doesn't mean you will save them. I didn't save my wife. I didn't save my son. The Cape did nothing. So, how can I wear the Cape? I wear it to create a culture that recognizes mental health issues as illness, and I'm going to stand up for you. I'm going to stand next to you, and I'm going to be proud to do that.

Many people overcome mental illness just as they do cancer, and they go on to lead amazing lives. However, we must create an atmosphere where they know it's okay to share their burdens without judgment. Empower the Cape to reinforce a can-do culture, in which you can help people in ways besides saving the day. Just stand next to them and say, "I love you. I believe in you." That is critical to the process, and more people need to role-model that behavior if we want to smash the stigma of mental illness.

We need to make it happen. We need to make it important. We need to make mental illness real and a priority. The Cape's a good thing. We just need to know when to put it on and when to take it off. We must always stand up to do the right thing so that people who are suffering realize we don't want to see them fail.

MENTAL ILLNESS ISN'T A WEAKNESS

This lesson I learned is the most important one my son Sean taught me:

Those who suffer from mental health challenges, no matter to what degree, are wonderful and courageous people. They are no more weak or responsible for their illnesses than someone who is diagnosed with a terminal physical illness. Their disease is not something you can see, like a tumor on an X-ray, but it is just as real and needs support and treatment.

Leaders of all types need to set up a system to provide help to those in need of treatment. I challenge you, if you are struggling, to take off the Cape for a moment and seek the assistance you deserve. Actively seek a qualified professional familiar with your profession who can provide the support you need personally or for the members of your organization.

Finally, make sure all know that your organization's values regarding this issue are clear: we support those in need of mental health assistance. You may not be Superman or Superwoman, but you can contribute to the world by being receptive to those who suffer from mental health challenges, seeing these as physical illnesses to be treated, not as weaknesses to be scorned.

Sean and I both thank you.

Chapter 29

Mental Illness Is a Physical Illness

It can't be said often enough: a mental health challenge is a physical illness, not a choice by someone too weak to move forward through life. Medically, the difficulties faced by someone with depression, anxiety, and bipolar disorder can be traced to actual chemical changes in the brain. This is not different from the chemical changes that lead to diabetes or high cholesterol. But somehow, we fail to make that connection and instead label those who have mental health diseases.

The stigma that only the weak are afflicted with mental illness is just a flat-out lie by people who don't understand that any mental illness is indeed physically based. Once we as a society in general and leaders, in particular, put our arms around and embrace that concept, we will finally move toward genuinely caring about our brothers and sisters who suffer from mental health diseases.

People with diabetes, as well as those with depression, have good and bad days. A bad day is not a choice people make because they're not strong enough to "power through" the day. It happens because what is going on with their body chemistry that day is overwhelming, and it is just too hard to maintain focus.

Somehow, leaders understand that a diabetic needs insulin, and not having that medication can negatively impact emotions and performance, and we have to quickly get what is needed to restore balance without subjecting the person to negative ramifications or character judgments. However, God forbid that a person forgets to take their anxiety medication and feels like they are crawling the wall: we look at that reaction as a choice they made and could quickly rectify. We harbor long-lasting judgments about them as a person and see them as somehow less than the rest of our workforce!

As the leader, approach resources for treating mental illness using the same model as you would for a physical illness. In our profession, back injuries are common due to the awkward way we have to lift heavy objects, including people. It's unavoidable. If the injury is physical and anticipated, as is the case for a back injury in the fire service, we have a model as a guide. I am proposing that we have similar mental health guidelines for all organizations and the human beings they employ.

The guidelines for any physical illness include pre-planning so that your response can be proactive, not reactive. Educate your people on the nature of the disease/injury and the reasonable expectation that they may be impacted. They need to know it is not something out of the ordinary, not something to be ashamed of and hide.

People around us are, for the most part, good people who have emotions. If they love someone who dies, they may experience loss and grief, which can lead to some depression and/or anxiety. That's not avoidable, either.

In both cases, you send the employee to a trusted healthcare professional whom you have already vetted. If a second opinion is needed for the back problem or if there is not a good connection with the therapist, you send them to another specialist. Both physical and mental illnesses may require medications or some therapy to heal. Some illnesses are temporary; some will last for life. Both physical and mental illnesses, if caught early, may receive a favorable prognosis. However, we know for sure that any physical illness, including a mental illness, if left untreated, can cripple you and eventually even become terminal.

LESSONS LEARNED

- **Mental health illness is physical illness.** It is not a choice made by someone too weak to face life. Medically, the challenges faced by someone with depression, anxiety, bipolar disorder, or any other mental illness can be traced to actual chemical changes in the brain. It's similar to the chemical changes in the body that lead to diabetes, high cholesterol, or cancer.

- **Both physical and mental illnesses should receive the same level of treatment.** Leaders of both families and organizations must be called upon to acknowledge and treat people who are mentally ill with the same care and concern as those who are physically ill, because they are.

Chapter 30

Proactively Find Resources

As the leader, be proactive about mental health, not reactive. Do not wait until something tragic occurs to get out in front of the problem. Investigate what resources, if any, are available in your business to deal with mental health challenges for both employees and their families. You need to know all the resources that are available to you, your co-workers, and their families locally, statewide, and nationally.

EMPLOYEE ASSISTANCE PROGRAMS

Remember, mental health issues can affect you. If there is nothing currently in place, be aggressive about pointing this out to those you report to and be part of the solution by helping to investigate viable resources in your community. If you do have programs, like an EAP (employee assistance program), don't be satisfied by its mere existence. Do your due diligence and investigate what they know about your business culture in general and your department specifically. They cannot help if they don't get it! In fact, they can make things worse. In the fire service, we deal with the deaths of children and fellow firefighters, and they need to understand that prior to an initial counseling session. If not, it won't be possible for the program to provide help that factors in the specific challenges involved. This holds true for any occupation; the EAP must understand what your people do.

Next, investigate what insurance will cover and for how long. Many EAP plans limit the number of visits that are covered. Picture your employee, who is just making a connection, being told, "Sorry, last visit." You know by this time what is most likely to happen next – that was their last visit!

OPTIONS FOR WHEN THERE IS NO EAP PROGRAM

If you don't have access to an EAP, what options are out there in your community?

- Some counselors will donate services or reduce their rates on a sliding scale if you seek their help and explain your situation.
- Many hospitals have psychiatric departments that offer assistance in the form of classes through counseling services.
- Local clergy can be approached to set up a type of chaplain program.
- Even local high schools have counseling departments that may lend some educational direction.

Remember, in all cases, no matter who offers to help, you are still responsible to educate them about the nature of your business, so they don't come in cold.

LESSONS LEARNED

- **Know how and where to find your resources.** As the leader, be familiar with the scope of resources that are available to you, your co-workers, and their families.
- **Research your resources.** Be familiar with their specialty, the insurance they take, and their limitations (how many visits are covered, whether they see the same counselor each time, what the counselor knows about their profession, and the like).

Chapter 31

Leading During a Crisis

Leaders are accustomed to being in control. If you want to see leaders feel defeated, place them in a situation in which they feel powerless. It was the emotion I struggled with most during Sean's and Eileen's illnesses: I was powerless to save them. Usually, you don't see a crisis coming, so you cannot forecast its devastating impact. You may not see it as it begins, and worse yet, you often can't predict when it will end.

What is a crisis? According to the *Merriam-Webster* dictionary, a crisis is:

- The turning point for better or worse in an acute disease or fever.
- An unstable or crucial time or state of affairs in which a decisive change is impending, especially one with the distinct possibility of a highly undesirable outcome.

As I write this book, we are in a pandemic caused by COVID-19. I started writing in earnest in April of 2019 with my talented and patient advisor/consultant/coach, Shannon. I've had the privilege to write a few articles, including a chapter for a book for a fellow fire chief, Chief Goldfeder, but never an entire book. I thought I would have this thing knocked out in a few months. I didn't realize I would still be working on it in the spring of 2020, right as the coronavirus struck.

This crisis has heightened the awareness of mental illness as a real illness, not a character weakness. People are quarantined in their homes and schools and churches are closed, creating limited human contact. In my career of almost thirty-eight years, leadership challenges related to mental health during a crisis were not on any political radar. Currently, the mental health of all involved (in this case, the entire population of the world) must be considered, and not just those on the front lines. Hotlines have been set up so that people can contact helpers to walk them through the pain of depression and anxiety, which are natural reactions to a crisis of this magnitude with the continuing isolation.

The pandemic has put most leaders into a difficult position. They not only didn't see it coming, but the end is not predicted any time soon. Organizations are having to furlough or fire people and wonder if they will survive even economically. The workers who are still active live in increasing fear of contracting the disease or taking it back home with them. Yes, this book is about mental health awareness, and it is now undeniable that this pandemic has made a substantial impact on the world's mental health.

It is hard enough for leaders to provide support for employees facing multiple mental health obstacles if they are on-premises and the interactions are face-to-face. However, the pandemic has led to a reduction in most face-to-face interactions to reduce the chance of spreading the virus. Therefore, we now must rely on video conferencing to communicate about even simple, everyday issues, such as medical appointments. When the pandemic hit, I didn't even know Zoom existed; however, I now have to rely on it daily as a leader to communicate and receive critical information.

TAKE A DAY-BY-DAY APPROACH

The challenge to leaders, whether you're a first responder like me or you run a small business, is to take a day-by-day approach. You must be okay with surrendering your Cape and living in the powerless zone for however long it takes. That does not mean you just sit back and take it; instead, you define objectively what you can affect, work within those constraints, and let everything else go.

In my case, that meant:

- Providing the most protective equipment.

- Providing the most comprehensive training.
- Communicating with fellow health providers.
- Monitoring daily the national health organizations.

This is the zone in which I can operate. It is extremely limiting and doesn't give me any power beyond assimilating information into a plan, but at least I can remain in a leadership role. I just had to re-define it. I don't know what stage this crisis will be in once this book is published, but I pray that the leaders who have the power to make impactful worldwide decisions realize their limitations and turn to the experts for guidance.

A time of crisis is no time for a leader to have an ego. This is the time to exhibit one quality of leadership I have always tried to follow, and that is a brutally honest self-analysis. Evaluate precisely what you don't know about the situation and then find the people who know as much as they can about that particular challenge. Remember that the Cape can choke you. You may feel like you have to do it all, but you can't know everything, so don't try.

Choose your advisors, get them on board, empower them to act, and then support their decisions, especially when those decisions aren't popular with the people you serve or those who serve with you. During a crisis, you are like a parent: you do what you think is right for your people even if they don't understand or are angered by that decision. As long as your heart is in protecting their well-being, whether financial or emotional, you are heading down the right path. If you want applause in a crisis, please turn the reins over to somebody else who will solve the problem, because you won't.

I always thought if I was an OB-GYN, I would tell women that their due date was a month past when I thought they were going to deliver. My intent would not be dishonest, as only God knows the date for sure, but I like the idea of providing the joy of something painful ending earlier than expected. Apply that idea to leading in a crisis. Don't promise people it's going to get better exactly when you think it will, because if it's delayed, your credibility will be gone. Positively forecast the future, but build in some cushion, so people have a chance to adjust to whatever this new "normal" is that they call life.

I have mentioned that there is no such thing as a parents' handbook for handling some of the issues we went through as parents when we were losing Sean. On the other hand, there were plenty of spousal handbooks for loss when my wife Eileen passed away. There is indeed something called *The Fire Chiefs' Handbook,* but it was not written to handle a pandemic like COVID-19 and the tremendous loss of life. Thousands of people worldwide are dying daily and the forecast is gruesome. Listening to those numbers day after day will affect your mental health regardless of where you live or what you do for a living. As of today, we still face an enemy that has no deadline, people are still being infected at alarming rates, and the death toll continues to rise, thus leaving us on this mental health marathon with no end in sight. It is emotionally exhausting.

People on the front lines who perform life-saving, emergency medical services, like our nurses, doctors, paramedics, and emergency medical technicians are put in frightening positions. They try to wear enough personal protective equipment "if it's available," as they deal with everything from the common cold to the deadly virus along with concern over a surge that will overload our EMS systems. This all adds up to affect everyone's mental health.

I wonder if this was God's way of telling me that this book may have some value after the pandemic is over, and that's why it's not ready to be published, yet. Of course, it could also be that I'm a terribly slow writer!

I have personally experienced the mental health impact that goes with feeling that your Cape not only can't help, but doesn't really exist, at all. I work on statewide plans and mutual-aid plans with our local fire departments and for our hospitals, along with other dedicated fire chiefs, to make the best out of impossible situations. Today, the plan is not to cure the virus, but to continue to slow down the spread and reduce the mortality rate. We try to reduce the exposure to our firefighter medics, not eliminate it. The burden of being the leader under these conditions can be crushing. I have a very small fire department compared to most communities, and yet, I feel the weight of fifty different families counting on me to keep them safe.

The news media is suffocating. In my thirty-eight years, I have been through several crises, both health-related, as well as the results from significant fires, but nothing like this. We didn't have the media coverage we have today, constantly bombarding the public with good information and, unfortunately, sometimes with misinformation using big spoons to stir anger and invoke panic. You must remember that your employees are people, and part of the general population. They usually reflect the makeup of that general public. So, if 10 percent of the public feels safe, and 10 percent feels that they are all going to die, the other 80 percent are appropriately concerned, and you can pretty much bet that reflects the feelings of your workforce.

I believe the same holds true for my peers. Honestly, I would put myself in that 80 percent, some days leaning more toward the fatalistic 10 percent view. Leaders find themselves physically and mentally exhausted as they plan all day and then listen to the news at night and wonder if they've done anything but lose ground. They look in the faces of their employees and do all you can to assure them that you are taking everything into consideration for their safety as they provide this invaluable service to the public. One of the new phenomena I have not had to deal with, surprisingly, is hoarding everything, from toilet paper to surgical masks and gloves. We can get away without the excess toilet paper in the firehouse, but we can't do our jobs without surgical masks, eye protection, gloves, and gowns. The frustration of trying to order what you need when it is not available, as simple as that sounds, can build on you.

I found myself waking up in the middle of the night with nightmares. These were not directly related to the virus but concerned being in a situation where I couldn't save somebody, either from a drowning or a building collapse. With my bachelor's degree in psychology, I self-

215

analyzed that dream (see Mom, I told you my psychology degree would pay off!), and the answer was apparent. I had to face the reality that, as diligently as I prepare, I can't promise everyone's safety.

WHEN THE CHECK ENGINE LIGHT IS ON

I heard a great analogy about life that is appropriate for mental health. Have you ever seen the check-engine light go on in your car and dismissed it, figuring it's probably just a sensor malfunction and no big deal? If you continue to ignore it until your engine seizes, you know what I am referring too. You know if you'd only paid attention to the light from the beginning, you would have saved a lot of wear and tear and expense.

Most leaders, when forced to the "wall," try to go to another level that allows them to push through until the crisis is resolved. It has been my experience that most leaders are Type A personalities and perfectionists, myself included. We ignore that personal check-engine light many times to our detriment physically, emotionally, and spiritually. It can destroy you. The key is to take care of the stress that light is indicating as soon as you recognize it, and get yourself some help. I am not very good at that.

I have been working straight through since March 2nd at five a.m. It is now the middle of October, and it was the beginning of May when I first realized I had violated everything I have been preaching in this book—taking care of myself. I sat on the couch with my significant other, Irene, listening to me as I was literally in tears because I felt so helpless and hopeless.

As I have for my whole life, I wanted so bad to be perfect, to show I could save the day. I think it all stems back to that little fat kid in grammar school who people made fun of and a mother who was seemingly never proud. Now as an adult, I was in a vicious cycle of perfectionism and depression. Many leaders can relate to falling into this cycle, either at work or at home. No one who wears a Cape is harder on himself than the leader, but that doesn't stop us from unjust self-criticisms or second-guessing, especially in an emotionally charged situation.

Often, only the leader is aware of all the facts, but that does not keep those on the outside from pointing out flaws, either to your face or behind your back. I am still shocked by how many rumors and questions about my actions and motives are still floating out there, years after Sean and Eileen have passed. Worse yet, they don't always come from your adversaries, but also from family and friends. As a leader, when you hear such rumors, remember they come from people who have never walked a day in your shoes.

A VICIOUS CYCLE

What do we leaders often do when facing an opponent that is an unknown challenge, like a pandemic? We push harder to prove them wrong and often spin into a depression because so many times in a crisis; you can't fix it! However, you can destroy yourself physically, emotionally, and spiritually if you don't recognize this spin cycle. With this pandemic, I should have recognized these unhealthy actions from my experience with Sean, but I didn't until I was on that couch in tears.

You see, the Cape itself is not a bad thing at all. What it really comes down to is this: How do you use it? What do you use it for? Do you know its limitations?

In a crisis, you have to make decisions to reduce or rectify the situation. If those decisions happen to be successful, the perfectionist in the leader is not satisfied. So, leaders look for the next mountain to climb. If they encounter more success, all it does is foster the belief that the Cape will always work and the next challenge will also be met with success. Basically, you have a closed-loop system. No opening to take a breath and enjoy accomplishments—or your personal life, for that matter. It appears on the surface that the Cape always comes through for you, leading to an unhealthy feeling of accomplishment that's just not realistic.

On the other hand, if you try to use the Cape against a crisis where you are faced with the unknown and have no experience, such as in a pandemic, the feelings you encounter are not those of success but what feels like failure. There is no objectivity here to evaluate whether you have the capabilities to manage the crisis or whether you are overmatched.

This is foreign to a leader. You are accustomed to using the Cape in every situation, no matter how complicated, and it has always worked. So, you conclude that the inability to solve the crisis must be a lack of effort. You don't take the time to examine that maybe you should be using the Cape instead to find the resources for handling a crisis outside of your abilities. As you sink deeper into the crisis, you lose the necessary awareness of self-care. You can sink into a depression that leads you to believe it is not the crisis that is overwhelming, but rather your lack of effort that is the problem, and that can lead to shame and guilt.

Realize that although the Cape is a wonderful tool under best-case scenarios, it can also be your worst enemy when you begin to disappear under it, lose yourself, and not take care of yourself. That is when it is critical to take the Cape off and seek professional counseling to clarify the purpose of the Cape and its limitations. It is not a complicated process, but one that allows you to get healthy again and return to a leadership role. Choosing to ignore that you need some help from professionals to straighten out your Cape can eventually lead to losing your leadership position. Even more devastating is the possibility of a disconnect from your family and suffering serious health implications that may be long-term.

I created the chart below after discussions with my friend, Dr. Cody Todd, who has her doctorate in Clinical Psychology from ISPP. She has done extensive and amazing work with first responders. The chart is an attempt to visually capture the path between perfectionism and depression. The Cape is a connector to both sides of the equation, because it can do remarkable or destructive things to you as a leader if you're not aware of why you put it on in the first place.

Objectively examine your understanding of your mission, the personal resources you bring to the crisis, and, most notably, the additional resources you may need to lead through this challenging situation. These factors will determine whether the Cape is a positive tool or something that suffocates you.

Here is a simple analogy we were taught early in the fire academy: a chainsaw is an excellent tool when used correctly and safely. However, if you don't realize the limitations of how and when to use it, it can cause serious injury. Your Cape is also a wonderful tool, and a gift. Just know how and when to use it.

PERFECTIONISM AND DEPRESSION PATH

```
                    ┌─────────────────────┐
                    │  Faced with crisis, │
                    │    don the Cape.    │
                    └─────────────────────┘
           ┌────────────────┴────────────────┐
┌──────────────────────┐        ┌──────────────────────────┐
│ Decisions made reduce│        │ Unable to make an impact  │
│  or rectify the      │        │  on the crisis. Can't     │
│  crisis.             │        │  understand why. Must     │
│                      │        │  be lack of effort.       │
└──────────────────────┘        └──────────────────────────┘
┌──────────────────────┐        ┌──────────────────────────┐
│ Look for next "crisis"│       │ Try again, push even      │
│  mountain to climb.  │        │  harder. Self-doubt and   │
│                      │        │  anxiety begin.           │
└──────────────────────┘        └──────────────────────────┘
┌──────────────────────┐        ┌──────────────────────────┐
│ Feel successful as   │        │ No success, blame         │
│  the leader. The Cape│        │  yourself, all your fault.│
│  worked! Motivated   │        │  Lose any awareness of    │
│  for next challenge. │        │  self-care. Where is your │
│                      │        │  Cape?                    │
└──────────────────────┘        └──────────────────────────┘
           ┌─────────────────────────┴─────────────┐
┌──────────────────────┐          ┌──────────────────────┐
│ Realize you need     │          │ Sink into depression. │
│  help. Seek out      │          │  All your fault       │
│  professional        │          │  because you weren't  │
│  counseling to walk  │          │  good enough. Feel    │
│  you through this    │          │  shame and guilt.     │
│  crisis.             │          │                       │
└──────────────────────┘          └──────────────────────┘
┌──────────────────────┐          ┌──────────────────────┐
│ Rebound and return   │          │ Lose leadership       │
│  to leadership role. │          │  position and suffer  │
│                      │          │  serious health       │
│                      │          │  implications.        │
└──────────────────────┘          └──────────────────────┘
```

By Patrick J. Kenny

MARATHON VERSUS SPRINT

My first grandchild, Caroline Eileen, turned one on April 18, 2020, and I hadn't held her since the last week of February before I left to go to Portland, Oregon, to teach a class. For fear of spreading the COVID-19 disease, I, like her other grandparents, was not able to do so on her first birthday. On her birthday, we went over and sat on one part of my son's driveway while they sat on the other, maintaining our social distance. We could at least see her, but as she started to come toward me, I had to get up and walk away for fear of passing on the disease.

The isolation might be the single most painful event of this crisis for me. It also caused me to reflect that while this vocation has given me so much, it also has taken away precious family time. I will not get back the hours and days I missed when Sean and Eileen were healthy and what I am missing now with my granddaughter's first birthday. The Cape giveth and the Cape taketh away! Talk about raising my Irish-Catholic guilt thermometer; that really hits home! You will read in the next section about my faith and "signs;" I believe I am doing what God wants me to do, but I'm not real happy right now about the cost of doing it.

As the leader, you have to decide whether what you're doing for your people is the right thing to do for them. Here is a separate and very different question: is it the right thing to do for yourself and your family? Right now, I am not sure, but I know from experience that uncertainty is normal in my leadership role. Being a leader is hard enough when things are going well. Up against a pandemic, and the social unrest that has followed, the crush of the weight on your Cape can cripple you. I can honestly say I've tried to use my own advice: I am not God, and all I can do is the best I can.

I had fully intended to be retired by January 1, 2021, just short of fifty years to the day my dad went to heaven. I had not shared that with anyone except my sons Brendan and Pat, my daughter-in-law Abbie, and my significant other Irene. Irene and I were scheduled to go to Ireland and be in Sean's pub on September 17, 2020, to celebrate what would have been his thirty-fifth birthday. On that day, I planned to announce my retirement.

Just as God did in January of 2016, he again drastically altered my retirement plan when COVID-19 hit. Not only was my department challenged with the most significant, life-threatening disease we had ever faced, but the nation's economy, unemployment, the education system, not to mention retirement plans, including mine, were taxed to the max or drastically impacted.

You cannot approach a crisis as you would train for a sprint. In the case of a sprint, you identify the target and go all out to finish. Instead, COVID-19 must be examined and attacked like a marathon. Most leaders, including me, are okay with sprints. Identify the problem, find the solution, implement the solution, problem fixed, and on to the next. In a crisis, you must go slow and be very methodical. Each day, what appears to be the problem can change, disappear, or increase in intensity. The stress level is not dispelled in a day or two, but sometimes over years, as with the 9-11 attacks. The mental and physical toll this kind of marathon takes on leaders is indescribable.

I've seen compelling examples of leaders who have acted in accord with what I believe is the hallmark of leadership, which is to stand up in front of people and be honest and confident in their statements. Following their example, do not promise what you can't deliver and make sure to assure everyone that you're doing everything you can. That may not make the situation better, but people will see and feel your sincerity and dedication as their leader, and sometimes that's enough of a life preserver to get you through a crisis.

I wanted no part of this pandemic fight. I wanted to ride off into the sunshine with an easy 2020 work year, enjoy my life, and retire content on January 1, 2021. But as I quoted Father Gavin before, "You are where you are supposed to be even when you don't want to be there." Well, I believe I am where I am supposed to be today—right smack in the middle of this crisis—and I certainly don't want to be here! I am praying my experience in other crises, albeit never this daunting, may help the people I serve both in my department and in the community.

To get through times of crisis, you cannot do it alone. And I believe you must feel that there is a higher power or meaning to your existence. In any crisis, personal or professional, you need a "sign" from somebody or somewhere to let you know that you are not alone and are on the right track. And in the next chapter, I'll show you my "playbook" of signs, which I believe has led me through all my crises.

LESSONS LEARNED

We learn lessons in any crisis. I was the fire chief on 9-11 in Hinsdale, Illinois. I was not in New York City, but that crisis affected everyone, and especially any man or woman who wore a fire department patch. We all stood speechless in our day room, watching as those heroes fought a battle to save even one life in the face of total destruction that would cost them their lives. Most crises impart similar lessons, so here are a few I am witnessing now and have witnessed in the past. If you want to make your own kind of "checklist," add from your own experience:

- **Have a trusted group of peers to vent with about the system.** During difficult times the most incredible leaders will step up, sometimes from the most unlikely spots, and they will stand out like bright lights.
- **Take care of yourself, and that means physically, emotionally, and spiritually.** Sometimes you have to know when enough is enough and make yourself the priority, not the crisis.
- **Know when to take the Cape Off.** You may want to put the Cape on for another fly around, again and again, but know when to take it off and let someone else lead. You need to be comfortable enough in your own skin to be a follower, at times. It is a sign of strength, not a weakness, to sometimes give your Cape away.

- **Surround yourself with good people who will tell you the truth in all situations without fear of retribution.** Sometimes the emperor truly has no clothes on, and if it's me, I want to know that.

- **Be aware of naysayers.** Some leaders shine during a crisis. You also see people who claim to be leaders shrink into the background or only weigh in to throw stones or personal criticisms at a process they don't understand. Recognize them for who they are, take steps to anticipate the objections before they come and neutralize them with facts to keep the mission in focus.

- **Handle obstructionists.** Lean on the intelligent command presence leaders and learn how to hold and keep obstructionists at bay by giving them meaningless tasks to keep them busy. That may sound harsh, but if you've ever operated an emergency operation center or a boardroom, you learn quickly that it's more important to know who you don't want in the center instead of who you do.

- **Be okay with not having a blueprint.** I think probably the hardest time to lead is in the middle of a crisis like this pandemic. There is no blueprint, no attack plan based on previous experience. This is shooting into the dark and hoping you hit something. There is concern about every decision you make having a domino effect. While that's not unique to this situation, it certainly is magnified when you're looking at a crisis that is worldwide and people of every country are suffering and dying.

- **Recognize early on when the perfectionist sets in and try to stop the cycle.** Those who wear the Cape are continually challenging themselves to find a way to avert the crisis. The magnitude of the problem increases when the crisis involves those you care about. In that case, it's even more important to know when to take a break or admit you can't solve the crisis, but only manage it. Notice when the check-engine light is on and get to a "mechanic" right away. Understanding your mission, the personal resources you bring to the crisis, and, most notably, the additional resources you are going to need to lead through this challenging situation will define whether the Cape is a positive tool or something that suffocates you.

Part 4

"SIGNS" AND FEELING THE PRESENCE OF THE DECEASED

Chapter 32

Passed Loved Ones and
My Signs from Beyond

As the leader of an organization, a fire department family, I rely on trends and signs to predict the future, reinforce decisions, or provide direction. Those "signs" can come through the end-of-year financial report, a trading prospectus, or an organizational analysis by a consultant. Obviously, none of these signs are foolproof, but I have enough confidence in them to make big life decisions, including some that are worth millions of dollars.

In terms of passed loved ones, there may also be signs, an occurrence that makes you think maybe, just maybe, one of your angels on the other side sent it to you. So why is it that when we get a "sign," we often dismiss it as a coincidence?

I learned early on as a leader that sometimes you have to trust in things you can't be 100 percent sure of. Ever heard "trust your gut"? I believe these signs are indeed the same as your gut feeling, that inner voice/feeling you learn to trust, but I also think the signs are tangible; you can see them. Whenever I catch myself being surprised by an occurrence, as in, "What are the odds of this happening?" I think, "I'll bet that was a sign."

So why are people hesitant to believe that those signs are real communication methods between the afterlife and you? Maybe they don't believe in God or a higher power, and perhaps they have had too much loss and pain to believe in a "plan" and that our loved ones are truly alive somewhere else. Whatever the rationale, I'm here to challenge your doubt or reinforce your belief with real-life examples.

As leaders, we often look for a significant impact or accomplishment to show that the ship is on course. But signs don't have to be earth-shattering; they can be as simple as a coin found.

FINDING DIMES

After we lost our son, a good friend shared that finding dimes is his sign to let him know his grandfather is nearby. He was amazed that in times of doubt or professional/personal struggle, a dime would show up somewhere totally unexpected, and he was comforted because he believed it was his grandfather letting him know he wasn't alone.

Sure enough, not long after that conversation, Eileen and I began to find dimes in our lowest moments and in the strangest, most inexplicable places. If you remember when I had my car accident, the only piece of my kneecap that was intact was said to be of a "dime shape." That sign carried over when Eileen passed, also. However, right before she passed, I asked her if her sign could be to send hundred-dollar bills instead of dimes. She smiled broadly and told me she'd see what she could do. To date, I have a drawer filled with nothing but dimes, no hundreds, and that will more than suffice.

The following are some significant signs that I have experienced.

DREAMING OF DAD'S FUNERAL

For me, signs started early in life, and that was probably a good thing. As the saying goes, it is at our darkest moments when our faith is challenged. When loss happens, whatever you have believed in (for me, it's Jesus Christ), it's going to either get stronger or go away.

I shared a bit of this story in the first chapter; however, I've expanded on it here. My first significant sign was when I was fourteen. I had a vivid dream of my father in a casket in a navy-blue suit. I could smell the flowers and see the arrangements, and I could see his face.

The day after Christmas in 1971, Dad started throwing up blood clots, and we called the ambulance. I had been so happy when I woke up two weeks earlier, realizing that seeing my father in his casket had been just a dream. Now, it appeared that the dream was getting closer to being a frightening reality. Five days later, on New Year's Eve, Mom allowed me to have a friend over since it was such an upsetting time. Just a little bit after midnight, we went outside to listen to fireworks. As people cheered in the New Year, Mom got a phone call and was looking for a ride to the hospital. Despite my mom telling me for the past five days that Dad would be fine, I never felt it was the case because of the dream.

I took one look at her, and I said, "Dad's gone."

She started to cry. "How did you know?"

Somehow, my dream had gotten me ready for my dad's death. It had sent me a sign that this life-altering event was on the horizon. Oh, some may argue that it was because I had been in a traumatic accident a few months earlier where I lost consciousness, so it was only a dream…just a coincidence. I call it my first sign, at least the first one that was so powerful I can remember its impact.

When I walked into the funeral home for Dad's wake, everything was precisely as I had pictured it in the dream: the suit, the casket, even the smell of the flowers. To this day, I don't enjoy the scent of flowers. At the wake, many people commented things like, "Well, you're the man of the family, now. You need to step up, do the right thing." I thought, "I'm a fourteen-year old kid who just lost his hero in a span of six days. I'm decimated, and I can't even cry because it would be seen as a weakness!" So, I would sneak off to the bathroom where I felt safe to cry and then come back. Occasionally when I came back, I'd hear somebody murmur, "Well, he must not have been very close to his dad because look at him—he's not showing any emotion." My first sign had warned me: emotional pain was now going to be my companion.

WHERE DID THEY GO?

When I was fourteen, I was in a car accident and told I might not walk normally again, and then two months later, I lost my dad. I wanted to die. I went to his grave, lay down, and waited to die. After a few minutes, I heard Dad's voice clearly say, "Get up and get out of here!" I felt it was a sign that there was more for me to do in this life. About three weeks later, I was due for my final diagnosis by the orthopedic surgeon. The previous X-ray in late December, just before my dad got sick, had shown that a dime-size bone fragment was still lodged in the joint of my knee and could cause further problems. Therefore, the debate was whether to remove that fragment now rather than wait for it to cause a problem. You must remember that in 1972 there was no arthroscopic surgery, as we know it today. Any type of surgery was full-blown and would take extensive, time-consuming rehab that would take me out of school, and I had just finished six months of that.

The surgeon redid the X-rays that day. As we were waiting for the results, my mom was distraught. I remember saying, "Don't worry, Mom, it's going to be fine," and she just looked down. I said, "No, it'll be fine."

"How can you be so sure?"

"Because Dad will fix it. He can do that, now." She just got teary and continued to look down.

Finally, the doctor walked in, put the X-rays up so he could read them, and I remember he just kept looking and looking. Eventually, he turned around. "Well, I don't know how it happened, but I don't see that bone fragment, now. So, whatever happened to it, we're not going to go in there and mess with it. If something goes wrong in the future, we'll deal with it. However, for now, you're good to go. You're released."

There's no doubt in my mind what happened to that bone fragment and who did it. It wasn't because I was somebody special who was supposed to get a gift that someone else deserved. It was because my mission in life was being carved out, and in order for me to carry it out,

I was going to need a little help, and I was going to need these legs to realize my vocation in life, to be a firefighter.

My dad and whoever else on the other side must have lobbied to get rid of that piece of bone. That was when I realized I was still alive for some reason. I could have died if I had stepped a little farther in front of that car. I could have died lying next to my dad in the cold cemetery, or frankly, may have lost my way back as the sun was going down and the gates were closed. I could have stumbled and fallen behind some headstone and not been found until the next morning. But there was some reason I was supposed to go on. I didn't know the reason, but I was confident there was one.

ONLY THREE OPEN SPOTS

It's at times like this that you either quit on your faith or it gets stronger, and for me, hearing his voice—Dad's voice—made me believe in my faith and put me on a mission for decades to make him proud. That passion drove me. I reshaped my future devoid of my dreams of being a professional athlete without my hero visible in the stands. I became a teacher and a coach. I loved coaching, hated teaching. Of course, I was teaching theology to an all-male high school class only three years younger than I was, so that was not exactly a formula for success!

My brother-in-law was a firefighter, and with his and my wife's encouragement, I started taking Fire Department tests. It's a competitive process and difficult to attain a position. I took out as many applications as I could to apply for any firefighter opening anywhere. Eventually, I found myself sitting in a gym with a couple of hundred men and women, and it seemed like every single one of them had a fire department t-shirt on except for me, this silly high school teacher. I thought there was no way I was going to pass the written exam that day, let alone all the other components, and pass all these people up to get one of only three open spots for that particular department.

The proctor, who was in his early sixties, said in a gruff voice, "You know what? If you miss hearing your name when you're called, you're automatically disqualified, so you'd better be listening."

Needless to say, I was intent and dialed in on what I needed to do. I listened keenly, and I thought I heard him call a Kenny, but it wasn't Patrick Kenny, that was for sure. Then, he moved on to Kowalski or whatever name came next. I immediately raised my hand.

"What?"

"Excuse me, sir. You didn't call my name."

"What's your name?"

"Patrick Kenny."

"Yeah, I called that name."

"No, sir, you didn't call Patrick Kenny. You called some other Kenny."

Not real thrilled with this interruption, the proctor said, "Come on up here."

You can imagine my embarrassment as I walked up there through all these people who were already aggravated that they were sitting there, waiting. I got to the front. He was looking at a manila envelope. "So, what's your name?"

"Patrick Joseph Kenny."

"I remember," he mumbled. "So, where did I get Michael from?" He shook his head. "Okay, here you go, kid. Take your packet and go sit down."

I walked back to my seat and very confidently sat down. I looked around the room before I opened the manila envelope, thinking, "You're all meat in this room, because I'm going to be one of those three." You see, my dad's name was Michael, and there was no question he was in the room! This was part of my destiny, part of that "Get up and get out of here" I heard at the cemetery. I had things I was supposed to do, and this was where I was supposed to be, for now. Sure enough, I ended up in the top three.

SEEING DAD'S DOUBLE

Okay, you may be thinking that I got lucky on the test, had extra self-confidence because of a "sign" that was *not* a sign. The proctor was old, maybe nearsighted, so that was it. Or perhaps not. How about this: I had been exposed to other signs (my Dad's wake, his voice in the cemetery, dream knee-healing), and I believe that this was, indeed, my dad, still looking after his son.

I had finished the teaching year and started with the fire department just as our first son, Brendan, was born. I loved the job, but it was long hours. It wasn't your regular firefighter's schedule of 24 hours on and 48 hours off. Instead, I was on duty from 6 a.m. until 6 p.m. Monday through Friday. I was averaging about 60-70 hours a week. I wasn't home very much. Our son had colic; my wife was up every night and exhausted.

Finally, we had that discussion at the kitchen table: "I love the firefighting thing, and I support you doing it 100 percent, but can you do it somewhere else where the hours are more regular?" So once again, I started testing at multiple agencies, and one I applied to take a test for was the Hinsdale Fire Department. I had taken a test there previously and had not passed, but the opening was coming up again. It was close to where we lived, and I really wanted to make my wife happy. However, I was coming close to the end of probation at the first fire department and was torn about having to start over again. "Do I want to do this?" I asked myself.

I pulled up in front of the Hinsdale station and debated about going in for the orientation. Eileen had flown down to Florida with Brendan to see her parents, and I thought, "You know what? So, what? I'll just go in. I'm here. Tomorrow, I'll be on a plane to Florida to meet them, and I'll be on a beach drinking beer. So, what can it hurt?"

I went in, and I sat down. This particular department had a tradition during orientation. The Hinsdale Fire Department had the culture of a very small, strongly knit family, so this was a little bit different than in a bigger organization in a place like New York or Chicago. At Hinsdale, they wanted you to understand that they were not like what you saw in movies or on television.

They would bring a couple out, in this case a firefighter and his wife, John and Carlean. The firefighter explained the specific requirements of the job. His wife talked about the impact on her: pager going off in the middle of the night; anniversaries left for later; birthdays missed; things like that. Using a real couple as an example is compelling, and I have made use of it over the years as a fire chief. What struck me most, though, and why I mention it here, is that when they came out and were introduced, I did a double take: The firefighter could have been the identical twin of my father. I looked again, and whispered, "Dad?"

No, it wasn't my dad. But oh, my God, did he look like my dad. And it was a sign. The next morning when I got on the plane to Florida, I knew I needed to see the process through at Hinsdale and see where it went. Sure enough, I finished first and moved to that department.

Are you seeing a theme here? Hard to argue that all these things I've shared were coincidences; maybe instead, my dad was still leading his son.

SOMEDAY YOU'LL BE CHIEF HERE

On the very first day at my new job, I was on the apparatus floor, looking at all the equipment, when the chief approached me out of nowhere. He had retired and therefore provided a "piggy move up," making an open spot at the bottom. "Hi," he said, "are you the new kid?"

"Yes, sir. I am."

"What's your name?"

"Patrick Kenny."

He said, "Did you know there was a chief of this fire department back in the 1800s whose last name was Kenny?" I said I didn't.

He said, "Someday, you'll be the fire chief here," and walked away.

I didn't even know where the bathroom was in that station. Well, anyway, so maybe this chief's a little loony, but okay, very friendly. I didn't think much more about it. Almost ten years later, to the date, I became the fire chief of that organization and, in fact, delivered the eulogy at Chief Leo Musch's funeral. It was a true "what are the odds?" situation that again reinforced for me that, indeed, I was where I was supposed to be.

Getting harder to call these things coincidences?

SEAN'S MESSAGES FROM THE OTHER SIDE

If these so far are not proof enough to get you at least thinking that maybe signs do exist, let's move to Sean. In Chapter 4, I relayed the story about Sean coming out of a coma. He had seen my father and described him to a tee. You may want to go back and re-read it, as it was a powerful sign.

Little did I know that not only would Sean be the messenger for the most powerful sign we had ever experienced, but someday, way too soon, he would take the place of my dad in delivering a powerful sign to me under the worst circumstances.

Well, in 2015, I thought I had a lot of things figured out. I was going to retire on my birthday in May of 2017 in the oldest pub in the tiny town of Athlone, Ireland, a place called Sean's Pub. With Eileen sitting on my lap, I was going to call in to work and say, "I've retired!" She loved the idea of sharing it with Sean, so we agreed to do it.

Also, two years earlier, we had created a slide comparing mental illness to physical illness using brain cancer as an example. After the diagnosis of inoperable brain cancer, I was crying as I said, "Did we know? Did we know that this was going to happen? Why did we pick that disease? Why did we make it the comparable?" I've got a lot of whys in my life. This was the biggest one I had been faced with: Why? Why her?

We were told upfront that this was non-operable and terminal. Our middle son was getting married in November that year, so the goal was to get Eileen there, as good as she could be. For the next 11 months, the goal was November 12, 2016, the wedding day.

On October 31ˢᵗ, Pat and Abbie came to the house. In a very emotional exchange, Pat asked Eileen straight out, "Mom, do you have thirteen days left in you?"

"I didn't fight this hard not to make it." We prepared a hotel room at the reception site with room for a hospital bed for Eileen and a wheelchair that my brother-in-law Terry decked out in green lights and shamrocks. It was going to suck, but we were going to make it the best we could.

The next day was All Saints Day. I went for a run. It was an unseasonably warm and bright day. As I got to the Forest Preserve, I was already drained and not in the mood to run. Also, Sean's Walkman, which I was using, had run out of battery previously, so all my preset stations were gone. I turned on the FM as I began to run. Of course, the first station I found was a religious station! Right then, it was the last thing I wanted, since I felt there was only the slimmest chance that Eileen would make it to that wedding. Even if she did, it would not be what she wanted it to be—about Abbie and Pat. It would be about her. However, the song hit me with these words: "…if you feel like you have no answers and you are looking for help, drop to your knees and ask God to help you."

In my desperation and pain, I did just that. I dropped to my knees right in the middle of the trail and cried, literally. I asked God, "Please help me. I cannot save or even help my wife, anymore!" I can't say I felt that much better, but I did feel more peaceful.

As I walked in the door later, Eileen's good friend and Sean's godmother, Tess, who had been taking care of her, said, "There's been a change. You need to talk to her."

Alarmed, I said, "Why didn't you call me?" She said Eileen was fine, that she just needed to talk to me.

"So, what is going on? I hear there has been a change?" I said as I walked into the bedroom.

Eileen said, "You can tell everyone I won't make the wedding, as I'm going to make my transition."

"Wait a minute, you just told Pat and Abbie last night that you were going to make it. What changed?"

"I saw Sean."

"What! Where?"

"Right there," she said, pointing to the end of her bed.

"How did he look?"

"So happy and so healthy."

"Did he talk to you?"

She said, "Yes. He said, 'Mom, I'm coming to get you.' "

Yes, you might say that this was a woman whose brain was full of cancer on her deathbed, hallucinating. I am telling you that the way she looked at me, her clarity and peace, made me know that Sean indeed had come to let her know she was going home before the wedding.

Later, from conversations with Tess, I figured that Sean's appearance had occurred at about the same time I was on my knees asking God for guidance. I believe God sent Sean.

Pat and Abbie returned that night. Abbie and I huddled and cried in the kitchen. Pat and Eileen talked alone, a son who so badly had wanted his mom to see him get married and a mom who had fought hard for almost eleven months to be there for him. They agreed that it was time for Eileen to go home. It was the most loving conversation I had ever heard. Pat gave her permission to go and told her, "Mom, you've waited ten years for that Sean hug, go get it."

Later, Eileen shared that she had seen her dad, too, on that day, so now things were clear. No more praying to survive, but prayers for a smooth trip home. For the next few days, people came to say goodbye. The Cubs were in the midst of making history that Wednesday night, playing Cleveland in Game 7 of the World Series. When she went to bed in about the 6th inning, the Cubs were winning. Eileen was a huge Cubs fan, and Anthony Rizzo had sent her a signed jersey and note early on in her illness. Before she went down, Bill O'Rourke and I had some Black Bushmills Irish Whiskey with her. She asked for a second, something she never did, so we enthusiastically joined her. My heart sank; I knew it was one of our last toasts together. I did not even stay up to watch the end of the game. We had both dreamed of a Cubs' World Series, and now here it was, almost in our grasp, and I could not care less. In fact, given the circumstances, it hurt like hell.

About midnight I was awakened by yelling and fireworks, and so I assumed the Cubs had won. I did not know that they had blown the lead, and it went to extra innings. It looked like, once again, the loveable losers would blow it. But there was a rain delay of exactly 17 minutes (yes, 17, Eileen's lucky number throughout her ordeal), and when they came back, the Cubs scored and hung on to win. The nurse caring for her during the night told her, "You made it. They won!" Again, a coincidence, no doubt.

The next day, Thursday, November 3rd, Father Gavin stopped by. We sat on our driveway with friends, drinking her favorite Starbucks as she entertained, making sure all were fed and had beverages, especially my nephew Brian's banana bread. At one point, a bright cardinal flew low right over Eileen's head. For Eileen, the cardinal had always been a sign that her dad and her mom's spirits were around.

Father Gavin noticed the cardinal. He asked Eileen, "E, did you see that beautiful cardinal?"

Eileen smiled and said yes. "Next week," he told her, "you will be at that wedding in a much healthier state, able to dance and laugh, because you will be home." I had to get up and walk away. That thought killed me. But she seemed so good in that moment that I thought maybe she would survive until then.

The next morning, she was very different, very weak, and the hospice nurse said, "It will be today." She tried to rise to go to the bathroom, but he said no, it was dangerous, to lie back down and not worry as she had a diaper on. She complied, but you need to know in all eleven months of her illness, she never had an accident. She did not want to soil herself, and she didn't. Now she was told that it was okay, and that it needed to be that way. She should not get up. An hour later, she went into a coma right about the time the Cubs' victory parade started. As they marched down Michigan Avenue, Eileen began her march to heaven. The irony was not lost on me.

Around five p.m., we closed ranks to only our family. Tough call to ask her family and friends to leave, but the hospice folks said she needed calm to make her way home. It made sense because Eileen had always been the *last* person to leave a party. I never realized that creating calm is a common technique to help a person be at peace on their final journey. The evening was the worst part of that journey. Her breathing was labored and very fast and went on for hours, but she received exceptional care from her best friend, Carlean, a nurse, and our other nurse, Aurora.

Here is advice for family leaders in a terminal situation like this: ask the hospice provider what they can do for your loved one, and more important, what they cannot do to make that person comfortable. Not all hospice agencies can provide the same level of comfort management, and I did not know that. So, do your homework ahead of time to find out exactly what they will or will not do. For hours, I held her hand and tried to coach her home. I used the baseball analogy that she was running the bases and heading for home, where Sean was waiting. "Just reach for him. You are almost home, and he is standing there." Eileen had been an outstanding softball player and fast as the wind. This night, she defied all odds; her respiration was so fast that she nearly choked with each breath. It was so painful to watch. I told God she deserved so much better after this life of giving to others; why couldn't she just go to Sean? At about two-thirty a.m., I could not take it anymore. We called hospice, who sent out a nurse who helped her clear her airway. By three a.m., she became peaceful for the first time since late afternoon on the previous day.

At about three-thirty, her breathing was almost nonexistent, but she was hanging on. Why? She would not cross home plate until 3:43 a.m. The hospice nurse proclaimed aloud, "Time of death 3:43 a.m." I asked her to repeat the time.

"Why?"

I said, "Do you know how many firefighters died on 9-11? Three hundred forty-three." She knew that I would know she was home by picking a time that meant something to me, because I *knew* it was a sign! She was home with all those other heroes, the wife of a firefighter for thirty-five years. It was her first angel sign to me.

The circle of signs was complete: from my Dad to Sean, from Sean to Eileen, and now from Eileen to me. If you wish, you can try to defeat my notion. You can say that these were not signs, but instead the work of a pain-damaged mind seeking desperately to find a positive meaning in these tragedies. I, as the leader of my family, chose to rely on those signs. I believe such signs are sent to me from the other side to predict the future, reinforce my decisions, and provide direction. I believe we all have loved ones who send out those signs, our guardian angels, and we are all capable of reading them. I'm certainly not gifted or special. Many times, I think, we choose not to read those signs or dismiss them by labeling them coincidences. I'll bet that's pretty frustrating even for an angel!

> **Signs have led me along throughout my entire life, pointing to paths, reaffirming directions I've chosen. Some were easy to recognize. Some I had to learn to follow. I certainly don't like where some of those signs have taken me, but I believe I truly am where I'm supposed to be all the time, even when I don't want to be there, and those signs let me know.**

I will finish with my two most recent signs, which were powerful.

MEMORIAL GOLF TOURNAMENT

Eileen and I had decided to have a memorial golf tournament to make it through Sean's first anniversary in 2007, and then continued every year. We added my brother-in-law Bob to the event after his passing in May of 2007 from ALS. Eileen had told me as she was dying that our

2016 outing should be the last one. I didn't need to do it anymore after she passed; we had done enough. Then, after she died, I just didn't have it in me to stop. Instead, I would add Eileen's name to the outing for one last tournament, our 13th.

One hundred twenty golfers signed up and we scheduled a meal at a pub for afterward, as we had done on the other twelve occasions. On those, we'd had a few rain showers, but nothing much. However, the weather forecast for this tournament was all-day rain due to a tropical storm remnant.

I spent the day before figuring out a Plan B because of the forecast. A good friend who helped every year as our starter/comedian told me, "It's going to be fine. Have faith in your angels."

"Bob," I said, "the percentage chance of rain is never less than 90 percent all day."

The night before, the forecast was a 100 percent chance of rain during the night followed by a 90 percent chance of rain from seven a.m. until six p.m. I tossed and turned. I could hear the rain pounding, and I was so sad to think that this last outing, when all the rest had been fine, would be rained out. There must be a reason.

I told all in an e-mail the night before that I would go to the course at eight a.m. to meet the owner and make a final decision, but I figured that we were likely going to cancel. When I awoke at six-thirty, there was no rain, just clouds. I wiped the sleep out of my eyes and checked the weather. It said 20 percent chance of rain at seven a.m., then *zero* percent from eight a.m. until one p.m., 40 percent until two p.m., and then 60 percent after two. All golfers would be pretty much done or on the course by one, so I sent out messages that it was a go.

When I got to the course at eight, the sun peeked out from the clouds. The owner said, "Boy, have you got some powerful angels up there!" Sean, Eileen, and Bob would not let the last outing be rained out! We all played. Only the final two foursomes got a little soaked, and fittingly, they were all our family members! As we said that day, the heavens opened up!

This small family outing had raised over $170,000 in those thirteen years. It benefited many worthy charities that deal with mental health and cancer and a scholarship in Bob's name to educate future police officers. No way, the weather should have been good enough to play that day, but we did. Almost every player had ruled out the tournament the night before, but that day, they could only laugh, shake their heads, and say, "The angels were at work." Yes, the weather can change on a "dime," but not to that extreme. At least that's my version, and I'm sticking to it.

SURPRISE GUESTS

After Sean's talks, I've had the great honor of hearing many wonderful stories, sometimes for long after the program is over. Unfortunately, like any other speaker, I sometimes have to hurry off to catch a plane or get back to work. This was the case recently when I did a program in Montana. I needed to drive ninety minutes to catch a flight home for a wedding, so I asked the organizers to make sure I could leave quickly. The plan worked perfectly, and out the door I went. As I was in the parking lot, I got a text from a fire chief friend in the venue saying that I had left Sean's glasses there. I always bring Sean's glasses with me when I do my presentation, more for his presence than to see, so reluctantly, I ran back inside to get them. I was waylaid in the hallway by a chief who said he needed to talk to me.

I have to admit I was annoyed. The conference host stepped in and offered to go get the glasses while I talked to the chief. This "annoyance," without a doubt, turned into one of the most powerful sign events that have occurred to me to date.

The chief was very kind in his remarks about the talk. He referred to it as a sermon, which I found kind of humorous given I didn't make it through seminary. However, what he told me next was the most powerful thing I've ever heard at a Sean's talk.

He said, "As you were speaking, I got annoyed because I could feel somebody standing behind me, over my shoulder, and there were still available seats. I waited a few minutes, and again, I could feel someone there, so I turned around to say something." The chief's eyes filled with tears. I told him to slow down; that I had plenty of time.

He continued, "I looked, and then I glanced back again to make sure that it was who I thought it was. And standing behind me was Jesus. He was watching you, and somebody was next to him, someone I didn't recognize. He was intently looking at you, not down at me or at anyone else. I am not a very religious man, but I know what I saw."

Stunned, I asked, "Why do you think that, of all the people here today, he stood behind you? It was because he knew you'd tell me while others might be hesitant. And if I hadn't left Sean's glasses in here, I wouldn't have come back and met you. So obviously, somebody on the other side was at work."

"However, there's more to it than this," he said.

"How could this get any more powerful?"

"Later in your presentation, when you talked about your wife passing from cancer and you put her picture up on the screen, I recognized her. She was the one who was standing next to Jesus, intently watching you. It was just like you said about Eileen when she was alive, always standing in the back when you spoke."

This is a kind of drop-the-mic story. I have no explanation. It did tell me that I'm not finished sharing Sean's message, whether I like it or not. Although the presentation centers on mental health, the part of the presentation dealing with Eileen's journey and signs provides hope for people in their belief that their loved ones are safely somewhere else, regardless of religious affiliation. It's such a huge piece of our resiliency.

Chapter 33

Other People's Stories and Signs

DAD APPEARS ALONG THE TRAIL

I am certainly not the only one to have been blessed with signs. I think we all get them but do not acknowledge them for several reasons. One of my favorite stories is from a friend who was very close to his dad, who passed away from lung cancer. An avid hiker, he was hiking in the mountains with his son and other friends. He went ahead to scout the trail, and suddenly, as he turned a corner, there in the middle of the trail stood his dad.

As you can imagine, my friend was stunned and excited at the same time. Looking extremely fit and healthy, his dad just smiled and told him not to worry, that he was okay, and disappeared. Again, you may think it was wishful thinking or some kind of mind game, but I can tell you the emotion that filled his eyes when he shared his story with me left no doubt in my mind: he saw his dad, and his dad had come to ease his pain.

I believe that many times signs come for exactly that reason, to ease our pain. If you've ever seen the movie *Field of Dreams,* you can understand what I'm saying. An angel came to ease the pain of Kevin Costner's character, Ray, who had not been able to say goodbye to his dad, having left on bad terms. Not everyone gets something as powerful as a vision, but when you do, it's no mind game, it's a gift, and I believe it is intended to ease your pain.

THE LIGHT SHINES ON

At the same time my wife was battling cancer, a paramedic, Fred, in my department was already over a year into his wife Ruth's fight with a very aggressive cancer. This couple had always had a relationship as best friends to each other, and so they shared the pain. I had talked to Fred countless times about my belief and the signs I had been blessed to receive from Sean, and then from Eileen, too, after her passing. Shortly after his wife passed, Fred called me. "I know you believe in signs, so I'm going to share this story with you."

He had been seated next to his wife's bed in mid-afternoon. The family was all in their home, knowing that her hour was near. "I fell asleep in the chair," he said, "and all of a sudden I was awakened by an incredibly bright light. It was warm. Then, an incredible feeling of peace came over me. I looked over at Ruth and realized that she was about to cross over." His chair faced the window that looked out to the east of the house. The sun had already passed over his home, so the light couldn't have been from the sun, and there was no other source of light to come through that window.

I asked, "Do you think she sent that to you?" and he agreed. I have no doubt that she wanted him to feel at peace for doing such a great job of taking care of her and to give him just a glimpse of what heaven feels like. I believe that most signs are designed to provide you with hope in the middle of your despair. In this case, literally, it brought light to the darkest moment Fred had faced.

I COULD HAVE DANCED ALL NIGHT

In our relationship, my mom and I had a rough go. I now realize that she had a number of her own mental health challenges. Very late in life, she told me that she had been sexually abused by her father, in addition to having had a rough life in Ireland before coming here. It seems to me that those experiences led to a feeling that nothing was ever good enough. She was a negative person. Our relationship was incredibly strained, especially once I got married. She never accepted Eileen and constantly badmouthed her to other people behind our backs, never realizing that these people were Eileen's friends, and that it came right back to us one way or another.

When my mom became ill, and I was forced to find a nursing home for her, it was a difficult transition. She wished then that Eileen and she were closer, something she expected to happen overnight, and it wasn't realistic. While Eileen was always gracious whenever I brought Mom to our home, she was not going to be visiting her daily at the nursing home. As the only child, that was my job. And so, at least three days a week for several years, I went to the nursing home. If you have ever had a relative or friend in a nursing home, you realize it's not much of a life, and you start to pray for them to go to heaven. I couldn't understand why she was hanging on so long. I look back now, and I realize that it was God's plan to allow us to at least put a Band-Aid on the wound of our relationship. By the time she was diagnosed with an abscess in her stomach and decided against surgery and to go into hospice, we were in an okay place.

I had come into this world with her alone, and I would stay by her alone until she went to the other side. Originally, only a day or two in hospice was predicted, but it stretched on day after day, despite not making sense medically. On about day three, a nurse asked me what Mom liked to do. I told her that she had loved to dance with my stepdad Gene.

The nurse said to bring the music to her hospice room and play it; that maybe she needed to relax. I can't say enough about the nurses in Elmhurst Hospital's hospice unit. Any moment I stepped out to catch a catnap or grab a cup of coffee, if the CD ended, they'd immediately put on a new one. Friends came to the room loaded with Guinness, and we included her in every conversation. She wasn't going anywhere.

Finally, after five straight days of not much sleep for me and no real reason for her body to still be functioning, one of the hospice nurses suggested at around ten p.m. that I go home. I told her no, we've come this far, her breathing is shallow, I'd hang out. Politely, she said, "If she wants you here in the morning, your mom won't leave. I have a feeling that she's not leaving while you're here." So, I kissed her goodbye and drove home, which took about thirty minutes. The phone rang when I walked in the door. It was the nurse saying that Mom had passed. Eileen and I got back in the car and drove to the hospital.

It was almost midnight. All the doors were closed except through the emergency room. We entered there and walked through the very quiet hallway. Elevator music was playing in the background. I needed to stop and use the bathroom before we went upstairs, and when I came out, Eileen had an odd look on her face. "Do you hear that music? Do you know what this song is?" I said it was that crummy elevator music.

"No!" she said. Now, I have no musical aptitude, at all. I think Bruce Springsteen sang every song written.

"How in the world would I know what this is?"

"The name of the song is, 'I Could Have Danced All Night.' What do you think your mom's telling you?" Eileen continued. "She loved to dance, and you played music for the last four days because of that. She's home, and more important, you and your mom are okay."

We went up to the room, I said my final goodbyes, and we came back down. By the way, I thanked the nurse who had advised me to go home. She had been right. If I hadn't, my mom would probably have still been there, waiting for me to leave!

By then, it was almost one-thirty in the morning. The parking lot was empty except for my car and, annoyingly, another car that was next to my vehicle. There were probably five hundred spaces in that lot, and that car had parked right up against mine! I opened the passenger door and Eileen climbed in.

I glanced back at that other vehicle. "Get out of the car," I said. She looked at me, puzzled. "Please get out of the car," I said, so she did. "Look at the back of that car."

She looked at the bumper for a sticker, then asked, "What am I looking for?"

I directed her to look at the back window. A big, black Superman logo covered the entire window. I had never seen the logo in black. Why in black? My mom knew the story I often told about Sean and taking my Cape off, and the correlation I made between Superman and me—and there it was, in my face, right up against my car.

Eileen smiled and shook her head. "Well, I guess she knew you were lousy at music, so she wanted to make sure you got the point; let's go home." No doubt, Mom had her way to the end, and it gave me peace.

GRANDPA SAID IT'S OKAY

My father-in-law Robert used to live with us Monday through Friday because he and his wife lived in Crystal Lake, about forty-five minutes from where he was working in Chicago. He'd had two serious heart attacks, and we had an in-law apartment in the basement, so it just made sense.

Robert's relationship with my wife and oldest son Brendan, who was only about three-and-a-half at the time, was powerful. It always made me feel good to know he was there for Eileen when I was working a twenty-four-hour tour of duty at the firehouse. When my father-in-law left for work in the morning, Brendan always stood in the front window, and they exchanged a military salute.

On December 11, 1985, my father-in-law went downstairs with my brother-in-law Terry to finish building a train set for Brendan. Later, Terry continued working on the train set and my father-in-law went to his room to watch the nine-o'clock news. Terry heard a gurgling sound, went to check on his dad, and found him unconscious. He came running up the stairs. "I think Dad had a heart attack." Sean was an infant then, so Eileen put him in the crib and we ran downstairs. Sure enough, I knew by the look on Robert's face that he was in full arrest. We pulled him off the bed, and I started CPR.

In all the times I've done CPR, I've never wanted it to work so badly, but it didn't. My father-in-law was probably in heaven before I even hit the bottom stair. Probably the most heartbreaking moment at the wake was when we took Brendan up to the casket, and he gave his grandpa one last salute.

In the spring of that year, we experienced a typical thunderstorm, the kind that wakes your kids. We heard Brendan talking in his room, so we got out of bed and went in. He was standing on his bed. We asked if he was okay. He said, "I'm okay; Grandpa told me it would be okay."

Eileen's eyes lit up. "Where did you see Grandpa?" she asked. Brendan pointed to the end of the bed. "Did Grandpa talk to you?" Eileen asked. He just lay down. He didn't say another word and went back to sleep.

Children are still innocent at that age, so they don't know that when somebody passes to the other side, you're not supposed to be able to see them! I've heard many similar stories that children have shared with their parents. So, if your children tell you that they have seen somebody who has passed on and you have decided it was impossible—think again!

LIFE MARCHES ON WHETHER YOU LIKE IT OR NOT

In July of 2006, one of Eileen's best friends and a nurse, Joanne, who helped deliver two of our kids was diagnosed with lung cancer that had already grown aggressively, seemingly overnight. Eileen helped her on her journey for the next five months against my wishes. I knew what the outcome would be, and on the heels of Sean's passing, I thought the heartbreak would be too much. Nevertheless, Eileen said she had to do it.

During that time, Joanne became obsessed with the fact that when Sean died, we buried him with one shamrock earring on, and Eileen wore his other one every day. Joanne wanted to give Eileen another piercing so she could wear a matching pair. It never happened; Joanne got too weak to pierce Eileen's ear.

Ironically, Eileen was now wearing the Cape; I knew it was a losing battle and she would be devastated again. As Christmas grew near, my dread increased exponentially. I had flashbacks of my Dad, and now knowing that Joanne could die any day, I was afraid of the hole it would leave for Eileen. Sure enough, on Christmas morning, Eileen was called to Joanne's bedside, as she was close to the end. She left me sitting on the couch with Sean's photo album, alone. I was shocked, hurt, and angry, but I said nothing. Joanne did indeed pass that morning on Christ's birthday, very fitting for a nurse who helped deliver thousands of babies.

What happened over the next three days steered us to a course on which we could move forward without Sean. As Joanne was passing in and out of consciousness, at one point, she grabbed Eileen's hand and kissed it, something she had never done before. She gave Eileen a huge smile.

Eileen asked, "What are you looking at?" Joanne's smile became even more prominent. "Do you see Sean?" Joanne's head nodded. "Was that kiss from Sean?" Again, she nodded.

Well, my anger was quickly replaced with amazement. It was no coincidence on this powerful holiday of eternal life that this message came to Eileen, but it gets better! On the day of Joanne's wake, I was at work. I told Eileen I would meet her at the wake. She called that morning, crying inconsolably.

"What's wrong?"

She yelled at me. "Did you take the shamrock off Sean's coat?"

"Of course not. Why would I do that? He had it on when we closed the lid."

That morning, Eileen had decided to wear matching earrings to honor Joanne's wishes. Eileen had removed Sean's shamrock from her ear before going into the shower and put it on the bed. When she came out, she went to her earring box to find a pair and saw the shamrock earring. She thought it was strange, since she knew she had put it on the bed. Turning to look, she did indeed see a shamrock earring on the bed. Now, she had both shamrock earrings and no way to explain it.

If we buried Sean with one shamrock earring, how did Eileen have two of them? Simple: Joanne's wish that she wear matching earrings had been granted in heaven and in the form of a most potent sign that told her, "Mom, that kiss was from Joanne and me, and we are here. It's okay!"

You can always find a way to explain away what I call a sign. But there was *no other* explanation for what happened that morning, except that Sean sent his earring back to his mom. If you have a different explanation that holds water, contact me!

I challenge you to recognize these signs from the other side in your own life. Maybe you blew them off to coincidence, or perhaps it was just too soon in your grief to recognize them. But make no mistake about it, they are there. Now, go find yours.

LESSONS LEARNED

- **Everyone gets signs from the other side.** Your loved ones let you know that they're okay or maybe provide some guidance. It's a matter of being open to believing that's what they are.
- **Pay attention to signs in your own life.** Allow yourself to be open to receiving them. There are angels on the other side who will try and send you signs. When you find yourself saying, "What were the odds of that?" do a self-check. Ask yourself, "Could that have been a sign?"
- **There are no coincidences.** Don't dismiss signs from the other side as coincidences. I truly believe there are no coincidences. Each sign I received gave me purpose at a turning point in my life and guided me to the next step of my mission, even when I didn't realize it at the time. Recognize that sometimes you get what you pray for, just not in the way that you expected.
- **Signs can happen at any time.** There is no particular point in life where the light goes on, and you understand that signs have been given to you. You can receive signs at any point along your life path. Some people get more than others, but everyone gets signs. You just have to be open to them, and sometimes you need to know how to translate them.

- **Signs come in all forms and sizes.** Be open to all of them. Signs can come in the form of a specific type of bird, a specific song on the radio, a particular coin, and so on. There's not just one way our loved ones communicate. They can be significant, like Sean going to the afterlife and describing a conversation with a deceased grandfather he never met. Signs can be small, like finding a dime. The magnitude of the sign is not important; what's important is your belief in what it signifies. Remember, if we knew about the afterlife's existence for sure, we would have no need for faith.

- **Share your signs.** When you have been blessed to receive a sign, make sure you share it. Many people out there are struggling to get affirmation that what they believe to be a sign is real. You might be just the voice someone needs to hear that day to give them the special gift of hope. What are some of your examples of receiving signs? Were you afraid to acknowledge them to others for fear of ridicule? Another great blessing of signs is the opportunity to pass them on so that others may have hope, too. Signs from beyond are not just for you; they are meant to be shared.

Chapter 34

Talking to Passed Loved Ones

After my wife passed away, going back into our home was the single most challenging thing I had to do, and I had to do it daily. That act alone caused so much pain because it was a constant reminder that she was in heaven, and I was not going to see her until the good Lord called me home.

The last week she was alive, Eileen warned me that I would want to sell the house. As usual, she was right. I was more than ready to get rid of what was causing me the pain. When I shared with my counselor that I was dying every day over and over again when I walked into that house, she asked me to explain what my routine used to be.

I didn't know what she meant, so she spelled it out. "Tell me exactly what you used to do when you crossed the threshold into your house."

"I would say, 'Hey, I'm home.' "

"That's fine, so what are you doing now?"

"I walk in, hang up my keys, and turn on the lights."

"Why don't you say you're home? Why don't you announce that you're back?"

"Because there's nobody there."

As usual, she hit me square between the eyes with her next comment: "I thought you said you believe they are now angels, and therefore they can be anywhere!"

I hate it when she's right.

"If you truly believe that, then from now on, I want you to walk into the house and greet both of them with, 'Hey guys, I'm home. Hi Sean, hi Eileen, you can't imagine the crappy day I had.' Talk to them; they need to hear from you because they want to, and you need to keep that line of communication open."

I know it probably sounds silly as I share this, and I did indeed feel silly the first day I tried it. It's amazing how freeing that became. Not just walking into the house, but also driving in the car, laughing about a poor golf shot that went awry or seeing some great sports play they would both enjoy. I verbalized these thoughts, and it helped me to feel their presence.

When I do Sean's talks onstage, I am often asked how I do it. I always tell them I'm not up there alone. They can't see the army of people behind me, not only my family but all those firefighters who have taken their lives. I believe they are listening and whispering in my ear when I screw something up or I'm about to forget a significant point. They also talk to me when I lose my composure, especially Sean and Eileen. Over and over, I hear Sean saying, "Dad, you've got this. Take your time. Don't lose them on your emotions."

If they are talking to me, it's only polite to return the conversation! I encourage you, wherever you need to focus, whether it's at the cemetery or in the front seat of your car with the radio blaring, have that conversation and keep that line of communication open with the other side until you are reunited again. I'm sure I don't always get the message accurately, but of course, Eileen would tell you that I wasn't very good at hearing things accurately when she was on this side, too!

In this way, you can carry not only their memory, but their soul with you, and when you need to feel that thing they call a gut feeling, it's their souls kicking in, letting you know which direction you need to go. I like to think they're pretty excited when they can make that impact, and I want to believe they still love to hear our voices as much as we miss theirs.

LESSONS LEARNED

- **Reach out and talk to your loved one.** No matter how you cut it, losing a loved one, regardless of the cause, is crushing. You can't see their face or touch their hand. They speak to you with signs, so don't be afraid to talk to them. If you listen hard enough, you may hear their voice or recognize their advice through the signs.

- **Listen.** What we refer to as a "gut feeling" could indeed be one of your loved ones from the other side, connecting with your soul to transmit a message. Don't dismiss it. They have to work pretty hard to get through our thick human skulls.

Part 5

MOVING FORWARD

Chapter 35

Moving Forward as a Couple

There are many challenges you face as you try to move forward without your child, each of you personally and as a couple. People asked if Eileen and I were upset with Sean, angry about "what he did to you, what he did to your family?" No, nothing could be farther from the truth. We watched a hero battle an illness just as if he was battling cancer, and finally, when it got too bad, when it got terminal, he chose to escape the pain and went to heaven. He taught us so much about mental illness and what it really is, and that was the impetus to speak on this topic and share with you in this book. We must defeat the stigma attached to mental illness.

Regardless of what you think about Sean's decision to end his life, the result is the same as with cancer: a child is gone, a family is devastated. So, how do you go on?

First, you realize the harsh reality that life goes on for everyone else. Happy things occur around you while your fog of pain endures. We had been warned about two things by our counselor: One was that friends and maybe even some family members would avoid us. The second was that over 50 percent of marriages that lose a child end up in divorce. I didn't buy either one, but I was quickly educated that the counselor knew better.

Not one week after Sean passed, I was in the grocery store. I was a known figure in the community, probably more for volunteer coaching baseball at the local high school than for being a fire chief. It was not unusual to run into people in the store. In fact, sometimes it was aggravating, as I'd end up in there for thirty minutes more than I wanted to. On this day, I was aimlessly walking down an aisle to get something

I couldn't remember. I looked up and the mom of a kid I had coached for four years in high school was approaching. She did not see me at first, but when she did, she ran the other way out of the aisle and the store.

I know now she was not trying to be rude; instead, she had no idea what to say to me. So please, if you are ever confronted with a similar situation, do not flee; just give a hug. If you feel like it, say, "I'm so sorry for your loss." That's enough. Running away only intensifies the feeling in the bereaved that you are somehow at fault for losing your child, and that other people are afraid to "catch" whatever has infected you.

The danger for marriages the therapist had warned us about became apparent after I went back to work. I spoke about this earlier under communication and teamwork being especially important for couples enduring a trauma involving their children. Trauma leaves all impacted in pain, and emotions are raw. About three weeks after Sean passed, I went back to work, which is not uncommon for leaders faced with a crisis they can't control at home. I soon realized I shouldn't have, as I went back against my wife's wishes. Her predictions of ongoing triggers at work given how many memories of Sean existed there were right on the money. Once when I'd had an okay day, one in which I didn't cry all day or want to kick somebody's butt, I came home and Eileen asked me how my day was. I said, "Good."

In twenty-five years of marriage, Eileen and I had gotten into a handful of shouting matches, but the tone she hit me with that day was nothing I had heard before. "So, that's just great! How the heck can you have a great day? Must be nice when I'm dying here. Glad you could get over it so fast." As she yelled, I could almost hear our counselor's voice echo that warning. I thought, "Oh, no! Here it comes." I did something I had never done before. I walked away and went outside. I waited for about five minutes, then came back in. I said, "We need to start this over again. Remember what Sue warned us about? It just happened."

When I'd said my day was "good," I meant that I didn't feel like a loser all day, I didn't sob all day, and I didn't spend all day with regrets about what I should have done as the leader of my family to save Sean. Instead, I spent only 75 percent of the day dealing with those feelings. *Good* was a relative term, not an absolute. We talked. We hugged, cried, and vowed to keep our radar up so this did not occur again. We were *not* going to lose our son *and* our marriage, and we didn't, thanks to Sue's advice.

In organizations, as well as in families, there is the tendency to identify responsibility and affix blame when nasty things happen. The truth is, when a child dies, there is no place for blame. Instead, resolve to live for your child's memory, not without it. There isn't always someone to blame. Life just happens.

The reality is that you as a couple will grieve and, eventually, hopefully, you will heal well enough to move forward at different rates. Just be aware of that and how sensitive communications can be. The key is to handle angry emotions without aiming them at your spouse.

Not comfortable at home and not comfortable being alone, I did what I had done all during Sean's illness. I dove back into what I knew I was good at, since, as a dad, I felt like a failure. Of course, for me, the answer was to put the Cape back on and get back to my comfort zone as the fire chief, where I was the leader of an organization. Couples need to seek out professional help to make their way forward through this painful experience. It's easy to ignore the pain and race back to areas where you feel safe, but the pain won't go away until you hit it head-on. You will face triggers as individuals and as a couple, and you will need guidance to recognize and address them in a healthy manner.

LESSONS LEARNED

- **Let go of "Why."** Losing a child puts tremendous stress on even a great marriage. There is always a search for the answers to the question of why? Often, that unfulfilled question leads to blaming your spouse.

- **Get professional help as a couple as well as individually.** Couples need to seek out counseling to make their way through this painful experience. It's easy to fall back into areas in which you feel comfortable and ignore the pain, but it won't go away until you hit it head-on.

Chapter 36

Moving Forward after Loss of a Spouse

On the day of the wedding of my son Pat and Abbie, my brother-in-law Pat wandered by. As the wedding party boarded the bus to go take pictures, he handed me an article from the local newspaper. "You need to read this. It's incredible. It's about today." Honestly, I just threw it on the desk in my hotel room, which was connected to the reception hall, and I didn't read it until during the reception. Eileen had challenged me to live after she passed, but that day I felt as close to emotionally dead as possible.

The author was Sharon Randall, who had lost her husband, and the "aha" moment for me was a quote from her friend:

> **"The challenge for you now, having lost your loved one, is to live a life that is honoring to his memory, while at the same time that life moves forward, so only one person has died, not two."**

Loads of people told me I needed to move on after Eileen passed, but only after she was gone did I truly know what it was like to be depressed and not care whether I lived or died. Many of her friends worried that I would take my life. I assured them it was not on my radar right then, but if God told me he was going to take me tomorrow, I would be all-in, and I would celebrate. The most comical line came from my oldest son Brendan, who told one of Eileen's friends: "I know my dad wouldn't kill himself; he's too Catholic."

At the time of this writing, it has been almost four years since I held Eileen's hand as she took her last breath and grabbed Sean's hand on the other side. I have been able to move forward, and not just move on. Aren't they the same? Not at all. In my mind, moving on meant leaving all those memories behind, abandoning them. Moving forward meant I could take those memories with me and cherish them, and also create new ones.

Moving forward started with forgiving myself for being unable to protect her. The feelings of inadequacy left over from Sean intensified. Eileen was so wise. She gave me specific instructions in her final week after seeing Sean in her room: You'll want to run away from all the memories, but don't sell the house. Don't retire on your birthday in May of 2017 as we planned; it is no longer the right time and you will be lost. Wait, and you'll know when it's time.

Finally, she said, "You need to move forward and find somebody, because you'll be too lonely."

"I'm an only child; you are one of thirteen! Who is going to be lonely if the other one dies?"

"You, because we have done everything together these past thirty-seven years."

I kept telling my son Pat that his mom was in my ear, telling me to do this or that. He let me go on for a while, then he challenged me: "Dad, you have to stop doing that! Mom's not here. It is not healthy for you. She's waiting for you somewhere else." I just couldn't move on.

The areas of concern she mentioned were not on my top-three list, but I found out quickly that she was correct about the house. Walking in the door every day, I felt like a lance was going through my side when I didn't hear her voice. I always had, even if she was sick and in bed. All the memories came racing back: kids running into the house, yelling, "Hi, Mom! I'm home." What helped me not sell, frankly, was all the solicitation calls from the likes of those I used to call "ambulance chasers," who prey on the ill. Those jerks knew I was newly widowed and feeling that everyday pain, and they were willing to do me a "favor" by taking the house off my hands. These calls ignited my Irish temper and helped me hold the line. My attitude was "screw you, you're not getting my house!" and got me through some tough months when I easily could have sold. Again, Eileen had been right on.

I didn't retire. In fact, I got busier doing Sean's talks or involved in outside activities related to work. My relatives commented that I was keeping an amazing schedule. It took at least a year for me to realize that the schedule was so busy because I was running away from the pain and just trying to stay occupied. I had put the Cape back on to do things I knew I could do well and also to forget that I'd had a second major trauma in my life, losing somebody I couldn't protect. I thought Sean's talks might save someone where I had failed.

KEEP TALKING TO YOUR LOVED ONE

If you are experiencing a great loss in your life, you can get through that hurdle by finding a counselor and telling that person precisely what you're doing. Let the therapist tell you what you are experiencing. In my case, I was trying to run from the grief and pain of being in that house by staying constantly on the go. It was tough for me to slow down, but counseling helped me do it. I'm still working on that process, but I am aware and a little better at it.

Here is an example of how a counselor can help you handle those difficult moments. As I wrote about earlier in talking to loved ones, and I think it is powerful advice to reinforce my counselor said: "When you walk into the house, do exactly what you've been doing for the last thirty-five years. Call out, 'Hi hon, I'm home.' You're a man of faith. You believe Sean and Eileen are in that house, so why aren't you talking to them? Is it just because you can't see them?" It was pretty simple advice, and luckily, I'm a pretty simple guy. Her advice helped because I do believe Sean and Eileen are there, watching over me.

DON'T JUST MOVE ON—MOVE FORWARD

It's vital to distinguish between moving on and moving forward. Moving on felt to me like I was leaving behind two wonderful people whom I loved so deeply in my soul and starting new. Moving forward is necessary and healthy. I was able to embrace the term *moving forward* after watching a YouTube video from a young woman who had lost her husband and later had remarried. She re-framed the term for me. She said she hadn't wanted to move on because she felt, as I did, that she was leaving her first husband behind. Instead, she had been able to move forward by bringing him along; her new husband had fallen in love with a woman whom her deceased husband helped to shape. This message brought into focus Eileen's final directive to find someone and live my life.

Once I flushed the Irish-Catholic guilt that moving forward didn't mean I had failed or I had abandoned Sean and Eileen, I realized that I had to work with my life as it was here on earth until I saw them again. Suddenly, before my eyes, someone appeared that I believe God sent to me to help me heal. I have opened my heart and moved forward, and she has provided the support and guidance for me to feel alive again. I bring Eileen with me to that relationship, and it strengthens—not threatens—it. God knows if you like the guy I am at all, you can thank Aunt Mary and Eileen for forming me, so why wouldn't I bring all that I have loved and all that I am as I move forward with my life?

As you try to move forward, remember those you've lost, and reframe the way in which they are still very much part of your life. Bring them along as you go forward. Use what they taught you and rely on their strength from the heavens for encouragement as you get back up on your feet and embrace the gift of life you still have until you see them again on the other side.

LESSONS LEARNED

- **Be open to possibilities.** Eileen challenged me in the week before her passing with a few assignments. Some were reasonably doable in my mind; others seemed impossible. The most impossible was to continue to live my life and be open to the possibility of enjoying it and finding someone else to share it with. At the time, that was the furthest thing from my mind. After some time, it seemed more like a possibility. Be open to having joy in your life in new ways without feeling guilty and thinking that you have abandoned your loved one.

- **Move forward.** I needed to differentiate between moving on versus moving forward before I was able to get out of the rut I had dug myself into. I realized that I was never going to move on, but I could move forward by bringing not only Eileen, but Sean with me, too. You don't leave them behind. You bring their memories with you. There is no set time for when it's time to move forward, but your angel, or in my case angels, will guide you.

Chapter 37

Dealing with Anniversaries, Birthdays, and Other Holidays

Anytime you lose someone you love, whether it's sudden and unexpected as it was with Eileen (from healthy to heaven in eleven months) or after a prolonged illness of almost fifteen years with Sean, anniversaries of all kinds produce difficult challenges: birthdays, your wedding anniversary, the day your loved one was diagnosed, the day he passed into heaven. Besides these, there are all the other holidays where everybody appears joyous, like Christmas, when you are supposed to be joyous as well, which, by the way, is nonsense. As you sit there feeling like your heart has been torn out of your chest, just breathing can be a challenge to survive the day.

In our family, the big holidays were Christmas, St. Patrick's Day, and Thanksgiving. Thanksgiving was huge. There were no presents, just loads and loads of family. Christmas was important. Eileen was one of thirteen children, so there were lots of families. St. Patrick's Day was the Irish New Year! Even birthdays were a big deal, as Eileen went to great lengths to celebrate everyone's birthday, and her own birthday would go on for months!

Once you lose somebody, you dread all those days as they approach. I have struggled with them because of both my losses, and I can tell you, sometimes the dread before the holiday is a whole lot worse than the day itself.

MAKE THE DAY POSITIVE

The one piece of advice I would give in dealing with anniversaries, birthdays, and other holidays is to find a way to make those days positive. It certainly has helped me because, initially, my whole experience of special days consisted of flashbacks of what used to be or the loneliness of here and now.

On Eileen's first birthday after she passed, I challenged her friends on Facebook to do something nice for a stranger without saying anything. However, if asked why, say, "Eileen did it for you." It might be something as simple as picking up a cup of coffee for someone or paying for someone's happy meal at the drive-through is taking care of others, which is what Eileen stood for. That tradition continues every year, now, making that day a "smiler" not a downer.

For Sean, we started a charity golf outing with the receipts going directly toward something he stood for. Specifically, the receipts helped to support a scholarship in honor of Sean's Uncle Bob Madden, who passed from ALS. Rosecrance, where he was a patient, now takes care of first responders with mental health and addiction challenges. When Eileen passed, we added her radiologist, Dr. Patrick Sweeney, to the donor list. He had become one of the family, and we wanted to encourage him to keep on doing for others in need what he had done for our family.

These suggestions for honoring your loved one's life instead of mourning their passing are helpful, but please realize that they don't always work. Not every pain is predictable. Sometimes something sneaks up on you that's not as obvious as an anniversary or holiday. It could be a song on the radio; it could be a sight or smell that reminds you of them. You can't avoid that, and it's okay, as my counselor Sue told me. It's all right to go back into that dark, painful place and feel it. Just don't stay there!

MY BIRTHDAY

For some reason, even after therapy, I still don't understand why I have never enjoyed the thought of my birthday. It is not that I dread those age milestones. Instead, the day has had a sick feeling to it since I can remember.

In 2005, almost a year before Sean took his life, he typed me a birthday note, which I have placed at the end of this chapter. When I received it, I did not know I would never get a birthday card from Sean again. I didn't get one in 2006 for my last birthday while he was here on earth, as things were going badly at that time. I have read his letter on every birthday since then. Sometimes, I read it in a park or at the baseball field or the cemetery. Wherever I am across the country, the note is with me. I keep it in a sealed plastic cover. I could put it on my phone, but I want to touch the paper as he did. I have never missed that tradition.

Now you may ask why I would put myself through that every year when it must be so painful. I think Sean knew when he threw in his P.S. that, while humorous, it would be correct for eternity. Yes, I get emotional, just carrying it in my pocket. I get emotional even though I know precisely what it says as I open it, and I sob as I read it. Why read it? Sean gave me the greatest gift he could have, not some stupid t-shirt, but a snapshot of who he was in his own words on paper he touched and held. Sean was not defined by his illness, as no one with a mental illness should be, instead, he is remembered for his wonderful character, which shines brightly in his note. That thought is captured best in a movie that continues to inspire me, *Brian's Song,* about a young football player for the Chicago Bears who dies tragically of cancer. It came out in November of 1971 as I was trying to recover from my broken legs, and Brian Piccolo's courage inspired me. So did Sean's. Both battled terminal illnesses with so much to give and so much to lose. His coach, George Halas, was credited with this statement in the movie:

273

"Brian Piccolo died of cancer at the age of 26. He left a wife and three daughters. He also left a great many loving friends who miss and think of him often. But when they think of him, it's not how he died that they remember— but how he lived. How he did live!"

—Coach George Halas

You never met Sean, but read this letter, and you will know how he lived, which is more important than how he died. You will feel his caring heart and his keen sense of what was going on around him even in his excruciating pain. He saw the efforts of those around him—his mom, brothers, family, and friends—trying to save him. Most important, I think he knew the devastation and guilt I felt that I couldn't save him, and that, once he was gone, it could finish me as a dad, husband, and leader. He knew that he needed me to know he loved me so that I could put the Cape back on and move forward as the leader of the family and my firehouse. Even in my perceived failure to save him, he needed me to know he loved me.

I read it each birthday, not to remind me that he is no longer within arm's reach, but instead so that I may be thankful to God for the gift of a wonderful son who, despite his own pain, thought to take the time to ease my pain every year on my birthday. I remember how he lived.

Dear Dad, Happy 48th birthday. Sorry I could not afford a present for you however I felt that a note would be more heartfelt than some stupid T-shirt or gift card. I want to thank you for all the support that you have given to me over the years. Even though you aren't around much because of work, you always make up for it with your support. I am very proud of you and your achievements although I may not show it. Hopefully when all the medications are figured out I will be able to accomplish things as you have been able to. Thank you for cooperating with all my crap, I don't intentionally try to disappoint you guys but sometimes things get so bad that I make impulsive decisions that I regret. However you always seem to forgive me and give me another chance. You are the staple of this family, the extra work you put in to make sure that the family is taken care of means a lot to me and the other boys. I cannot tell you how much I appreciate your hard work to keep this family stable. Have a great b-day and I love you very much. P.S. please don't get all emotional, just kidding.

Love Sean

LESSONS LEARNED

- **Not everyone feels joyful about holidays.** When someone passes away, it seems like the whole world goes on at full speed right after the funeral, and everyone else's happiness seems magnified. The reality is that normal holidays, anniversaries, and birthdays do not always make people happy, even without the pain of loss. In fact, they can make some people depressed or melancholy. Loss magnifies the hole left behind and brings to mind memories of loved ones on the other side. Remember, though, they are not gone. As my son said, "We didn't lose Mom. We know exactly where she is!" If you know someone who is grieving during the holidays, you can be supportive and sensitive by acknowledging the loss with a hug and letting them know you will remember them on that day, along with their loved one on the other side. It reinforces the fact that while they may not be able to see and touch their loved one, that person is still a part of their life until they meet again.

- **Make the special occasion positive.** The key to handling certain special days is that you can see them coming, unlike other triggers that make you sad, so use that to your advantage. Make the occasion positive by celebrating the person's life or doing something to enhance their legacy. It doesn't have to be big; something as simple and anonymous as buying somebody a cup of coffee in their honor.

- **Command the holiday.** Don't let the anniversary, birthday, or holiday control you; you have to control it. Once you feel in charge and take command of how that holiday is going to be, your emotion may even switch from despair to an occasional smile.

Chapter 38

Sean's Team

When doing a keynote, very early in my talk, I instruct the audience to put all their electronic devices, including their phones, away. I have found that as I get deeper into the talk, many people want to distract themselves from looking at me because it's just too emotional. I challenge them. "If, by the end of my talk, all you get out of it is that you feel bad for me and the losses in my life, then I have wasted my time as well as yours." My goal is to motivate people to act. Now I am asking you, who are kind enough to take your valuable time to read this book, to realize that you can make a difference in how mental illness is perceived. I want you to be proactive, taking actions aimed at crushing the stigma associated with this complicated disease. I want you to feel in your heart that you would like to join Sean's team, because he would love to stand behind you and support you, as would I.

What does it mean to join Sean's team?

- **It's an open invitation**. You are invited to join Sean's team to help remove the stigma regarding mental health in your workplace and family just by having open conversations about the disease at the kitchen table or in the break room.

- **Your commitment is on the honor system**. I won't know if you accept my invitation or even whether you believe a word I have written. You are on the honor system for normalizing mental illness so that it is treated like any other physical illness, and not as a character weakness. I trust you will, and so does Sean. He longs for all to be his teammates, carrying forward his message on earth to eradicate the stigma of mental illness. I believe that was his life's mission.

- **You have faith that your message will be heard**. Sean was never afraid to speak his mind, even challenging psychologists who said they knew what his problem was when they had no clue. He fought for others' rights in the hospital when they did not have a voice. Trust that your message on mental illness will be heard, too. It may be only one person at a time, but that's how you lead to build your army of hope.

- **Spread the message of this book**. If you choose to join his team, Sean will be elated. Your goal is to elicit disciples of his message who will spread it around the world and continue to grow his team. I like the term *disciple* because it implies that someone will spread the word. I mean, even Jesus needed disciples to spread his message. Sean knows I need help!

SEAN'S TEAM IN ACTION

Since Eileen passed, I now ask people to be disciples of Sean and Eileen's team. Just like anybody, I have an ego, and sometimes leaders have an even bigger ego than the rest, but I am not naive enough to think that I was the one and only person who could save the day. I am, however, confident that one person can start a message that takes off like wildfire. I started doing Sean's talks in 2009, and some eleven years later, I have seen the message that mental illness is a health concern increase across the general public and specifically in my industry. I am convinced that one reason is those wonderful disciples of Sean's team are spreading the word. I take no credit for it; I'm just delivering Sean's and Eileen's message. The true heroes of Sean's team are those who had the courage to move me forward by giving me the platform to start spreading the message.

There are so many to mention that I could probably fill a book on just that alone. It began with Janet Wilmoth of *Fire Chief* magazine, who encouraged me to write an article about my journey. That occurred in 2009 after I had read a similar article by a young man chronicling his battle with cancer. Sean's team then spread to my good friend Ed Kaplan, who was on the administration team of the National Fire Academy. I like to say that Ed tricked me into doing my first Sean's talk. He challenged me to turn the article into a presentation, which I reluctantly did on Sean's third anniversary day in 2009. He did not tell me that I would be doing it three times in one day!

That experience grew. An attendee in that class asked me to present it to one of the true legends of my profession, Chief Alan Brunacini. I was so nervous that I thought my message had been incomplete, but at the end, he told me, "Okay, Chief, you've got my attention. What are you going to do about it?" That presentation led to an educational-track presentation at the International Association of Fire Chiefs Volunteer and Combination Committee Symposium in the Sun Conference. The talk was so well received that the conference committee, led by Vickie Pritchett, brought me back the following year to be the keynote speaker. To my knowledge, at that point, mental health had never been a keynote topic at any of the fire industry conferences.

Respected Fire Service leaders became members of Sean's Team. Chief Billy Goldfeder trusted an idea I presented in a parking lot at a conference to have a web page on mental health even though he had never met me before. Chiefs Bobby Halton and Tim Sendelbach then invited me to address huge audiences across the country, delivering Sean's message and then the combined topic of mental illness and cancer awareness.

Many more people I have not mentioned have become part of Sean's team and, ultimately, part of Sean's and Eileen's team. I owe all of them a debt of gratitude on behalf of both Sean and Eileen. They are the disciples. They are the true heroes in this story, not me. It takes courage to embrace something you may not completely understand, but in your heart, you know is something that needs to be moved forward. Nothing brings a bigger smile to my face than to get a random e-mail, text message, or Facebook message from somebody who signs off as, "Proud member of Sean's team."

I am certainly no one special and I don't have any unique gifts; instead, I have a passion for this message. Every one of you has something that burns deep inside, too, so don't be intimidated by the size of the message; just get it started, light the fire, and build your team to watch it grow. The angels will help you, trust me.

LESSONS LEARNED

- **There is a ripple effect.** One person can start a message that takes off like wildfire. When you join Sean's team, you bring that message into your workplace and family and they, in turn, share the message, and so on. The ripple broadens out, reaching people you have never even met.
- **There is a reason for everything.** This book would not have come to pass if certain people had not been placed in my life long before Sean or Eileen passed. I spoke earlier about signs, and I also believe there's a reason for everything. You don't have to like it. Sometimes, you understand the *why*, and sometimes you don't.
- **Be open to others' help.** I can look back now on my mission to share Sean's message and see that I could not have been successful on my own. Special people I never imagined I would meet, through circumstances, became friends who could help me with my platform. God may have taken away my two angels a little early, but he put a lot of other angels in my life to help me move forward and keep the message going.
- **Look for those special helpers/angels in your life.** God has put them there. Sometimes the reason for their presence in your life is apparent. Other times you have to dig to find it, but it is always there. Remember no coincidences? There is a reason you read this book. Sean knows why, and he hopes it helps you or someone you love.

Chapter 39

Own the Story

"Own the story, and you get to write the ending.
Deny the story, and it owns you."
—Brené Brown, *Dare to Lead*

While reading the above quote, I said out loud, "Yeah, that was me!" It perfectly describes where I was and where I moved to in my journey.

For so many years, I denied that Sean was as ill as he was. I denied that mental illness was indeed a physical illness and not a decision based on weakness. I did it with my family as well as with my work family. I shut them out. I couldn't reconcile being a leader with being such a failure as a dad. Once I owned it, I recognized that, as a leader, it's important to keep your significant other and your family involved. You need to share with them what you do. Don't assume they wouldn't be interested or understand. As in my case, don't cut them short regarding their ability to absorb your anxiety and sadness over anything from bad experiences/traumatic calls to perceived shortcomings in your ability to lead. If you deny they exist to your family, they will eventually own you and negatively affect your ability to lead.

Remember, your family stands beside you to support your mission as a leader. The people who work with you stand beside you, too. Never for a minute think of them as walking behind you; if you do, the only view of you they will ever get is from the rear. It becomes a lot easier to call your leader an ass when that's the view you're consistently providing them. Some would argue that's my best view, anyway, but I try not to make that the norm! If you want to create a strong line of solidarity in your organization or family, it's got to be horizontal. If the group is not standing next to you, you will be alone, especially in times of crisis, and it's not a good feeling. Instead, make the culture of standing beside you the expectation from the very beginning.

Joseph Campbell said,

> *"The cave you fear to enter holds the treasure you seek. Own the fear, find the cave and write a new ending for yourself, for the people you're meant to serve and support, and for your culture, choose courage over comfort, choose whole hearts over armor and choose the great adventure of being brave and afraid at the exact same time."*

For me, moving forward meant gaining the courage, through therapy, to enter the cave of darkness that mental illness created. I had to clarify and heal that which would inhibit my ability to lead. Specifically, I had failed to create a culture in my firehouse of accepting that mental illness is the same as any other physical problem, because it was easier. Once I put down that "protective armor" and took my Cape off, I could look mental illness squarely in the eye, as much as it frightened me. Being brave and afraid at the same time eventually led me out of the cave. Then, I could put my Cape back on with my ability to serve and support those around me not only intact, but enhanced.

The big difference? I realized I had to take the Cape off sometimes, and that was indeed the brave thing to do.

And you can, too!

LESSONS LEARNED

- **As a leader, allow others to stand next to you.** A robust line of solidarity in your organization or family has to run horizontally. People need to stand next to you, not behind or in front but at your side, especially in a time of family or organizational crisis.

- **Exude self-confidence.** Your job as leader is to provide a culture in which your family or co-workers are peers when they need to be. Do not feel intimidated by that decision; your ability to include them in the fight is empowering.
- **It's okay for a leader to be brave and unsure.** As a leader, you can be both brave and unsure at the same time. With that combination, you know that sometimes you have to take the Cape off, and that is the bravest thing you can do.

Chapter 40

Stand Up and Be the Best!

The phrase, "Stand up and be the best," is from a scene in the movie *The Natural,* where Robert Redford, a baseball player, is struggling to hit the baseball. The scene has him performing on the road in front of a hostile crowd that is all over him. With two strikes on him, he steps out of the batter's box. When he glances into the stands, he notices a woman standing in all-white, the glow of the sun behind her like a halo surrounding an angel.

I have probably watched *The Natural* a thousand times. Still, I never noticed the figure that looked like a glowing angel standing there until I watched it again on the Christmas Eve after Eileen passed away. You can see Redford's character struggling to clarify what he has seen, but he gets back into the batter's box, and in typical Hollywood fashion, not only hits a home run but shatters a clock tower in doing so.

Later in the movie and, indeed, at the most critical point in the film as far as my talk goes, he asks her "Why did you stand up that day?"

"Because I didn't want to see you fail."

For me, the message is unmistakable: we all have that ability to make a difference! We can all give someone facing a hostile crowd the hope and faith that they can succeed. We can all be that person for someone who needs it. If you think about it, you could probably name at least a handful of people who were angels for you at some point in life, who stood up for you in a difficult situation to let you know they didn't want to see you fail.

From the time I began doing Sean's talks until the time she passed away, Eileen was that angel in the "stands." Standing in the back of the auditorium, she stood up for me when my emotions hit me. Countless times in our marriage, when it looked like nobody believed in me, Eileen stood up to let me know she was there. I knew she didn't want to see me fail; I knew that I had that support.

In the movie, the character played by Glenn Close stood up, but it did not guarantee that Redford would succeed. It was a statement of fact: somebody believed in him. People who struggle with mental health issues in your family or your workplace need people to stand up for them, so they know that at least one person doesn't want to see them fail.

Standing up for them is our job as human beings, and I believe it is our responsibility. Be aware that no matter what you do, there will always be people who suffer from a mental illness that is terminal, people like Sean whom you can't save no matter what you do, but you will escape the horrible cloud of guilt after they head to heaven when you know that at least you cared and tried. You stood for them, and that does count. At the end of your career and your life as a leader, you can know that, indeed, you cared enough to "stand."

LESSONS LEARNED

- **Never underestimate the power of one person to affect your organization or family.** Sometimes, it only takes one person to stand up for someone struggling and let him know that you don't want to see him fail. As a leader, you can be that person.
- **Don't hesitate to be the only one to stand up.** Standing up for someone is no guarantee that they will succeed, or in the case of mental illness, that they will be healed. The struggle can still lead to suicide. You can only do so much. However, through it all, that person will know that you didn't want to see them fail. You may be the only one, and that might just be enough.

CONCLUSION

I have prayed to take something positive from losing my son. Sean taught me my final lesson, and it is the most important one.

> *Those who suffer from mental health challenges, no matter to what degree, are wonderful and courageous people. They are no weaker and no more responsible for their illness than someone with a life-threatening physical illness. You cannot see their disease, like a tumor on an X-ray, but it is just as real and needs support and treatment.*

Leaders and employees alike need to set up a system to provide help to those in need of treatment.

Now, you may be thinking, "Thanks, Chief, for the advice, but most of what you talked about is out of my control. That's the job of the chief, CEO, or president, and I am *just* a firefighter, just an employee. Where would I start?" I'm sure that sounds familiar to any leader.

Well, my friends, we are all *just* employees, regardless of vocation. We have different assignments and titles, but the bottom line is we are all human beings who can make a difference in how mental health is regarded by starting with the one thing we have total control of—our own actions.

- Be Open
- Be Positive
- Be Supportive

If you think anything I have said in this book has merit, I urge you to go back to your workplace and your family and foster a culture in which mental health challenges have the same level of acceptance as physical diseases. The stigma of mental health is that it is perceived as a personal weakness, something someone can control unlike other diseases, such as cancer. That stigma must be eradicated.

You can speak openly with your co-workers and family about the struggles we have as a society with mental illness. Recognize the impact of your profession on your family's mental health. Your personal struggles relative to mental health as the leader with the Cape will pave the way to change the culture that labels mental illness as a personal weakness.

These suggestions do not require money or creation of a standard operating procedure or permission from your administration. They require the personal courage that you all have inside to just speak up. Duck into a nearby phone booth, if you can find one today—or a cubicle will do—and summon your Cape to do battle with this injustice that has persisted for centuries.

Sean's life mission was to teach our family and the fire service about mental illness, and I believe his mission extends to all leaders and all employees and their families. I believe Sean gave his life so others might live.

So, do me a favor as you continue your exciting career in your field: become a member of Sean's Team. Go back to your workplace and family and make a difference in how mental health challenges are accepted. Embrace learning about the subject in depth, the same way you learn about any part of your trade, profession, or business practice. For that, Sean, Eileen, Brendan, Patrick, and I will be eternally grateful.

RESOURCES

As the leader, there is no excuse for you not to get out there and assemble the resources for your people or yourself *when*, not *if*, the Cape fails.

I have always believed that good leaders surround themselves with people who are smarter than they are and then stand back and let them do their thing without fear of being upstaged. Besides the people, you need to know where to get the resources necessary to assist your organization, as well as yourself.

Both things and people are resources. A resource can be anyone or anything from a powerful, nationally accredited source to the guy you meet sitting next to you on the plane when you aren't in the mood for conversation. Sometimes a resource crosses your path and you don't immediately see how it can assist you as the leader, but it becomes apparent further down the line.

Mental illness resources are sometimes hard to find, and that's because mental illness is so complicated that you may not know what you are looking for. It's not as simple as finding a doctor or medication through a search on the internet. Reliable sources are so important to leaders, and those blind internet searches can be frustrating because there is usually no way to validate the information. However, when you are desperate to help a loved one, co-worker, or yourself, it seems like the first and only place to start. Remember, sometimes a resource is as simple as someone you can trust to be your sounding board or help guide your decision-making. Many significant decisions throughout

289

history have been made by talking through an idea out loud with another person: Is it doable? Will it accomplish what it must? With mental illness, usually you're not sure what you're looking at or looking for, so it helps to have recommendations for internet sites to guide you.

How do you figure out who to trust, who to try? Compared to the early 1990s, when Sean started his journey, there are many more programs and places to turn to, resources I didn't have as the leader of our family and my fire department. You can now identify loads of resources under the category of mental health that were not in existence ten, let alone twenty, years ago.

That is good news. The bad news is that mental health has become, all of a sudden, a sexy topic. What do I mean? As a good leader, you have to examine the motives of the supplier. Since mental health prevention, intervention, and treatment are now okay to talk about, some people have jumped on it as an economic opportunity to grab an untapped market.

In the fire service alone, we have added to our job descriptions emergency medical services, hazardous materials mitigation, technical rescue, and now even terrorism. In each new field, vendors come out of the woodwork to market the latest and brightest. Some are helpful, and others are like used car salespeople, trying to capture a quick dollar. As you select mental health resources, always be careful to do your research. When seeking a therapist/clinician, get referrals from friends or colleagues of people whom that person has treated. Ask for feedback on the person's personality, success rate, charges, insurance coverage, age limitations on who they will see, and diagnosis limitations, such as only treating specific illnesses. This kind of information is not only vital for leaders to make good decisions, but really, it should be standard protocol whenever you are venturing into uncharted waters, and mental illness certainly qualifies.

I will share a few resources I have used personally and professionally for both mental health and cancer. Some are for the public, and many are specific to the fire service. I have included them all to make the point that such resources are out there in various forms. The ones I will briefly outline are not meant to form a comprehensive list or to imply that I endorse these over others; instead, these are resources that were useful to me.

Leaders, if you truly mean it when you say you care about your people, whether family members or employees, you have a responsibility to know what is out there to help *before* a crisis. In the area of mental health, society in general and the fire service in particular are terrible! We are reactive, not proactive. My theory as to why we just wait and react is that we are afraid of mental illness, and we do not understand it. Therefore, we ignore the problem or even the possible existence of one until it bangs us over the head. Unfortunately, many programs are the direct result of a tragedy.

As a leader, try to get in front of the issue. Good leaders are visionaries. They see the horizon and put things in place proactively to avoid pain for the individual and the organization. Good leaders should not have a "clean up on aisle five" mentality, because mental health challenges will certainly affect your organization and/or family. This is not about *if;* it's about *when.*

PEER SUPPORT

I first want to mention peer support and support groups in general. The stigma of mental health drives all of us into shutdown mode. We are afraid to acknowledge it, let alone seek help until it is a huge problem that threatens our job or our marriage. One of the most basic, proven, successful, and cost-effective resources out there for dealing with mental health struggles of any kind is talking with a peer.

I am a test case for both denying Sean's condition early in his life and also for not sharing his illness in my fire department later due to the stigma associated with having a mental illness. Candidly looking back, I also think I didn't share it because, as the leader, I was afraid I'd be seen as a failure as a father; how could I possibly lead an organization when I couldn't even help my son? The sad part is that, had I been open and discussed it with my people, I now know that Sean and my family would have had the support I tried to provide all by myself, wearing the Cape.

I also missed an opportunity to educate my people about mental illness, how I felt about it, and how desperately I, too, needed their help and support. I had an opportunity to remove a lot of that stigma surrounding mental health by normalizing it as just another physical disease befalling my child. As a leader, please don't make that same mistake. Many people face this illness every day, just as they do cancer, and talking about it should be commonplace, not the exception if you genuinely want the peer concept to work.

When our son died, we were encouraged to join a support group. This is "peer" support within a group of people who are in the same situation. When I became a new chief, my former boss encouraged me to seek out peers to talk with about my new position. The theory is that only someone who is in your shoes can converse with you intelligently about it and provide both empathy and direction. He was right-on, but I must advise you that it doesn't always work. Not all situations that appear the same have the same circumstances. Frankly, I didn't think I would be using any kind of peer support group for my son's suicide or later when my wife passed.

Peer support can be just a matter of talking to someone you know, someone you trust and care about who is not necessarily a medically trained professional. That's why peer support has been such a powerful resource, especially in the fire service. Simply framed, peer support is a bridge from where you are to where you need to be. It may lead to professional counseling, but that does not always need to be the first line of defense.

So what mental health awareness, intervention, and support come down to is one human being caring about another, leaders and employees, without judging why help is needed. Why they are suffering is not the issue; the issue is how we can help, and better yet prevent, a personal crisis.

Sean and Eileen stood for helping those in need. Both had their lives taken by a terminal physical illness. They did not die in vain; instead, they gave us the map for defeating the prejudices about mental health illnesses and the encouragement to work proactively to help all in need, especially those who battle the physical disease of mental illness.

SUICIDE PREVENTION, HOPE, AND SUPPORT

National Suicide Prevention Hot Line

We can all help prevent suicide. The Lifeline provides 24/7, free and confidential support for people in distress, including suicide prevention and crisis resources for you or your loved ones and best practices for professionals.

suicidepreventionlifeline.org

1-800-273-8255 (TALK)

The National Action Alliance for Suicide Prevention

This action alliance is working with more than 250 national partners from the public and private sectors to advance the National Strategy for Suicide Prevention. It currently focuses on three priority areas, selected from the national strategy, based on their potential to save lives:

- Transforming health systems.
- Transforming communities.
- Changing the conversation.

theactionalliance.org

National Alliance on Mental Illness. (NAMI)

There are also several national organizations that you can turn to that deal with all types of mental illness, including suicide. This is one of the most prominent.

nami.org

Hope Squad

Peer support is not only a fire service or military tool. It needs to be available to all groups at almost any age. What is too young? Sean was diagnosed with clinical depression at five. The discussion to normalize mental health challenges never starts too early. Young children are dying by suicide in junior high and sometimes earlier. This wonderful peer-support model for schools rose out of the tragedy of a young child who took his life. The critical components are the same: an aware environment, peer support, and resources for getting help.

hopesquad.com

Hope Research Center – University of Oklahoma – Tulsa

The center is interested in both the science and power of hope as a psychological strength, especially among those experiencing trauma and adversity. Three questions guide their work:

- Does hope buffer adversity and stress?
- Do hopeful children and adults have better psychological, social, and behavioral outcomes?
- Can hope be increased and sustained by targeted interventions?

ou.edu/tulsa/hope

Compassionate Friends

Compassionate Friends deals with surviving the pain of a child's suicide and will put you in touch with others who already have traveled this painful road. Everyone's journey is unique, but there are commonalities that are helpful to hear about so you don't feel that they are only happening to you (e.g., being avoided in public).

compassionatefriends.org/surviving-childs-suicide

MENTAL ILLNESS AND SUBSTANCE ABUSE RESOURCES

Mental illness often coincides with substance abuse as people seek to self-medicate. That was true with Sean; he used every substance he could to get temporary relief from his pain and suffering. Treatment centers that recognize and treat both illnesses at the same time are powerful. Here are a couple of examples:

Rosecrance

Rosecrance has a board-certified psychiatrist and addictionologist who is trained and experienced in treating firefighters and paramedics for co-occurring disorders.

rosecrance.org/substance-abuse/florian-firefighter-treatment-center

IAFF Center of Excellence for Behavioral Health Treatment and Recovery System

Many centers like this are establishing programs, not just for firefighters, but for first responders, the military, etc. The problem of self-medicating crosses all professions.

iaffrecoverycenter.com

FIREFIGHTER RESOURCES

Other organizations seek to educate across multiple platforms, from co-workers on up to the leader and clinician. In the case of firefighters, the clinician needs to know about our culture. We are indeed a different breed. If you ignore what the real atmosphere is, you are sending the clinician in blind. The fire service recognized this need for access in many organizations.

I will highlight a few:

Illinois Fire Service Institute Resiliency Program

First Responders experience unavoidable stress and traumatic events in the course of their vocation. If these challenges are not dealt with in a productive manner, they can lead to emotional and behavioral health problems. Since many of the current ways to deal with these challenges revolve around assistance and treatment after the event, the Illinois Fire Service Institute has sought to change the fire service culture relative to mental health and resiliency by adding training to many of its courses. This culture change will occur by helping First Responders to be aware of the components of resiliency when they encounter stressful events.

fsi.illinois.edu

Illinois Firefighter Peer Support

Illinois has a special network for firefighters, and such networks are present across the country and the world. Almost all large metropolitan fire departments (New York, Chicago, Boston, Phoenix, etc.) have them.

ilffps.org

The International Association of Firefighters (IAFF) Peer Support Program

This is another outstanding program. If you are not a firefighter, don't be afraid to contact any of these organizations to ask for guidance and suggestions on starting a support group in your company. In fact. I recently read of the "crisis" the New Zealand Fire Service was facing in mental health. This is a global challenge. Peer support is not a substitute for specialized services, but it may act as the liaison between peers and needed professionals in complex cases.

iaff.org/peer-support

Share the Load

This is a joint effort between the National Volunteer Fire Council and American Addiction Centers, offering a free 24-hour hotline for firefighters and EMS workers nationwide. When first responders call the line, they will be able to talk to another first responder who understands the nature of their work and can guide them to the resources that work. It's a powerful combination of peer support and professional referral.

nvfc.org/programs/share-the-load-program

Firefighter Close Calls, Personal Survival Page

This is a website with many pages. One is dedicated to mental health stories of loss, survival, and recovery, as well as resources and contact information. It is a page of hope, with many success stories, so that those suffering from mental health challenges know that they are not alone. We just haven't been very good about sharing success stories because it means admitting that you had an illness! Yet, it is the sharing that gets folks to be open to the view of mental illness as a physical illness.

firefighterclosecalls.com/personal-survival.php

Medical University of South Carolina

When we talk about 24/7 accessibility, some programs can be provided as apps that may be more appealing to the younger generation. This is one that has the support of significant fire service leaders.

pocketpeer.org

National Fallen Firefighters Foundation

Curriculum development for educating people on what is and is not mental illness is crucial to reducing and eventually removing the stigma. Many fire service organizations have added this to their mission, including this one. They provide the curriculum to train those who will treat responders, including what to do in the event of a tragic suicide (i.e., Fire Service Behavioral Health Rapid Response). Also, training modules are set up for line firefighters on stress first aid and curbside manner.

firehero.org

International Association of Firefighters

iaff.org

International Association of Fire Chiefs

Both of the above international organizations represent labor and management and provide educational opportunities in the form of classes, symposiums, and position papers on the topic of mental health. Again, while aimed at the fire service, the concepts are universal.

iafc.org

CANCER RESOURCES

National Hospice Web

In our experience, hospice was a great resource for talking about the mourning process and a better understanding of the illness. When Eileen was sick, hospice provided information about the inevitable, what to expect, what kinds of things to talk about, etc. Ironically, there is no hospice for a mentally terminal patient; there is, instead, a painful feeling of loneliness. Not all hospices are created equal, so it is good to do your homework sooner rather than later. One site with much information is:

hospicefoundation.org/Hospice-Care/Hospice-Services

The Firefighter Cancer Support Network

Even though the network is aimed at firefighters, the information is still valuable for some guidance on Eileen, including what to ask, what to expect, etc.

firefightercancersupport.org

SUGGESTED BOOKS

The following is a list of books I found especially helpful as I navigated through and continue to work on my personal losses, leadership, and resiliency. In addition, there are hundreds of books in many of these areas that you may find helpful to you; these just happened to really hit home with me.

After Loss of a Child

- *Heaven Is for Real: A Little Boy's Astounding Story of His Trip to Heaven and Back,* by Todd Burpo and Lynn Vincent.

After Loss of a Spouse

- *Option B,* by Sheryl Sandberg and Adam Grant.

Leadership

- *The Mentor Leader,* by Tony Dungy and Nathan Whitaker.
- *The Trust Edge,* by David Horsager.
- *Turn the Ship Around!: A True Story of Turning Followers into Leaders,* by L. David Marquet and Stephen R. Covey.
- *The Carpenter: A Story About the Greatest Success Strategies of All,* by Jon Gordon.

- *Pass it On,* by Billy Goldfeder and Friends.
- *Dare to Lead,* by Dr. Brené Brown.

Resilience

- *Supernormal,* by Meg Jay.

Mental Health

- *Why People Die by Suicide,* by Dr. Thomas Joiner.

NOTES

While I have brought my own personal insight and experience to these subjects, I also understand my knowledge is limited. Therefore, I reached out to a variety of sources to provide resources for this book beyond what I have shared.

Note: Any failure to give full and proper credit is purely unintentional.

PART 1: DEALING WITH MENTAL ILLNESS

CHAPTER 2: Child Diagnosis of Depression

Page 15, Clinical Depression: Mayo Clinic, "What does the term 'clinical depression' mean?" by Daniel K. Hall-Flavin, M.D. https://www.mayoclinic.org/diseases-conditions/depression/expert-answers/clinical-depression/faq-20057770

Page 16, Childhood depression: *CHOC Children*, "What Parents Need to Know About Childhood Depression," posted by Caryn Bailey. https://www.choc.org/news/what-parents-need-to-know-about-childhood-depression

Page 16, Symptoms of childhood depression: *Healthline*, "What does depression look like in a child?" https://www.healthline.com/health/mental-health/childhood-depression#symptoms

Page 17, Family history: "Mental Health Myths and Facts." https://www.mentalhealth.gov/basics/mental-health-myths-facts

CHAPTER 5: Exhausting All Options

Page 44, Electroconvulsive therapy (ECT): *Mayo Clinic,* "Electroconvulsive therapy." https://www.mayoclinic.org/tests-procedures/electroconvulsive-therapy/doctors-departments/pdc-20393895

Page 45, Cognitive Behavioral Therapy (CBT): *Mayo Clinic,* "Cognitive behavioral therapy." https://www.mayoclinic.org/tests-procedures/cognitive-behavioral-therapy/about/pac-20384610

Page 48, Experimental Vagus Nerve Implant: *Elemental,* "Science Confirms That the Vagus Nerve Is Key to Well-being: The mysterious nerve network that quiets pain and stress — and may defeat disease," Markham Heid, Dec 19, 2019. https://elemental.medium.com/science-confirms-that-the-vagus-nerve-is-key-to-well-being-c23fab90e211

CHAPTER 7: Parent Survival Tips

Page 58, Divorce rates: "The Myth of Divorce Following the Death of a Child," by Stephanie Frogge, March 1, 2015. https://www.taps.org/articles/21-1/divorce

Page 59: "Bereaved Parents: Particular Difficulties, Unique Factors, and Treatment Issues," by Therese A. Rando, Ph.D., January 1, 1985. https://academic.oup.com/sw/article-abstract/30/1/19/1942856?redirectedFrom=fulltext

CHAPTER 8: Mental Health Myths

Page 63, First Myth: *HelpGuide,* "Suicide Prevention," by Melinda Smith, M.A., Jeanne Segal, Ph.D., and Lawrence Robinson. Last updated: October 2019. https://www.helpguide.org/articles/suicide-prevention/suicide-prevention.htm

Page 64, Second Myth: Nevada Division of Public and Behavioral Health (DPBH), Office of Suicide Prevention, "The Myths and Facts of Youth Suicide." http://suicideprevention.nv.gov/Youth/Myths

Page 64, Third Myth: *Independent,* "Intelligent People More at Risk of Mental Illness Study Finds," by Henry Austin, October 17, 2017.

https://www.independent.co.uk/news/health/intelligence-mentalillness-iq-study-findings-depression-a8005801.html

Page 64, Fourth Myth: *Mayo Clinic,* "Q and A: Suicide and genetics — a complicated association," by Liza Toborg, April 15, 2017. https://newsnetwork.mayoclinic.org/discussion/mayo-clinic-q-and-a-suicide-and-genetics-a-complicated-association

Page 64, Fourth Myth: Nevada Division of Public and Behavioral Health, Office of Suicide Prevention. "The Myths and Facts of Youth Suicide." http://suicideprevention.nv.gov/Youth/Myths

Page 65, Fifth Myth: *Mental Health.gov,* "Mental Health Myths and Facts," August 29, 2017. https://www.mentalhealth.gov/basics/mental-health-myths-facts

Page 65, Sixth Myth: *Healthline,* "Depression: What You need to Know," by Jamie Elmer, November 14, 2018. https://www.healthline.com/health/smiling-depression

Page 66, Seventh Myth: *WalesOnline,* "There is no magic pill to 'cure' mental illness – instead we need to take a look at society," by Dr. Julian Tudor Hart, August 4, 2008. https://www.walesonline.co.uk/news/health/no-magic-pill-cure-mental-2156088

Page 66, Eighth Myth: National Alliance of Mental Illness, "Treatments," 2020. https://www.nami.org/About-Mental-Illness/Treatments

Page 67, Ninth Myth: "Suicide Prevention," by Melinda Smith, M.A., Jeanne Segal, Ph.D., and Lawrence Robinson, last updated October 2019. https://www.helpguide.org/articles/suicide-prevention/suicide-prevention.htm

Page 67, Tenth Myth: "Suicide Prevention," by Melinda Smith, M.A., Jeanne Segal, Ph.D., and Lawrence Robinson. Last updated: October 2019. https://www.helpguide.org/articles/suicide-prevention/suicide-prevention.htm

Page 67, Eleventh Myth: National Alliance of Mental Illness, "Mental Health by the Numbers, September 2019.
https://www.nami.org/mhstats

Page 68, Twelfth Myth: *Psychology Today,* "Common Myths About Suicide Debunked. Fact: Suicide is not always about mental illness," by Kristen Fuller, M.D., June 12, 2018.
https://www.psychologytoday.com/us/blog/happiness-is-state-mind/201806/common-myths-about-suicide-debunked

CHAPTER 9: Mental Illness Isn't a Choice

Page 73: *The Valedictorian of Being Dead: The True Story of Dying Ten Times to Live,* Heather B. Armstrong, Gallery Books, April 23, 2019.

PART 2: SUICIDE, GRIEF, AND LOSS

CHAPTER 16: The Power of Professional Help

Page 117: *Compassionate Friends*
https://www.compassionatefriends.org/surviving-childs-suicide

PART 3: LEADING WITHOUT A CAPE

CHAPTER 17: Experiencing Grief and Loss as a Leader

Page 129: "Lessons in exercise neurobiology: The case of endorphins," by Rod K. Dishman and Patrick J. O'Connor.
https://www.sciencedirect.com/science/article/abs/pii/S1755296609000039

CHAPTER 19: The Cape Can Choke You

Page 142: The National Fallen Firefighters Foundation, "16 Life Safety Initiatives." https://www.everyonegoeshome.com/16-initiatives

CHAPTER 20: War Veterans and PTSD

Page 147: *On Killing: The psychological cost of learning to kill in war and society, by* D.A. Grossman, New York: Little, Brown and Company. Hale, C. R., 1997

CHAPTER 22: Mental Health Myth Busters for Leaders

Pages 155-158: *Mental Health.gov*, "Mental Health Myths and Facts," August 29, 2017. https://www.mentalhealth.gov/basics/mental-health-myths-facts

CHAPTER 23: Leadership and Spotting Signs of Mental Health Issues

Page 159: National Alliance of Mental Illness, "Warning Signs and Symptoms," 2020. https://www.nami.org/About-Mental-Illness/Warning-Signs-and-Symptoms

CHAPTER 24: The Question to Ask and What to Do

Page 170: "ACE, Suicide Prevention for the Army by the Army," by Lt. Col. Blain S. Walker, Ph.D., U.S. Army Public Health Command, September 1, 2011. https://www.army.mil/article/64796/ace_suicide_prevention_for_the_army_by_the_army
Page 170: *AIRFORCE RESILIENCE,* 2020. https://www.resilience.af.mil/Tools/ACE/

CHAPTER 26: Why People Die by Suicide

Pages 185-188: *Why People Die by Suicide*, By Dr. Thomas Joiner, Harvard University Press, September 30, 2007.

CHAPTER 31: Leading During a Crisis

Page 211: Crisis Definition, https://www.merriam-webster.com/dictionary/crisis

Page 219: "Perfectionism and Depression Flow Chart."
Created by Patrick J. Kenny with input from Dr. Cody Todd, doctorate in Clinical Psychology from ISPP.

PART 5: MOVING FORWARD

CHAPTER 36: Moving Forward after Loss of a Spouse

Page 265: "Celebrate Life," by Sharon Randall, Nov. 8, 2016.
http://sharonrandall.com/2016/11/celebrate-life-nov-8-2016

CHAPTER 37: Dealing with Anniversaries, Birthdays, and Other Holidays

Page 273: *Brian's Song,* by Gale Sayers and William Blinn, November 30, 1971.

CHAPTER 39: Own the Story

Page 281: *Dare to Lead,* by Brené Brown, Random House, 2019.
Page 282: "Face Your Fears & Find Your Potential: 5 Life Changing Joseph Campbell Quotes," by Chiara Gizzi, August 11, 2015.
https://www.fearlessmotivation.com/2015/08/11/5-life-changing-joseph-campbell-quotes

CHAPTER 40: Stand Up and Be the Best

Page 285: The Lady in white from the movie, "The Natural," 1984, story by Bernard Malamud and Roger Towne.
https://www.youtube.com/watch?v=J0lof7tFKtE

ACKNOWLEDGMENTS

I believe that angels have been sent into all of our lives, whether we recognize them or not, to help us along the way. When Eileen challenged me to write a book about Sean's story, I had no idea how hard it would be, both physically and emotionally. There are so many people to thank along the way that these acknowledgments could be as long as the book. I have kept this as short as I can, but I am not willing to trade brevity for omitting anyone I need to thank. No doubt I am bound to miss many, and so I apologize ahead of time.

I have already mentioned many angels who helped me along in the book, so I won't repeat their names here, but there are few more who helped me keep on track. Some I won't mention by name, but instead by their groups or affiliations.

Whenever you're faced with a challenge in life, you always need at least one person who believes in you. Even if that person is the only one who does, it is enough to provide you with the confidence to succeed. My first acknowledgment goes to my dad, "Galway Mike," who was the family's role model for hard work. In Ireland, he had been an exceptional athlete, and my memories of him reflect what the leader of a team looks like, which was clear in the respect he got. He could command a room!

My next angel was my Aunt Mary, who was my godmother. From my struggles as a chubby little kid through a significant car accident and numerous disappointments, she never lost faith in me. She reinforced that I could do whatever I needed to do, and, in fact, what I was destined to accomplish. She personified for me the power of one person's faith in another to carry him forward to his goal. I am living proof. I pinned my original Chief's badge on her dress before they closed her casket, as she had earned it as much as I had.

I have an incredible group of friends from grammar school, high school, and college with whom I played baseball until we were into our late twenties on a team called the Eagles. Joe Cieslak and I were only children when we met in grammar school and we bonded, so Joe became the brother I never had. They and their significant others have remained lifelong friends. They gave me the confidence that I could lead, even as a peer. They helped me develop abilities I've used as a leader in the fire service for the last thirty-eight years.

We had a wonderful neighborhood that supported Sean and number one on that list was the Basco family. Kathy Basco was another mom to Sean, from listening to late-night cell calls to always welcoming him in her home, Sean loved Mrs. Basco.

I was incredibly blessed to meet a young lady named Eileen Madden, who became my wife and who brought me into her family. I hated being an only child, and through Eileen, I was embraced into the fold of thirteen Madden brothers and sisters. True, it was a bit of a culture shock, but it was also incredibly supportive to be part of a big and loving family.

I had a new role model in the person of Robert Madden, Eileen's dad and my surrogate dad—Bucko, as I referred to him. While I only had him for a few years, he made a tremendous impact on my life before he died suddenly of a heart attack. He showed me what it was to be a good husband and dad.

My inspiration to become a firefighter came from Eileen's family, reinforced by a couple of her brothers who were in public service. But make no mistake about it, without thirty-seven years of Eileen always having my back, I wouldn't have succeeded at tying my shoes, let alone writing a book. She was the real hero in our family, not me. I was gone so much as a firefighter, and on my off-days, I was back at school or teaching. Too often, I was missing in action, and she never complained.

She raised three wonderful children—Brendan, Patrick, and Sean—men I am very proud of for who they are. I am nobody without my family. The love I got when I walked up the driveway after being gone for sometimes forty-eight hours or more, my three boys running toward me is a memory that still gives me chills.

I was blessed in my fire service career to cross paths with a lot of great people at the Hinsdale Fire Department, co-workers and their wives who became family members and supported me as I moved up the chain to Chief. Besides helping my professional development, they kept Eileen and me sane through Sean's illness and his passing. And although I had moved on to the Western Springs Fire Department family by the time Eileen was diagnosed with brain cancer, my Hinsdale family was at the front, building wheelchair ramps, sending meals, and so on. I called them "Eileen's angels," and they and the incredible people at Western Springs had my back until Eileen made her trip to heaven.

Sean was blessed with a great godmother, Tess. She reached out when he was hospitalized and was one of only two people (Eileen's mom was the other) to whom he would respond. Again, it is an example of how one person's belief in you can help you keep fighting.

My therapist Sue Wilkie took care of Sean and eventually our whole family. She kept Sean alive for more years than expected, given his pain, and what a gift that was! Sean loved and respected her. She, too, is family.

For over twenty years, I've been a volunteer coach at Downers Grove South High School, coaching baseball. I've met exceptional people and functioned as an assistant coach under Bill and Darren and Tim. In my youth and again in later years, baseball became my escape. These people truly understood both Sean's and Eileen's struggles and stood side-by-side with me.

As you can see, even though some would say my life has been kind of rough, I also have been blessed by a lot of angels. When it comes to the book, however, it's pretty easy to see the line of succession of those angels. It started with the boss, Eileen, telling me shortly after Sean passed in 2006 that I needed to write the book about his life to share his journey for the sake of helping others. She continued that push for almost ten years right up until the day before she passed.

During that time, I met a firefighter who was working part-time for Hinsdale when I started there, and he became a close friend and colleague. Tim McElroy took up the torch along with Eileen and pushed for this book to be written. He has been relentless, and without many a good kick in the butt, I probably would've given up on the idea four years ago, right after Eileen passed. Tim continued to push even harder with Eileen in heaven.

One day, while discussing an unrelated item with our HR director Ellen in her office in Western Springs, our conversation turned to "signs" and our belief in them. That led to Ellen telling me about a friend, an author named D.D. Marx, who wrote about signs. She suggested we meet and share stories. We did meet, and I asked Marx if she thought I had a story that people would want to read. Much to my chagrin, she said, "You have to do it." She sent me to the angel, counselor, friend, and taskmaster who has brought me to this point, and that is Shannon O'Keeffe.

Shannon has been my consultant throughout. She quickly became a member of Sean's team, and we are both sure Sean has made some visits to her house in a demanding fashion, saying, "Let's finally get this thing done!" I can't thank her enough for her patience and guidance. This book would never have seen the light of day without her passion.

Shannon led me to Sarah Aschenbach, who has edited the book. If you think it is well written, no need to go any farther to ask why. She took the manuscript on with a mission—another member of Sean's team.

Finally talk about angels being sent when you least expect it. I was a physical and emotional mess after Eileen passed and along came an amazing person named Irene. We had been friends, as she was a physical therapist who helped me with multiple fire department related injuries. Years later, Irene also became a friend to Eileen and even took her to some of her radiation treatments. Neither of us expected, so many years after we met, to become bonded in such a supportive relationship.

I didn't deserve one angel in my lifetime, let alone two, but I think God felt sorry for me. Many of Eileen's friends believe that Eileen sent Irene to me. I'm sure part of it was that Eileen knew I couldn't finish the book alone, so she sent the right companion!

I have learned that writing a book is a daunting endeavor. I've also found that when you are rehashing incredibly painful moments, it's easy to see this as a valid excuse to quit. I've had many moments over the last eighteen months when I wrote myself a permission slip to stop. Irene has watched me laugh but more often watched me cry, agonizing over flashbacks and nightmares at night as I relived much of this journey. I am here to tell you I would have quit for sure if she wasn't in my life, and so she shares in seeing that Sean's story finds the light of day.

Finally, to my little boy Sean, my "Boomer." Son, when I wanted to quit because it hurt so much, I thought of you. When I felt depressed and alone, reliving your pain and how helpless I was as your dad, I thought of you. When I saw the stigma of mental illness put on so many good people, when I saw them judged as weak, not ill, I thought of you.

You never quit! That word was not in your vocabulary. Then, you decided enough with this "terminal illness," and you sought healing and comfort with God. Having witnessed your courage and your fight for fifteen years, there was no way I could quit. I didn't want to let you and your mom down.

I hope you are both proud of what you read here, and that I got the story right. I pray it helps many in the multiple ways you both envisioned.

I kept my promise!

ABOUT THE AUTHOR

PATRICK J. KENNY has been a member of the fire service for over 38 years, a chief officer for over 25 years, and before retiring was the Fire Chief in Western Spring, Illinois. A popular speaker, he has presented throughout the US and in multiple countries on *Mayday for Mental Health*® for more than a decade. He has written articles on mental health,  leadership, fire safety, and fire code challenges. In 2004, he was awarded the Fire Chief of the Year by the Illinois Fire Chiefs Association, in 2020–2021 he was awarded the George D. Post Instructor of the Year by the Fire Engineering/International Society of Fire Service Instructors (ISFSI), and in 2021 he was awarded Fire Chief Emeritus status by the Executive Board of the Illinois Fire Chiefs Association.

For more information on Pat Kenny and to book him for speaking engagements, you may contact him at:

PatrickJKenny.com

ADDITIONAL MATERIALS & RESOURCES

Access your additional materials & resources
referenced throughout this book at:

https://patrickjkenny.com/bookbonus

Made in the USA
Monee, IL
17 August 2022

11851082R00188